Gastric Sleeve Bariatric Cookbook

500 Quick, Easy and Delicious Recipes to Avoid Regaining Weight after Surgery.

Overcome Food Addiction | 8-Week Healing Meal Plan for your Stomach & Weight Loss

Dr. Alan Williams

Table of Contents

Introduction 12

Chapter 1: Basics of Sleeve Gastrectomy 13

    1.1 Gastric Sleeve and Gastric Bypass 13

    1.2 Benefits of Gastric Sleeve Bariatric Surgery 13

    1.3 Risks With Sleeve Gastrectomy 14

Chapter 2: Steps and Strategies 15

    2.1 Before the Surgery 15

    2.2 After the Surgery 16

    2.3 The Five Stages of Eating After Bariatric Surgery 17

    2.4 Nutritional Concern 17

    2.5 Exercise Guidelines for Each Stage of Weight-loss Surgery 18

    2.6 How to live better 19

    2.7 Foods to avoid after surgery 20

Chapter 3: Meal Plan 21

    Week 1 21

    Week 2 21

    Week 3 22

    Week 4 22

    Week 5 23

    Week 6 23

    Week 7 24

    Week 8 24

Chapter 4: Liquid Recipes 26

    Strawberry-Banana Protein Smoothie 26

    Chunky Monkey Smoothie 26

    Spinach Super food Smoothie 26

    Berry Blast Protein Shake 26

    Tropical Mango Smoothie 26

    Vanilla Apple Pie Protein Shake 27

    Protein-Packed Peanut Butter Cup Shake 27

    Very Vanilla Bean Probiotic Shake 27

    Double Fudge Chocolate Shake 27

    Pumpkin Spice Latte Protein Shake 27

    High-Protein Milk 28

    Berry Cheesecake Protein Shake 28

    Root Beer Float Protein Shake 28

Tangy Orange Protein Shake 28

Vanilla Strawberry Protein Shake 28

Chocolate Covered Banana Protein Shake 28

Chocolate Covered Cherries Protein Shake 28

Dreamscicle 28

Choco-Vanilla Protein Shake 29

Buttercream Toffee Vanilla Latte 29

Pumpkin Spice Shake 29

Protein Fruit Smoothie 29

Hazelnut Cappuccino 29

Cinnamon Nag 29

Cafe Kahlua 29

Banana Protein Nog 30

Nectar Protein Cocktail 30

Chocolate Peanut Butter Smoothie 30

Banana Rum Smoothie 30

Banana Cream Pie Shake 30

Butter Almond Latte 30

Peach Almond Italian Soda 30

Cinnamon Roll Latte 30

Cream Dream Latte 31

Hot or Cold Chocolate Drink 31

Creamer Recipe 31

Hot Chocolate Drink 31

Jingle Java Latte 31

French Twist Mocha 31

Cafe Caramel Mocha 31

Chocolate Covered Caramel Mocha 31

Creamy Fuzzy Navel 32

Pumpkin Protein Shake 32

Boysenberry Smoothie 32

Buttermilk Fruit Shake 32

Snickers bar Mocha Protein Shake 32

Hazelnut Mocha Cappuccino Shake 32

Strawberry Protein Smoothie 32

Protein Fruit Smoothie 33

Tropical Fruit Breeze Protein Shake 33

Chapter 5: Breakfast Recipes 34

Cheesy Veggies Pancake.................................. 34

Turkey Bacon and Avocado Scramble 34

Puréed Black Beans with Scrambled Eggs 34

Veggie Muffins.. 34

Steel Cut Oat Berries Pancakes 35

Blueberries and Strawberries Muesli 35

Peach and Raspberry Sauce Sandwich 35

Shakshuka.. 35

Italian Eggs in Purgatory 36

Denver Egg Muffins 36

Mushroom, Lentils and Tomato Scrambled Tofu 36

Protein Breakfast Burritos 36

Soft Peachy Cream of Wheat................................. 37

Cheesy Mushrooms, Broccoli and Eggs Bake 37

Puréed Black Beans and Pumpkin Soup 37

Turmeric Leek, Broccoli and Tofu Quiche.................... 37

Cheese-Filled Tofu Acorn Squash 38

Cheese Spinach Bake 38

Apple Cinnamon Oatmeal 38

Creamy 2 Cheese Grits 38

Berries Parfait and Greek Yogurt............................. 39

Italian Style Tomatoes and Scrambled Eggs 39

Mexican Scrambled Eggs 39

Spinach and Mushrooms Omelet 39

Almond Protein Porridge 39

Egg and Mashed Avocado Toast............................. 40

Tomato, Feta and Leek Frittata 40

Egg Scramble with Lox, Olives, and Avocado 40

Spinach Frittata and Bean Cream 40

Protein Breakfast Burrito................................... 41

Turkey Hash Mini-Cakes 41

Smoothie Bowl with Greek Yogurt and Fresh Berries ... 41

Slow Cooker Apple-Carrot-Raisins Oatmeal 41

Cherry-Vanilla Baked Oatmeal Muffins 42

Banana Protein Pancakes 42

Pistachio Zucchini Muffins with Orange Glaze 42

Pumpkin Zucchini Muffins 42

Marinated Salmon Pancake Rolls 43

Turkey Frittata with Arugula and Gouda Cheese 43

Curry Lentils and Sunny-Side Up Egg with Yogurt.......... 43

Avocado Sauce Cauliflower Scrambled Burrito 44

Chicken, Broccoli, Cheese and Mushroom Casserole 44

Berry-Lemon Greek Yogurt Pancakes 44

Banana Strawberries Oatmeal with Almond Butter 45

Vanilla Cinnamon French Toast 45

Vegetarian Savory Bread Pudding 45

Fully Green Shakshuka with Beans 46

Protein-Packed Breakfast Bars.............................. 46

Spinach, Tomato and Cheese Soft Omelet 46

Salmon and Artichokes Scrambled Eggs 46

Chapter 6: Soups and Salads 48

"Left Over "Turkey Salad 48

Chestnut Chicken Salad.................................... 48

Poached Chicken Salad 48

Chicken Grilled Cesar Salad 48

Waldorf salad 48

Bahamas Shrimp Salad 49

Southern Tuna Salad 49

Black Bean and Chicken Salad.............................. 49

Cottage Cheese Salad 49

Chicken Caesar Salad 49

Tossed Blue Cheese Salad 50

Greek Style Egg Salad 50

Pasta Salad Recipe 50

Black Bean Salad 50

Grilled Steak Salad 50

Smoked Chicken Salad with Raspberry Balsamic
Vinaigrette 50

Garlic-Roasted Radicchio 51

Cantaloupe and Avocado Salad 51

Chicken Salad Sandwich................................... 51

Luncheon Salad 51

Marinated Shrimp Salad 52

Tennessee Chicken Salad 52

Roasted Grape, Chicken, and Vegetable Salad 52

Georgian Egg Salad 52

Wilted Spinach Chicken Salad 52

Veggie Soup Base Mix................................. 53

Post-Op Soup 53

Thanksgiving Leftover Soup 53

Garden Gazpacho 53

Turkey-Sausage and Seafood Gumbo.................... 53

Taco Chili Soup 54

Jambalaya 54

Heavenly Hearty and Healthy Soup 54

Fireside Beef Stew 54

Chili 55

Low Fat Chicken Cacciatore 55

Low Carb Chili 55

Chicken & Mushroom Stew 55

Beef - Vegetable Casserole (Crock-pot)............... 56

Pinto Bean Puree 56

Salmon Chowder 56

Taco Soup 56

Lentil Barley Stew 57

Artichoke Feta Quiche 57

Creamy Black Bean Soup 57

Meatball Minestrone.................................. 57

Meatball Stew 58

Creamy Broccoli Chowder 58

Red Lentil Soup with Kale 58

Cheesy Broccoli Soup 58

Chapter 7: Side Dishes and Snacks 60

Spinach and Artichoke Dip 60

Slow Cooker Boston Beans 60

Scalloped Potatoes 60

Green Beans Greek Style 60

Marinated Mushrooms 61

Cauliflower Purée 61

Minty Summer Squash and Mushrooms Mix 61

Puréed Classic Egg Salad............................ 61

Maple-Mashed Sweet Potatoes 61

Basil-2 Cheeses Chips 62

Thyme-Radish Chips 62

Rosemary Cheese Biscuits 62

Kohlrabi Chips 62

Daikon Chips 62

Parmesan Herb Muffins 63

2 Cheese Cauliflower Patties 63

Mozzarella Mushroom Caps 63

3-Cheese Bake.. 63

Crusted Mozzarella Sticks 63

Light Almond Cookies 64

Raspberry Gelatin Tea 64

Cinnamon Vanilla Coconut Milk........................ 64

Yogurt, Chocolate and Chia Pudding 64

Vanilla Frozen Yogurt 65

Italian Salad Bites 65

Greek Salad 65

Eggs and Veggie Cauliflower Rice 65

Healthy Roasted Vegetables 65

Asian Cabbage Salad 66

Southwest Deviled Eggs 66

Turkey Cajun Roll-Ups 66

Parmesan Chips 66

Edamame Hummus....................................... 66

Spicy Roasted Chickpeas 67

Mashed Beans and Cauliflower 67

Chicken and Pickle Roll-Ups 67

Baked Zucchini Fries 67

Eggplant Pizzas 67

Tomato, Basil, Cucumber and Feta Salad 68

Roasted Root Vegetables 68

Cauliflower Rice 68

Tomato and Mozzarella Skewers 68

Baked Homemade Potato Chips 69

Baked Brie with Apricot 69

Chocolate Energy Protein Bites 69

Hummus... 69

Seasoned Cheese Chips 69

Cabbage and Plums Salad 70

Cinnamon Fried Bananas 70

Melting Tuna and Cheese Toasties 70

Smoked Tofu Quesadillas 70

Chapter 8: Dressings, Sauces, and Seasonings 71

Greek Salad Dressing 71

Creamy Peppercorn Ranch Dressing 71

Seafood Sauce 71

Homemade Enchilada Sauce 71

Mango Salsa 71

Basil Pesto 71

Marinara Sauce with Italian herbs 72

Baba Ghanoush Dip 72

Homemade BBQ Sauce 72

Mixed Bean Salsa 72

Spicy Lentils 72

Parsley Hummus 72

White Cheese Sauce 73

Cheesy Vegetable Dip 73

Sugar-Free BBQ Sauce 73

Layered Mexican Dip 73

Cinnamon Applesauce 73

Italian Herb-Roasted Chicken in Tomato-Basil Sauce 74

Steamed Fish with Yogurt Dill Sauce 74

Beef Kabobs with Peanut Dipping Sauce 74

Turkey Tacos with Avocado-Corn Salsa 75

South Beach Barbecue Sauce 75

Roma Tomatoes Salsa 75

Jalapeno Salsa 75

White Chicken Chili 75

Party Curried Chicken Rice 75

Pasta with Chickpea Sauce 76

Lemon Avocado Salad Dressing 76

Creamy Avocado Cilantro Lime Dressing 76

Creamy Avocado Dressing 76

Southwestern Avocado Salad Dressing 76

Mango Salsa 77

Zoodles with Basil and Avocado Sauce 77

Roasted Tomato Sauce 77

Avocado Mayo 77

Applesauce 77

Beef Roasted in Applesauce 78

Beet and Arugula Salad with Parsley Dressing 78

Short Ribs and Beer Sauce 78

Short Ribs and Special Sauce 78

Beef Patty in Mushroom Sauce 78

Beef Brisket and Onion Sauce 79

Turkey Wraps with Thai Sauce 79

Cod Steaks and Plum Sauce 79

Steamed Salmon and Yogurt Sauce 80

Salmon and Coconut Sauce 80

Salmon and Chives Sauce 80

Lobster Tails with White Wine Sauce 80

Chicken Wings with Alfredo Sauce 81

Zucchini Strips with Marinara Dip 81

Chapter 9: Poultry and Meat Recipes 82

Artichoke and Spinach Chicken Rolls 82

Avocado Turkey Blt 82

BBQ Chicken with Avocado 82

Chicken and Water Chestnut Wraps 82

Cucumber Turkey Rolls 82

Mexican Salsa Chicken 83

Salsa Verde Chicken Bowl 83

Turkey and Spinach Burgers 83

Veg and Chicken Meatballs 83

Apple Braised Pork 84

Beef and mushroom Stroganoff 84

Beef Brisket Roast 84

Creamy Horseradish London Broil 84

Hearty Beef Bordelaise 85

Madeira Pork Tenderloin 85

Pork Medallions with Mushrooms 85

Pork Tenderloin Asian Style 85

Ritzy Beef and Veg Stir-fry 85

Chicken Soup 86

Mexican Chicken Chili 86

Herbed Turkey Purée 86

Greek Yogurt Chicken 87

Herbed Turkey Breast	87
Thai Chili Chicken Wings	87
BBQ Chicken Wings	87
Chicken Jalapeño Poppers	87
Chicken Alfredo	88
Cauliflower Chicken Burgers	88
Crispy Honey Garlic Chicken Wings	88
Garlic Honey Chicken	88
Roasted Duck Breasts with Endives	89
Chicken Sausage with Nestled Eggs	89
Cornmeal Mush with Mushrooms and Chicken Sausage	89
Mozzarella Turkey Rolls	89
Spinach, Zucchini, and Sausage Pasta	89
Thai Chicken Satay	90
Butter and Orange Fried Chicken	90
Lemon-Pepper Chicken Wings	90
Honey and Wine Chicken Breast	90
Chicken Paté	91
Turkey Breasts with Mustard Gravy	91
Dry-Rubbed Chicken Wings	91
Herbed Roast Chicken	91
Za'atar Chicken	91
Spicy Asian Chicken	92
Air Fryer Turkey Bites	92
Cheesy Turkey Calzone	92
Turkey Juniper Paté	92
Korean Chicken Wings	93
Curry Chicken Wings	93
Chapter 10: Vegetarian Recipes	94
Chickpeas Salad	94
Quinoa, Avocado and Mango Salad	94
Sweet Potato and Bell Pepper Soup	94
Pumpkin and Black Beans Soup	95
Lentils and Quinoa Stew	95
Sweet Potato and Kale Stew	95
Barley and Lentil Stew	96
Mushroom and Corn Curry	96
Chickpeas and Pumpkin Curry	96
Beans and Sweet Potato Chili	97
Arugula Lentil Salad	97
Tomato Avocado Toast	97
Classic Tofu Salad	97
Moroccan Couscous Salad	98
Eggplant Curry	98
Baked Zucchini Fries	99
Best Eggplant Parmesan Pizza	99
Tomato, Basil, and Feta Salad	99
Easy Black Bean Chipotle Dip	99
Easy, Classic Roasted Root Vegetables	100
Healthy Cauliflower Rice	100
Roasted Vegetable Quinoa Salad	100
Taco Stuffed Summer Squash Boats	101
The Best Broccoli Cheese Soup	101
Turmeric Red Lentil Soup with Kale	102
Mushroom Barley Risotto	102
Coconut Curry Tofu Bowl	102
Eggplant Rollatini	103
Onion Soup	103
Baked Parmesan Herbs Tomatoes	103
Greek Chickpeas Cucumber Salad	104
Roasted Veggies	104
Cabbage Salad	104
Potato Salad	104
Spaghetti Squash Chow Mein	104
Italian Zucchini Roll-Ups	105
Roasted Vegetable Quinoa Salad with Chickpeas	105
Mexican Stuffed Summer Squash	105
Tomato Bruschetta	106
Roasted Garlic Zucchini and Tomatoes	106
Stuffed Acorn Squash with Cheese	106
Carrot, Zucchini and Leeks Purée	106
Chickpea and Feta Salad	107
Eggplant Pesto Mini Pizza	107
Lentil Vegetarian Loaf	107
Spinach Lasagna	107

Vegetarian Frittata 108
Seitan Buffalo Bites 108
Veggie Sloppy Joes in Lettuce.................... 108
Backed Brussels Sprouts with Parmesan 109

Chapter 11: Seafood Recipes 110
Shrimp, Zucchini and Cherry Tomato Sauce 110
Monkfish with Olives and Capers 110
Baked Garlic Scallops.................................... 110
Ranch Tilapia 110
Easy Crab Sticks 110
Vinegar Spice Prawns 111
Herbed Baked Shrimp.................................. 111
Breaded Coconut Shrimp 111
Lemon Cod Meal... 111
Oregano and Thyme Scallops 112
Crispy Breaded Tilapia 112
Sweet and Sour Glazed Salmon 112
Fried Catfish... 112
Baked Tilapia Cheese 113
Breaded Cod Sticks 113
Honey Glazed Salmon 113
Crumbled Chives Sole 113
Lime Marinated Salmon 113
Cod Fish Nuggets 114
Creamy Yogurt Salmon 114
Baked Onion Cod 114
Mussels with Pepper 114
Cajun Salmon... 115
Lemon Juice Salmon with Quinoa 115
Breaded Flounder 115
Puréed Tuna with Chives 115
Salmon Butter Crumbed............................. 115
Seasoned Fish Fry Shrimp............................ 116
Halibut with Vegetables and Egg................ 116
Air Fried Prawns 116
Salmon with Pistachio Bark 116
Grilled Herbed Sardines 117
Rangoon Crab Dip....................................... 117

Perfect Crab Dip 117
Herb-Crusted Salmon................................... 117
Shrimp Kabobs 117
Crab-Stuffed Mushrooms 118
Yogurt Salmon Paté 118
Pesto-Topped Swordfish............................... 118
Baked Halibut Mediterranean Style............. 118
Cod with Leek, Bell Pepper and Kalamata Olives......... 118
Cucumber Tuna Salad 118
Creamy Salmon Salad 119
Baked Dijon Salmon 119
Broiled Fish Fillet 119
Baked Lemon Tilapia 119
Garlic Shrimp 119
Chili Garlic Salmon 120
Salmon Salad with Marinade 120
Salmon Mini Patties 120
Salmon Lime Cream 120

Chapter 12: Dessert Recipes 122
Brown Sugar.. 122
Powdered Sugar.. 122
Healthy Amazing Dessert 122
Plain Peanut Butter Cookies 122
Protein Rich Dessert 122
Cream Cheese Nibblers................................. 122
Tropical Dream 122
Butterscotch and Pumpkin Pudding 123
Fruit Smoothie Cheesecake 123
Yogurt Parfait 123
Fudge Brownies 123
Strawberry Angel Pie 123
Sugar-Free Graham Cracker Crust 124
Strawberry Cheesecake 124
Blueberry-Peach Crisp.................................. 124
Peanut Butter Oatmeal Protein Balls............ 124
Peanut Butter Protein Balls........................... 124
Vanilla & Peanut Butter Cookies 125
Flourless Chewy Oatmeal Cookies................ 125

Amazing Pecan Pie.. 125

Crestless Pumpkin Pie 125

Chocolate Peanut Brittle 125

Spritz Cookies 126

Rum Balls 126

Almond Flour Cookies 126

Sugar-Free Peanut Brittle 126

Gingerbread Cookies 126

Beatrice's Apricot Cream Cheese Cookies 127

Almond Cookies.. 127

Chocolate Truffles 127

Cinnabliss Lace Cookies 127

Double Chocolate Protein Pudding 128

Cinnamon Bliss Pumpkin Mousse.............................. 128

Ricotta Apple Pancake 128

Cappuccino Custard.. 128

Black Forest Mocha Cake.. 128

Ricotta Swirl... 129

Peanut Butter Pie 129

Vanilla Egg Custard 129

Sweetened Condensed Milk 129

Pecan Pie 129

Cinnamon Caramel Custard..................................... 130

Cheesecake Tarts with Berries 130

Almond Shortbread 130

Old-Fashioned Apple Crisp 130

Lemon-Blackberry Frozen Yogurt 130

Chocolate Brownies with Almond Butter.................... 131

Easy Peanut Butter Cookies.................................... 131

Chocolate Chia Pudding.. 131

Super food Dark Chocolates 131

Caramel Custard 131

Chocolate Cheesecake... 132

Crème Brûlée 132

Pears with Coconut Butter 132

Green Beans with Lemon 132

Peppermint Cheesecake 133

Strawberry Sorbet 133

Pumpkin Balls.. 133

Smooth Peanut Butter Cream................................... 133

Vanilla Avocado Popsicles.. 134

Cocoa Chocolate Chips Cookies 134

Amazing Rice Pudding.. 134

Mini Molten Lava Cakes... 134

Raspberry Compote... 135

Chocolate Popsicle.. 135

Raspberry Ice Cream... 135

Chocolate Frosty... 135

Wrapped Pears with Vanilla Bean Sauce 135

Chocolate Almond Butter Brownie 136

Peanut Butter Fudge.. 136

Banana Chocolate Cake 136

Blueberry Muffins... 136

Chia Pudding 136

Lean Green Smoothie 137

Light Ice Cream Sandwich Cake 137

Carrot Gelatin Salad.. 137

Vegan Chocolate Almond Milk Ice Cream Fudgsicle Style
.... 137

Avocado Pudding 137

Strawberry Granita 137

Peanut Butter Coconut Popsicle 138

Brownie Bites.. 138

Peanut Butter Brownie Ice Cream Sandwiches 138

Homemade Bounty Bars 138

Tiramisu Protein Pancakes.. 139

Mixed Berry Popsicles.. 139

Choco Frosty 139

Cheesecake Fat Bombs 139

Matcha Ice Cream 140

Moist Avocado Brownies 140

Mix Berry Sorbet 140

Chia Almond Pudding... 140

Chia Raspberry Pudding... 140

Pear-Cranberry Pie with Oatmeal Streusel 140

Blueberry Frozen Yogurt No Bake Cake 141

Chocolate Almond Ginger Mousse 141

Apple Crisp 141

Red Energy Wonders 141

Chocolate Protein Pudding Pops 141

Lemon Mousse.. 142

Watermelon-Basil Granita 142

Conclusion 143

Introduction

The sleeve has superseded the gastric bypass and adjustable gastric band as the most popular kind of bariatric surgery by a wide margin. In the last five years, the number of people who have had a sleeve gastrectomy in the United States has grown.

When all other methods have failed, bariatric surgery is the most effective method for achieving and maintaining significant weight loss. Persons who have been obese for a long time, people who have uncontrolled obesity-related health problems that limit their ability to enjoy life fully, and people who need to lose a significant amount of weight in a reasonable amount of time may benefit from bariatric surgery.

After a sleeve gastrectomy or other type of bariatric surgery, this device could be life-changing. Following specific dietary instructions for the rest of one's life is essential for post-operative success. These techniques can assist you in achieving physical and mental goals, as well as making you healthier rather than just leaner. When you search for "bariatric surgery diet" on Google, you'll get about 350,000 results. It's understandable that many people are puzzled about what to eat after weight-loss surgery, given the abundance of information accessible.

This cookbook also includes food suggestions for the first few weeks following surgery. If you've had the VSG, this cookbook will ensure that you never have to worry about what to eat or when to eat it. This book provide more than just a compilation of recipes. From day one to 10,001, it's a step-by-step guide to eating following surgery. We understand that eating requires much more than simply consuming food to keep our bodies alive. Eating is frequently emotional, and this book covers both the mental and nutritional aspects of eating to help people achieve short- and long-term success.

Finally, we'd want to send our sincere congratulations. You've finished the job! You've made the decision to abandon the latest fad diet, the latest eating craze, and the current weight-loss craze in favor of a healthy lifestyle for good. You've taken the decision to lose weight seriously and sought help.

You know you can accomplish it, but you also realize that you'll need to employ the best tool in the toolbox to create your new life. You've had it with yo-yo dieting and are ready to finally lose weight. The most important aspect is that you are deserving of it. Even the most fundamental things in your life ought to make you feel more energized, lighter, and at ease. Above all, you must improve your health. You deserve to benefit from the advantages of a healthy body and mind, whether it's easier breathing, avoiding certain medications, or better test results from your doctor's office. Let's get this party started!

Chapter 1: Basics of Sleeve Gastrectomy

1.1 Gastric Sleeve and Gastric Bypass

By forming a narrow gastric pouch from the upper portion of the stomach, the gastric bypass laparoscopic technique limits food consumption and shortens the digestive track. The intestine is surgically bound to this pocket, allowing food to flow into a small opening. The remainder of the stomach, as well as a part of the intestines, are bypassed. Gastric bypass surgery decreases the number of calories and nutrients absorbed from food by limiting the amount of food consumed.

A sleeve gastrectomy involves developing a sleeve-shaped tube from a small part of the stomach and removing the rest of the stomach. Food enters the intestines directly through the new stomach tube. Nutrients and calories are absorbed naturally from food, but patients feel full faster and for longer. Sleeve gastrectomy is a laparoscopic procedure that may be used to permanently manage weight.

These two procedures are very similar; although the methods differ, it's all about reducing the size of the stomach and decreasing the amount of food a person can consume. They're both effective tools to lose weight in the long-term and improve obesity-related conditions such as diabetes, high cholesterol, high blood pressure, etc.

The gastric sleeve is a less complicated surgery, taking between 40 and 70 minutes to complete, whereas bypass surgery can take up to three hours.

Furthermore, gastric bypass patients may experience short-term complications such as bowel obstruction, ulcers, and internal hernias. The chance of sleeve patients developing any of these is close to zero.

If dietary constraints are the deciding factor for you, the changes you'll have to make will be the same for bypass and sleeve surgery. The main difference will be how much you can eat. If you opt for the gastric sleeve surgery, your stomach pouch will be able to hold up to three ounces. On the other hand, the gastric bypass will leave you with a stomach the size of a golf ball, which equates to 1 ounce.

Any decision of what bariatric surgery method to select should be made alongside your doctor. They will consider things like your age, overall health, weight, and expectations when making a decision. For example, gastric bypass surgery will usually be selected for patients with a Body Mass Index over 45, and not VSG.

1.2 Benefits of Gastric Sleeve Bariatric Surgery

The following are some of the reasons why individuals opt to get their arms sleeved.

Time spent in the operation room is reduced:

Any procedure carried out under general anesthesia has risks and the possibility of complications. These dangers may increase as the number of possible problems rises. These dangers may grow in proportion to the length of time it takes to perform the procedure. Although the VSG is more time-consuming than the adjustable band, it is less time-consuming and complicated than the gastric bypass and the BPD/DS.

Hunger pains are less frequent:

The hunger hormone ghrelin is reduced when the bulk of the stomach is removed. Feeling less hungry encourages you to eat less.

Portion control built-in:

Because just 15 to 25% of your stomach is left following surgery, the quantity of food you can consume at any one moment is restricted. Post-op, you can still consume various meals with a gradual change in texture consistency, but your stomach will send strong signals to tell you when you're full, causing you to quit eating

1.3 Risks With Sleeve Gastrectomy

Some bariatric surgery risks are:

- Anesthesia-related risks

- Chronic nausea

- Infection

- vomiting

- Acid reflux

- Dilation of esophagus

- Inability to consume certain foods.

- Failure to lose weight or weight gain.

- Blockage in stomach

Bariatric Surgery Long-Term Risks

Patients who undergo bariatric surgery face certain long-term complications., including:

- Low blood sugar

- Vomiting

- Malnutrition

- Ulcers

- Nausea and dizziness

- Hernias

- Bowel obstruction

How to reduce the risks associated with bariatric surgery?

Although all surgical procedures involve some risk, there are steps you should take to reduce the risk of adverse side effects from bariatric surgery. You will, for example, lower your body mass index (BMI), boost your workout, and stop smoking. To determine what is best for you, speak with your doctor regarding your options

Chapter 2: Steps and Strategies

2.1 Before the Surgery

This is a life-altering procedure. It can assist you with losing weight by altering you're eating habits before and after the treatment. You must pay close attention to your weight in the weeks leading up to the surgery. It's important not to gain weight because it would render the procedure's technical aspects even more complicated. You have to follow a strict liquid protein diet for two weeks before surgery. This lowers the odds of developing a fatty liver, which may render the treatment riskier. A fatty liver is caused by fat accumulation throughout the spleen and liver. Two weeks before the operation, you must adhere to a pre-operative liquid diet. The diet includes the following items:

- Meal replacement shakes, and protein shakes.

- Juice made from vegetables.

- Sugar-free beverages (You can use sugar substitutes)

- Soups and broths of no solid particles

- Extremely thin cream of rice or cream of wheat can be consumed.

- Drinks should be sipped steadily. Never take them with meals; instead, consume them 30 minutes after you've eaten a meal.

If you want to consume solids, you can have up to two portions of vegetables and lean meat, but your doctor must first know about it to give his or her approval. During this period, you can consume a variety of food substitutes, and protein shakes. It is safer to inquire about the products that your doctor suggests. To make a protein shake, combine 1 scoop of protein powder with 1 cup of skim milk or water in a blender. It's ready to drink after 60 seconds of processing. However, if you gain a considerable amount of weight over this period, the doctor will have to reconsider your candidacy for the operation. There is a decent possibility that the operation will be canceled and rescheduled. You can only have protein shakes the day before the treatment. After 5 p.m., stick to plain drinks like water, Jell-O, soup, ginger ale, and tea. Do not eat or drink food after midnight so that the stomach is empty for the operation. You must drop 10 to 15 pounds before the surgery. You must lose 10% of your body weight if your BMI is greater than 55. Before beginning the operation, make the following preparations:

- Be prepared for a significant improvement in nutrition after the treatment. Slowly eat. Limit yourself to three meals and one to two snacks a day. Make a habit of chewing the food thoroughly.

- Ask others to assist you with food preparation and vitamin supplementation during the first few weeks following surgery.

- Learn the types of workouts you may do during the operation. Select the forms that you would be able to adhere to and enjoy.

- Remain in constant contact with a licensed dietitian. Check with him to see if you can consume the food, you like or crave.

- Purchase the equipment you'll need to cook food and concoctions quickly following surgery.

- Do a thorough cleaning of your kitchen. Remove the foods that you won't be able to consume after the surgery and substitute them with the diet's prescribed foods. Purchase the following items prior to surgery:

- Meal replacement and protein shake that your doctor has approved.

- Vitamins and minerals recommended by the health team that is handling the

- Procedure

- Sugar-free flavors and sugar substitute

- Canned broth

- Jell-O, yogurt, popsicles, and pudding with no sugar added.

- Soups with a smooth texture

- Freezer bags, small food containers, kitchen utensils

- Food processor or blender

2.2 After the Surgery

The treatment will reduce the size of your stomach by up to 70%. This is a good way to lose weight because it suppresses your appetite and makes you feel satisfied even after limited meals. Since the surgery, you may not lose weight immediately. You could improve your eating habits and what you consume on a long-term basis. When it comes to your diet, you'll go through stages to make yourself recover. You will limit what you consume and how much you eat first, thus ensuring that you get enough vitamins and nutrients. Once your body has recovered, you may need to eat a more limited yet nutritionally healthy diet. To avoid complications after surgery, adhere to the following guidelines:

•   Take your time chewing your food. To be safe, chew your food until it has the same consistency as a liquid. If you do not do this, you will feel nauseated or vomit due to the blockages caused by food that was not thoroughly chewed.

•   Eat and drink in a very slow manner. The ideal time that you must allot for each meal is 30 minutes. You might vomit or get nauseated when you eat or drink too quickly.

•   Drink 30 to 60 minutes before and after meals. You cannot drink with your meals. Your stomach will become overloaded, which may lead to expansion and split.

•   Do not eat or drink more than what your doctor recommends. While you are still in the healing process, you have to avoid gaining weight. This can cause a rupture in the stomach, which will jeopardize your surgery.

•   Avoid food that has high sugar content and the kinds with too many calories but minimal nutrients. They can affect the number of nutrients you are getting, making it harder for you to lose weight.

•   Drink lots of fluids in a slow manner. Avoid dehydration at all costs. You need to consume 3 to 4 ounces of water in between meals. You can also take low-calorie beverages suitable for the diet. Once you become dehydrated due to the insufficient fluids that your body is getting, you will likely suffer from diarrhea and vomiting.

•   Take the recommended minerals, vitamins, and liquid supplements. Follow the kind of diet that is suitable for your recovery stage. The kinds of diet plans depend on your recovery stage.

•   Eat what your doctor tells you to eat after your surgery, which will consist of a lot of liquid. If you eat regular food too early or eat sugary or fat food, you may damage your stomach or harm yourself.

•   Depending on which kind of surgery you have and what type of work you do, you could be back to work as soon as two weeks after surgery if you do not lift anything heavy.

•   Wait about four weeks before you exercise or lift weights to decrease the chance that you will get a hernia in the wound.

•   Let your doctor check on your progress at the scheduled times. He'll see whether or not you are on schedule in your weight loss goals.

•   You should try out new recipes so that you can stay on your diet plan. It will not bore you with your food to turn you back to your old eating habits

2.3 The Five Stages of Eating After Bariatric Surgery

You should follow the surgical team's advice to the core as they know you, the treatment you've had, and the medical history. They do, however, suggest that you should consume in five stages:

•   Stage 1: Clear Liquids

•   Stage 2: Full Liquids

•   Stage 3: Pureed Foods

•   Stage 4: Soft Foods

•   Stage 5: Eating Well for Life

Food Cravings

In the days after surgery, you might notice that you've lost your cravings, meals don't excite you, and that the thought of trying new foods makes you feel nauseous. This is entirely normal; the body undergoes rapid hormonal and physical changes after surgery, and it can take some time before you revert to your former self and become interested in the foods you used to eat. However, this may be a positive thing since it allows you to wean yourself off unhealthy food options and train the body to crave nutritious meals, which can help you lose weight.

Maintain a strict diet regimen; food can be seen as nothing more than nourishment for the body. You will drop weight quicker than you think if you put a little effort and thought into what you put in your stomach, avoid high-calorie snacks, and adjust pre-existing meals to include nutritious ingredients. Consider your long-term progress.

2.4 Nutritional Concern

A big part of maintaining the healthy lifestyle changes you will see after your surgery in the long-term is ensuring that when you do eat, you eat the right things. This material does not replace what a trained health professional can offer but provides a general overview of what is generally prescribed and perhaps give you a little more insight into what the professionals are talking about.

Before we get into definitions and listings of nutrient-rich foods, let's review the guidelines for eating following surgery.

•   Consume three light meals a day as well as 1-2 snacks if you feel the need. This should include breakfast. This will total to eating a maximum of 5 times during the day.

•   Take the time to eat your food slowly. You have a new smaller stomach, so you need to be careful.

•   You need to limit your food consumption to 250 ml or 1 cup (approximately) of food for each meal.

•   Choose mostly solid foods with high nutritional value during these meals.

•   Foods that are tricky to chew, for example, foods that are tough, stringy, doughy, or very sticky, should be avoided as these can create discomfort and even vomiting. This is due to the obstruction in the pouch stoma (stomach opening).

•   Fluids should only be consumed more than thirty min before and thirty min after eating solid foods.

•   All liquids and liquid foods (i.e., soups) can be enjoyed between the consumption of solid food.

•   Soda pops or any carbonated drink should not be consumed. This is a waste of calories that provides no nutritional value to your body.

•   Do not consume foods or drinks with a high sugar content to assist in the prevention of dumping syndrome. This syndrome is a group of symptoms which can occur in some patients after the surgery when they eat. Discomfort in the abdominal area, weakness, and occasionally very rapid emptying of the bowels.

- Remember to take any prescribed vitamins and supplements. Generally, this will include one multi-vitamin, a mineral supplement, and perhaps some extra calcium and vitamin d if necessary.

- Consume approximately 60-80g of protein daily. If you are struggling to reach this amount of protein per day, you should have a low sugar protein shake daily to reach the required protein amount.

Remember that you have worked extremely hard to arrive at this place in your life. It is best to consider the above recommendations as a lifelong pattern and not a temporary measure. Patterns of behavior are created through repetition, and in the beginning, you will need to focus on the pattern created to avoid any negative behaviors creeping in.

The following lists are behaviors that can cause gradual weight gain and behaviors you must avoid. They may start as small as one or two-time indulgences that can increase in frequency through the months ahead. Stay vigilant about your goals for a healthy life.

Weight gain happens when:

- You start to choose foods which are dense in calories and not in nutrition.

- You increase how often you eat in a day. Eating more than five times a day is too many.

- You begin to 'nibble' between meals.

- You start to consume foods high in fat

- You start to consume foods high in sugar

- You start consuming drinks with more calories than what should be in your overall calorie goal for the day.

- Drinking soda pop or other high sugar carbonated drinks.

- You begin to ignore the thirty-minute rule about drinking pre and post meals.

- You are constantly over-consuming in one sitting and stretching your stomach.

Avoid these behavioral patterns at all costs. If you can feel yourself slipping into bad habits, you need to improve your mindset and re-align yourself with the desired end goal and why you want to achieve this goal. The notion of 'just this once' must be deferred indefinitely when it comes to eating and drinking.

Now let's look at what to eat.

Nutrient dense foods can be defined as food that is relatively low in calories and high in nutrition. When we consider what a nutrient is, these are foods that contain high amounts of vitamins and mineral. They are rich in complex carbohydrates, contain lean proteins, and only the healthy type of fats.

Some foods can amp up your nutrient consumption without increasing your overall caloric intake. These foods, such as fruits and vegetables, are the direct opposite of what is known as 'calorie-dense' foods.

Nutrient density can be used to distinguish different kinds of foods from each other, oatmeal versus frosted flakes, for example. It can also be identified as the nutrition arising from the quality of the soil it is grown in – the levels of mineral and nutrition in the soil itself. This is a complex relationship involving many dimensions to the creation of the food itself and rarely noted on any sort of food packaging. Foods grown in an organic or sustainable culture are denser in nutrition than other products.

2.5 Exercise Guidelines for Each Stage of Weight-loss Surgery

Your doctor may provide you with an exercise plan, or you may choose to consult with a personal trainer who has experience with patients with gastric sleeve surgery. Generally speaking, you can expect to begin with a moderate expectation, say ten min daily, increasing gradually over time. Once you feel confident that you are ready, you can look at several options available to you for increasing your strength, range of motion, and aerobic capability.

While you will certainly start to see results from simply not feeling as hungry in general and eating less overall, exercise will still play a crucial part in getting you to where you need to be. After all, diet can only take you so far when it comes to reaching your desired mi, weight, or body fat percentage. Exercise will also help to accelerate many of the other benefits associated with the surgery, including improving your cardiovascular health and reducing your blood pressure.

Getting started: first things first, it is important to never jump into any type of exercise immediately after your surgery has been performed. The simple fact is that healing takes time, and if you push too hard too fast, you will only end up doing more harm than good. Likewise, you will want to take great care to avoid adding any new exercise to your plan without consulting your doctor first.

Within the first month after having the surgery, it is common for many people to feel quite uncomfortable. During this time many surgeons recommend a simple walking program where patients are recommended to walk for 5 - 10 min, three times per day.

Other types of exercise should be avoided during this time with resistance training exercises being especially constrained.

2-3 months

The amount of exercise that can be undertaken during this period is often going to depend on your overall fitness before the surgery. Regardless, it is likely that sometime before 90 days you will be cleared for slightly more strenuous activities, with water-based exercises proving quite popular on average. Many people find this a great choice as it puts limited stress on the joins and many movements are easier to perform in the water. All activity level during this period should never become so intense that a conversation cannot be easily maintained at the same time.

By this point, you will be able to engage in a wide variety of normal activities which means that, with your doctor's permission, you can start working more on building your core strength and overall wellness.

Finally, it is also important to be cautious when it comes to activities that require significant coordination and balance because the surgery has likely led to a change in your center of balance which can make these exercises more difficult or potentially dangerous than they otherwise would be.

2.6 How to live better

When everything is new and strange, but also along your entire adventure, it can be helpful to use simple tools that support you in following the new rules that are unfamiliar and not yet part of your habits. Here are some simple kitchen tools that can make a difference in your task and help maximize your efforts.

• When you can, use a muffin tin: it will be useful to control portions and quantities (and avoid temptations!), but also to cook small meals or snacks that can be stored and consumed in the following days saving time. Adapt the ingredients to the muffin quantities and you can enjoy a great meal in small, moderate portions.

• At first, you can try eating with chopsticks: you'll be able to take smaller, more easily chewable bites and you'll slow down the pace of the meal by taking your time to eat. If you are very scrupulous you can also equip yourself with a timer to precisely calculate the time of each meal and adjust the speed at which you eat.

• In meal preparation a digital scale can be very useful to help you keep track of ingredient quantities and food portions.

• A smart trick is to use a spray oiler to grease pans when cooking but also to flavor dishes using the correct amount without the risk of overdoing it.

• You must pay attention to chewing, and therefore meals must be consumed taking the necessary time: it might be a good idea to use a cup warmer or a small food warmer that allows you to keep food or beverages warm without making you hurry up while eating.

- A tool that is as useful as fun is the spiralizer. With it you can create fantastic spaghetti and noodles with lots of vegetables and, in addition to eating a healthy and tasty meal, you can indulge your creativity in developing new dishes and recipes that are always different.

- If you're more tech-savvy types, and the stage of your diet (but more importantly your doctor) allows it, a great appliance is the air fryer. If you don't want to give up the pleasure of certain foods, for example the crispiness of fried food, the air fryer can make this meal much lighter than the traditional way of cooking it.

- Another great idea to keep food quantities under control is the use of plates with the portions printed directly on the ceramic, or plates divided into compartments that help to dose the right amount for each food. For the same purpose, it also works to use children's smaller plates to keep portion sizes down while still satisfying the eyes. Using children's cutlery can also help control the volume of your bites and consequently slow down the pace at which you consume your meal.

- Let's finish with one last clever trick that doesn't directly relate to cooking but to a consequential task that can be tedious and burdensome: cleaning and tidying up after cooking! It's a shortcut that's also used in professional restaurant kitchens, and can help boost your desire to get to the stove if tidying up is your concern. When you cook, get in the habit of lining your pots, your slow cookers, and your oven pans with aluminum foil (or baking paper, depending on the recipe you're cooking and the utensil you're using). You'll see that cleanup will simply result in replacing and tossing these liners.

2.7 Foods to avoid after surgery

Before you can start eating a healthy diet, you will need to know what is considered beneficial in the first place. It's possible to eat healthy foods and still gain weight if you eat way too much of them. Let's take a look at some of the things you should eat and the best left off your plate.

What to Eat for Weight Loss Before weight loss surgery; you may be able to take a pill that reduces your appetite and make you more likely to eat less. There are some types of bariatric surgery that do this, such as gastric banding. However, the type of bariatric surgery that lessens the calories in your diet is a gastric sleeve. This is because you will have a smaller stomach and will be able to eat fewer calories than before the surgery. In addition, you'll be able to adjust your diet and exercise habits to lose weight and keep it off. When you are making plans to lose weight, it is a good idea for you to talk with your doctor about improving your diet as much as possible. Whether you have surgery or not, eating less than 2,000 calories per is recommended for you. It is even better to eat a little less at first until you get used to your new lifestyle. Try cutting down on foods like:

- White bread

- Coke or soda

- Pasta

Markets such as Aldi's, Lidl, Sainsbury's, and Waitrose all feature a reduced-calorie version of chicken breast, salmon, potatoes, and fresh fruit. While you can find healthier versions of these products elsewhere (and are generally cheaper), you may not have the time to see them in a supermarket. In addition, these stores have weekly special offers and sales that can save you money on your regular healthy food shopping. What About the Food in Your Fridge? If your fridge is a treasure trove of fatty things that you crave every time you walk past it, then you will need to plan. It may be a good idea to give away what you will not be able to eat in the future, such as chips, cakes or cans of fizzy drink.Once You Are Ready to Begin Eating Healthy Before weight loss surgery, you will need to learn what foods are healthy for you & how much you should consume each . It is advised that you eat at least five portions of fruits and vegetables a , and a bit refers to the amount that fills your hand or a wine glass. Depending on your weight loss surgery, you may need to eat even more. After gastric bypass, you should be eating 60% of your daily calories in carbohydrates, 30% in protein, and 10% in fat. However, it's still recommended that you avoid fatty foods as much as possible. If you have a gastric sleeve, then 55% of your calories will be from carbohydrates, 35% from protein, and 10 % from fat.

Chapter 3: Meal Plan

You'll be weary after surgery from the abrupt changes your body is going through, and meal preparation will be just one more thing on your mind. Knowing what you'll eat ahead of time makes grocery shopping easier and reduces the stress of arriving home late from work with nothing to eat.

Some patients do not prepare meals before to surgery due to a lack of time or because it is not a priority. Some people skip meal preparation following surgery because they aren't hungry or don't want to eat.

It's critical to stick to a regular schedule to ensure that you get enough fluids, vitamins, and protein and don't skip meals and have to make up for it later. Between meals, take a four- to six-hour pause and snack on a glass of High Protein Milk or a protein shake. According to a crucial preparation advice, cook once and eat at least twice. The bulk of the recipes in this book serve enough food for the entire family, with leftovers for lunch the next day. Some recipes can be frozen in little amounts for later use.

The eight-week meal plans below can be used as a guide to make post-surgery food preparation easier. Feel free to change up your meal alternatives depending on your particular preferences and time constraints. Always follow the post-operative instructions provided by the operation center. These meal plans are meant to be used as a guide, and you need make sure you receive enough protein because the specific portions you eat will vary.

Week 1
Day 1:

- Breakfast: Commercial Protein Shake with at least 20 g protein

- Lunch: Guava Smoothie

- Dinner: Double Fudge Chocolate shake

Day 2:

- Breakfast: Protein-Packed Peanut butter shake

- Lunch: Commercial Protein Shake with atleast20 g protein

- Dinner: Double Fudge Chocolate shake

Day 3:

- Breakfast: High Protein Fruit Smoothie

- Lunch: Vanilla Bean Probiotic Shake

- Dinner: Commercial Protein Shake with atleast20 g protein

Day 4:

- Breakfast: Commercial Protein Shake with atleast20 g protein

- Lunch: Double Fudge Chocolate shake

- Dinner: Vanilla Bean Probiotic Shake

Day 5:

- Breakfast: Vanilla Bean Probiotic Shake

- Lunch: Commercial Protein Shake with atleast20 g protein

- Dinner: Protein-Packed Peanut butter shake

Day 6:

- Breakfast: High Protein Fruit Smoothie

- Lunch: Double Fudge Chocolate shake

- Dinner: Commercial Protein Shake with atleast20 g protein

Day 7:

- Breakfast: Commercial Protein Shake with atleast20 g protein

- Lunch: Vanilla Bean Probiotic Shake

- Dinner: Double Fudge Chocolate shake

Suggested Snack

Water / Calorie-free beverages

Week 2
Day 1:

- Breakfast: Double Fudge Chocolate shake

- Lunch: High Protein Fruit Smoothie

- Dinner: Commercial Protein Shake with at least 20 g protein

Day 2:

- Breakfast: Strawberry-Banana Protein Smoothie

- Lunch: Chunky Monkey Smoothie

- Dinner: Vanilla Apple pie protein shake

Day 3:

- Breakfast: Vanilla Apple pie protein shake

- Lunch: Commercial Protein Shake with atleast20 g protein

- Dinner: Guava Smoothie

Day 4:

- Breakfast: Commercial Protein Shake with atleast20 g protein

- Lunch: Berry Protein Shake

- Dinner: Double Fudge Chocolate shake

Day 5:

- Breakfast: Double Fudge Chocolate shake

- Lunch: Berry Protein Shake

- Dinner: Commercial Protein Shake with atleast20 g protein

Day 6:

- Breakfast: Pumpkin Pie Bliss Protein Shake

- Lunch: Fresh Mango Smoothie

- Dinner: Vanilla Bean Probiotic Shake

Day 7:

- Breakfast: Pumpkin Pie Bliss Protein Shake

- Lunch: Vanilla Bean Probiotic Shake

- Dinner: Fresh Mango Smoothie

Suggested Snack

Water / Calorie-free beverages

High Protein Milk

Week 3
Day 1: *Tuesday*

- Breakfast: Scrambled Eggs

- Lunch: Tuna salad

- Dinner: Noodle less lasagna with Ricotta cheese

Day 2:

- Breakfast: Cinnamon Oatmeal

- Lunch: Black Beans Salad

- Dinner: Slow cooker Barbecue Shredded Chicken and mashed Cauliflower

Day 3:

- Breakfast: Greek Yogurt

- Lunch: Tuna Salad

- Dinner: Chicken Salad

Day 4:

- Breakfast: Scrambled Eggs

- Lunch: Shrimp Cocktail Salad

- Dinner: Slow cooker Barbecue Shredded Chicken and mashed Cauliflower

Day 5:

- Breakfast: Cinnamon Oatmeal

- Lunch: Tuna Salad

- Dinner: Noodle less lasagna with Ricotta cheese

Day 6:

- Breakfast: Greek Yogurt

- Lunch: Chicken Salad

- Dinner: Shrimp Cocktail Salad

Day 7:

- Breakfast: Scrambled Eggs

- Lunch: Black Beans Salad

- Dinner: Slow cooker Barbecue Shredded Chicken and mashed Cauliflower

Suggested Snack

High Protein Milk

Protein Shake

Week 4
Day 1:

- Breakfast: Wisconsin Scrambler with Aged Cheddar Cheese

- Lunch: Tuna salad

- Dinner: Herb Crusted Salmon

Day 2:

- Breakfast: Greek Yogurt

- Lunch: Herb Crusted Salmon

- Dinner: Whole Herbed Roasted Chicken in the slow cooker

Day 3:

- Breakfast: Wisconsin Scrambler with Aged Cheddar Cheese

- Lunch: Chicken and Lotus Root Soup
- Dinner: Creamy Chicken Soup with Cauliflower

Day 4:
- Breakfast: Cinnamon Oatmeal
- Lunch: Creamy Chicken Soup with Cauliflower
- Dinner: Leftovers

Day 5:
- Breakfast: Greek Yogurt
- Lunch: Cottage Cheese with peaches (without skin)
- Dinner: Tuna Noodle less Casserole

Day 6:
- Breakfast: Wisconsin Scrambler with Aged Cheddar Cheese
- Lunch: Tuna Noodle less Casserole
- Dinner: Chicken and Lotus Root Soup

Day 7:
- Breakfast: Cinnamon Oatmeal
- Lunch: Slow cooker Turkey Chili
- Dinner: Lemon-Parsley Crab Cakes

Suggested Snack

High Protein Milk

Protein Shake

Week 5
Day 1:
- Breakfast: High Protein Pancakes
- Lunch: Lemon-Parsley Crab Cakes
- Dinner: Curried Zucchini Soup

Day 2:
- Breakfast: Souffle Omelet with Mushrooms
- Lunch: Eggplant Rollatini
- Dinner: Baked fried Chicken Thighs and Roasted Root vegetables

Day 3:
- Breakfast: High- Protein Pancake
- Lunch: Chicken and Lotus Root Soup
- Dinner: Roasted Vegetables Quinoa Salad with Chickpeas

Day 4:
- Breakfast: Souffle Omelet with Mushrooms
- Lunch: Roasted Vegetables Quinoa Salad with Chickpeas
- Dinner: Chicken, vegetable, and barley soup

Day 5:
- Breakfast: High- Protein Pancake
- Lunch: Curried Zucchini Soup
- Dinner: Mexican Taco Skillet with red peppers and Zucchini

Day 6:
- Breakfast: Greek Yogurt
- Lunch: Mexican Taco Skillet with red peppers and Zucchini
- Dinner: Leftovers

Day 7:
- Breakfast: Souffle Omelet with Mushrooms
- Lunch: Cottage Cheese with fruit
- Dinner: Zoodles with Turkey Meatballs

Suggested Snack

High Protein Milk

Protein Shake

Week 6
Day 1:
- Breakfast: Scrambled eggs
- Lunch: Zoodles with Turkey Meatballs
- Dinner: Seafood Cioppino

Day 2:
- Breakfast: Cherry Vanilla baked Oatmeal
- Lunch: Seafood Cioppino
- Dinner: Italian Eggplant Pizzas

Day 3:
- Breakfast: Greek Yogurt
- Lunch: Italian Eggplant Pizzas
- Dinner: Baked fish with pea puree

Day 4:
- Breakfast: Cherry Vanilla baked Oatmeal

- Lunch: Red Snapper Veracruz
- Dinner: Leftovers

Day 5:
- Breakfast: Scrambled eggs
- Lunch: Cottage cheese with fruits
- Dinner: Slow Cooker White Chicken chili

Day 6:
- Breakfast: Greek Yogurt
- Lunch: Slow Cooker White Chicken chili
- Dinner: Fried-less Fish fry with Cod and baked Zucchini Fries

Day 7:
- Breakfast: Cherry Vanilla baked Oatmeal
- Lunch: Fried-less Fish fry with Cod and baked Zucchini Fries
- Dinner: Mediterranean turkey Meatballs

Suggested Snack

1 cup Milk

High Protein Milk

Protein Shake

Week 7
Day 1:
- Breakfast: Berry Wrap
- Lunch: Mediterranean turkey Meatballs
- Dinner: Baked Halibut with tomatoes

Day 2:
- Breakfast: Greek Yogurt
- Lunch: Baked Halibut with tomatoes
- Dinner: Coconut Curry Tofu Bowl

Day 3:
- Breakfast: Scrambled eggs
- Lunch: Coconut Curry Tofu Bowl
- Dinner: Baked fish with pea puree

Day 4:
- Breakfast: Andre's Hangry Eggs with Cauliflower
- Lunch: Mexican Stuffed Summer Squash

- Dinner: Leftovers

Day 5:
- Breakfast: Smoothie Bowl with Greek Yogurt and fresh berries
- Lunch: Cottage cheese with fruits
- Dinner: Chicken Cordon Bleu

Day 6:
- Breakfast: Andre's Hangry Eggs with Cauliflower
- Lunch: Chicken Cordon Bleu
- Dinner: Chicken nachos with sweet bell peppers

Day 7:
- Breakfast: Smoothie Bowl with Greek Yogurt and fresh berries
- Lunch: Chicken nachos with sweet bell peppers
- Dinner: Tuna Salad

Suggested Snack

1 cup Milk (High Protein Milk)

Week 8
Day 1:
- Breakfast: Boiled eggs and Avocado on Toast
- Lunch: Tuna Salad
- Dinner: Slow roasted Pesto Salmon

Day 2:
- Breakfast: Cinnamon Oatmeal
- Lunch: Slow roasted Pesto Salmon
- Dinner: Leftovers

Day 3:
- Breakfast: Boiled eggs and Avocado on Toast
- Lunch: Cottage Cheese with fruits
- Dinner: Baked fish with pea puree

Day 4:
- Breakfast: Cinnamon Oatmeal
- Lunch: Ranch Seasoned Crispy Chicken tenders Cheesy Cauliflower Casserole
- Dinner: Butternut Squash and black bean Enchiladas

Day 5:
- Breakfast: High protein Pancakes

- Lunch: Butternut Squash and black bean Enchiladas
- Dinner: Buffalo Chicken Wrap

Day 6:

- Breakfast: Greek Yogurt
- Lunch: Buffalo Chicken Wrap
- Dinner: Cauliflower Pizza and caramelized onions and chicken sausage

Day 7:

- Breakfast High protein Pancakes
- Lunch: Cauliflower Pizza and caramelized onions and chicken sausage
- Dinner: Tuna Salad

Suggested Snack

1 cup Milk (High Protein Milk)

Chapter 4: Liquid Recipes

Strawberry-Banana Protein Smoothie

PREP TIME: 5 min / **COOK TIME:** none / **YIELD:** 2 Serves

INGREDIENTS:

- 5 ice cubes
- 1 cup of low-fat milk
- ½ cup frozen strawberries
- ⅓ ripe banana
- 1 scoop (¼ cup) vanilla or unflavored protein powder

DIRECTIONS:

- Pulse the protein powder, milk, frozen strawberries, banana, and ice cubes in a high-powered blender for 3 to 4 minutes, or until the contents are thoroughly mixed and no more visible.
- Half of the shake should be poured into a glass and enjoyed. Any smoothie that you don't consume or use right away may be stored in an airtight container for up to a week. Before serving, re-blend.

NUTRITION:

131 Cal; 16g Protein; 1g Tot Fat; 14g Carb; 2g Fiber; 11g Sugar; 154mg Sodium

Chunky Monkey Smoothie

PREP TIME: 5 min / **COOK TIME:** none / **YIELD:** 2 Serves

INGREDIENTS:

- 2 tbsp. powdered peanut butter
- 1 cup unsweetened almond milk
- 1 scoop (¼ cup) chocolate protein powder
- ½ cup of low-fat plain Greek yogurt
- 1 cup ice cubes
- 1 small banana, frozen

DIRECTIONS:

- Beat the powdered peanut butter, milk, banana, protein powder, yoghurt, and ice cubes together in a blender. Blend on high for 2.5 minutes, or until the shake is completely smooth and free of lumps.

cup mixed frozen berries

- 1 cup of low-fat milk or unsweetened soy milk

DIRECTIONS:

- Mix the protein powder, berries, milk, and ice cubes in a mixer. Blend for 2.5 minutes on high speed, or until the powder is completely dissolved and no longer evident.
- Half of the shake should be poured into a glass and enjoyed. Any smoothie that you don't consume or use right away may be stored in the refrigerator for up to a week. Before serving, re-blend.

NUTRITION:

126 Cal; 15g Protein; 1g Tot Fat; 14g Carb; 3g Fiber; 10g Sugar; 153mg Sodium

Tropical Mango Smoothie

PREP TIME: 5 min / **COOK TIME:** none / **YIELD:** 2 Serves

INGREDIENTS:

- Half of the shake should be poured into a glass and enjoyed. Any smoothie that you don't consume or use right away may be stored in an airtight container for up to one week. Before serving, re-blend.

NUTRITION:

194 Cal; 20g Protein; 4g Tot Fat; 23g Carb; 4g Fiber; 11g Sugar; 245mg Sodium

Spinach Super food Smoothie

PREP TIME: 5 min / **COOK TIME:** none / **YIELD:** 2 Serves

INGREDIENTS:

- 1 scoop (¼ cup) unflavored or vanilla protein powder
- 1 kiwi fruit, peeled and cut into chunks
- 1 cup unsweetened almond milk or low-fat milk 1 tbsp. ground flaxseed
- ½ small banana
- 1 tsp. chia seeds
- ½ medium cucumber, peeled
- 1 cup fresh spinach

DIRECTIONS:

- Add the chia seeds, kiwi, spinach, banana, cucumber, flaxseed, milk, protein powder, and ice cubes to a blender and mix until smooth. Blend on high for 2.5 minutes, or until the shake is smooth and lump-free. If the drink is too thick, add 2–4 tbsp. of water to thin it down to the appropriate consistency.
- Half of the shake should be poured into a glass and enjoyed. Any smoothie that you don't consume or use right away may be stored in an airtight container for up to a week. Before serving, re-blend.

NUTRITION:

148 Cal; 13g Protein; 4g Tot Fat; 17g Carb; 5g Fiber; 7g Sugar; 193mg Sodium

Berry Blast Protein Shake

PREP TIME: 5 min / **COOK TIME:** none / **YIELD:** 2 Serves

INGREDIENTS:

- 5 ice cubes
- 1 scoop (¼ cup) vanilla or plain protein powder
- ¾

- 5 ice cubes
- ¼ cup canned pineapple chunks in 100% natural juice or water, drained
- ½ cup of low-fat plain Greek yogurt
- ¼ cup frozen mango chunks
- 1 scoop (¼ cup) vanilla protein powder
- 1 cup unsweetened coconut milk

DIRECTIONS:

- Mix the yoghurt, protein powder, milk, and pineapple, mango, and ice cubes in a blender. Blend for 3.5 minutes on high speed, or until the powder is completely dissolved and no more visible.
- Half of the smoothie should be poured into a glass and enjoyed. Any smoothie that you don't consume or use right away may be stored in an airtight container for up to a week. Before serving, re-blend.

NUTRITION:

115 Cal; 15g Protein; 2.5g Tot Fat; 9g Carb; 1g Fiber; 7g Sugar; 136mg Sodium

Vanilla Apple Pie Protein Shake

PREP TIME: 5 min / **COOK TIME:** none / **YIELD:** 2 Serves

INGREDIENTS:
* 5 ice cubes
* 1 cup of low-fat milk
* 2 tsp. ground cinnamon
* 1 tsp. vanilla extract
* 1 small apple, peeled, cored, and chopped
* ½ tsp. ground nutmeg
* 1 scoop (¼ cup) vanilla protein powder

DIRECTIONS:
* Whisk the protein powder, milk, vanilla, apple, nutmeg, cinnamon, and ice cubes together in a mixer. Blend for around 3 to 4 minutes on high speed, or until the powder is completely dissolved and no more visible.
* Half of the shake should be poured into a glass and enjoyed. Any smoothie that you don't consume or use right away may be stored in an airtight container for up to a week. Before serving, re-blend.

NUTRITION:
123 Cal; 14g Protein; 1g Tot Fat; 14g Carb; 1g Fiber; 14g Sugar; 153mg Sodium

Protein-Packed Peanut Butter Cup Shake

PREP TIME: 5 min / **COOK TIME:** none / **YIELD:** 2 Serves

INGREDIENTS:
* 2 tbsp. powdered peanut butter
* ½ cup of low-fat plain Greek yogurt
* 1 scoop (¼ cup) chocolate protein powder
* ¼ cup nonfat ricotta cheese
* 2 tbsp. cocoa powder
* 1 cup of low-fat milk

DIRECTIONS:
* Mix the powdered peanut butter, yoghurt, milk, protein powder, ricotta, and cocoa powder in a mixer. Blend for 3.5 minutes on high speed, or until the powders are completely dissolved and no more visible.
* Half of the shake should be poured into a glass and enjoyed. Any smoothie that you don't consume or use right away may be stored in an airtight container for up to a week. Before serving, re-blend.

NUTRITION:
215 Cal; 27g Protein; 3g Tot Fat; 18g Carb; 3g Fiber; 11g Sugar; 249mg Sodium

Very Vanilla Bean Probiotic Shake

PREP TIME: 5 min / **COOK TIME:** none / **YIELD:** 2 Serves

INGREDIENTS:
* 5 ice cubes
* ¼ cup of low-fat plain Greek yogurt
* ½ cup of low-fat plain kefir
* 1 scoop (¼ cup) vanilla protein powder
* 1 tsp. vanilla extract

* 1 cup unsweetened vanilla soy milk or low-fat milk

DIRECTIONS:
* Mix the vanilla, protein powder, milk, and yoghurt, kefir, and ice cubes in a blender. Mix for 3 to 4 minutes on high speed, or until the powder is completely dissolved and no more visible.
* Half of the shake should be poured into a glass and enjoyed. Any smoothie that you don't consume or use right away may be stored in an airtight container for up to a week. Before serving, re-blend.

NUTRITION:
153 Cal; 22g Protein; 3g Tot Fat; 8g Carb; 2g Fiber; 6g Sugar; 161mg Sodium

Double Fudge Chocolate Shake

PREP TIME: 5 min / **COOK TIME:** none / **YIELD:** 2 Serves

INGREDIENTS:
* ½ small banana
* ½ cup of low-fat plain Greek yogurt
* 2 tbsp. unsweetened cocoa powder
* 1 scoop (¼ cup) chocolate protein powder
* ½ tsp. vanilla extract
* 1 cup of low-fat milk or unsweetened soy milk

DIRECTIONS:
* Mix the banana, yoghurt, milk, cocoa powder, protein powder, and vanilla in a high-powered blender for 2 to 3 minutes, or until creamy and the ingredients are thoroughly dissolved.
* Half of the shake should be poured into a glass and enjoyed. Any smoothie that you don't consume or use right away may be stored in an airtight container for up to a week. Before serving, re-blend.

NUTRITION:
157 Cal; 20g Protein; 1g Tot Fat; 18g Carb; 3g Fiber; 8g Sugar; 156mg Sodium

Pumpkin Spice Latte Protein Shake

PREP TIME: 5 min / **COOK TIME:** none / **YIELD:** 2 Serves

INGREDIENTS:
* ⅛ tsp. ground cloves
* ¼ tsp. ground ginger
* 1 tsp. ground cinnamon
* 1 scoop (¼ cup) vanilla protein powder ¾ cup brewed decaf coffee
* ¼ tsp. ground nutmeg
* 1 cup of low-fat milk or unsweetened soy milk ½ cup pumpkin puree

DIRECTIONS:
* Mix the nutmeg, pumpkin puree, milk, coffee, protein powder, ginger, cinnamon, and cloves in a high-powered blender for 2 to 3 minutes, or until the drink is smooth and the powder is completely dissolved.
* Half of the shake should be poured into a glass and enjoyed. Any smoothie that you don't consume or use right away may be stored in an airtight container for up to a week. Before serving, re-blend.

NUTRITION:
125 Cal; 15g Protein; 0g Tot Fat; 12g Carb; 2g Fiber; 8g Sugar; 155mg Sodium

27

High-Protein Milk

PREP TIME: 5 min / **COOK TIME:** none / **YIELD:** 4 Serves

INGREDIENTS:
- 1 cup nonfat dry milk powder
- 4 cups skim milk

DIRECTIONS:
- Beat the milk and milk powder gently with a mixer or blend on high speed for approximately 5 minutes, until the powder is fully dissolved and no longer visible in a deep basin or blender.
- Keep any milk you don't drink or use straight away in an airtight container in the refrigerator. Overnight, the taste enhances. After 7 days, discard any leftover milk.

NUTRITION:
144 Cal; 14g Protein; 0g Tot Fat; 21g Carb; 0g Fiber; 21g Sugar; 218mg Sodium

Berry Cheesecake Protein Shake

PREP TIME: 5 min / **COOK TIME:** none / **YIELD:** 1 Serve

INGREDIENTS:
- 1 tbsp. fat-free cream cheese
- 2 tbsp. half & half
- 2 cups ice
- 1 scoop Protein Delight Vanilla Very Berry powder

DIRECTIONS:
- Blend using a blender until the mixture is completely smooth.

NUTRITION:
310 Cal; 21g Protein; 7g Tot Fat; 23g Carb; 4g Fiber; 5g Sugar; 108mg Sodium

Root Beer Float Protein Shake

PREP TIME: 5 min / **COOK TIME:** none / **YIELD:** 1 Serve

INGREDIENTS:
- 6 ice cubes
- 1 tsp. vanilla extract
- 2 tbsp. DaVinci of the root beer syrup
- 2 cups water
- 1 scoop Matrix Simply Vanilla protein powder

DIRECTIONS:
- Blend using a blender until the mixture is completely smooth.

NUTRITION:
200 Cal; 14g Protein; 6g Tot Fat; 16g Carb; 4g Fiber; 1g Sugar; 145mg Sodium

Tangy Orange Protein Shake

PREP TIME: 5 min / **COOK TIME:** none / **YIELD:** 1 Serve

INGREDIENTS:
- Ice
- 1-2 tbsp. DaVinci of vanilla syrup
- 1-2 cups prepared Crystal Light Sunrise Orange
- 1 scoop Matrix Orange Cream protein powder

DIRECTIONS:
- Blend using a blender until the mixture is completely smooth.

NUTRITION:
120 Cal; 13g Protein; 25g Tot Fat; 1.3g Carb; 1.7g Fiber; 2.8g Sugar; 114.5mg Sodium

Vanilla Strawberry Protein Shake

PREP TIME: 5 min / **COOK TIME:** none / **YIELD:** 1 Serve

INGREDIENTS:
- 1 tsp. Splenda
- 5 frozen strawberries
- 1/2 - 1 cup skim milk
- 1 scoop Vanilla protein powder

DIRECTIONS:
- Blend using a blender until the mixture is completely smooth.

NUTRITION:
120 Cal; 14g Protein; 6g Tot Fat; 11g Carb; 3g Fiber; 5g Sugar; 215mg Sodium

Chocolate Covered Banana Protein Shake

PREP TIME: 5 min / **COOK TIME:** none / **YIELD:** 1 Serve

INGREDIENTS:
- 1-2 tsp. peanut butter
- 1 cup skim milk
- 1-inch chunk banana
- 1 scoop chocolate protein powder

DIRECTIONS:
- Blend using a blender until the mixture is completely smooth.

NUTRITION:
130 Cal; 18g Protein; 15g Tot Fat; 23g Carb; 12g Fiber; 5g Sugar; 215mg Sodium

Chocolate Covered Cherries Protein Shake

PREP TIME: 5 min / **COOK TIME:** none / **YIELD:** 1 Serve

INGREDIENTS:
- 6 ice cubes
- 1-2 tbsp. DaVinci of cherry syrup
- 1-2 tbsp. DaVinci of chocolate syrup
- 6 ounces milk
- 1 scoop Nectar Cappuccino Latte protein powder

DIRECTIONS:
- Blend using a blender until the mixture is completely smooth.

NUTRITION:
230 Cal; 28g Protein; 5g Tot Fat; 13g Carb; 1g Fiber; 2g Sugar; 115mg Sodium

Dreamscicle

PREP TIME: 5 min / **COOK TIME:** none / **YIELD:** 1 Serve

INGREDIENTS:
- 1-2 tbsp. DaVinci of orange syrup
- 1 cup water
- 1 scoop Vanilla protein powder

DIRECTIONS:
- Blend using a blender until the mixture is completely smooth.

NUTRITION:

150 Cal; 12g Protein; 3g Tot Fat; 23g Carb; 5g Fiber; 3g Sugar; 215mg Sodium

Choco-Vanilla Protein Shake

PREP TIME: 5 min / **COOK TIME:** none / **YIELD:** 2 Serves
INGREDIENTS:
- Ice
- 1/2 cup water
- 1 cup milk
- 1 scoop IDS Cinnamon-Vanilla protein powder or any vanilla protein powder with 1/4 to 1/2 tsp. cinnamon to taste
- 1 scoop IDS Belgian Chocolate protein powder or any chocolate protein powder

DIRECTIONS:
- Blend using a blender until the mixture is completely smooth.

NUTRITION:
200 Cal; 14g Protein; 5.9g Tot Fat; 15g Carb; 4g Fiber; 5g Sugar; 112mg Sodium

Buttercream Toffee Vanilla Latte

PREP TIME: 5 min / **COOK TIME:** none / **YIELD:** 1 Serve
INGREDIENTS:
- 1/2 scoop Elite Butter crème Toffee protein powder
- 2-3 ounces crushed ice
- 1/2 packet Big Train Vanilla Latte mix
- 2-3 ounces water
- 4 ounces Micellar Milk Vanilla, vanilla ready to drink protein, or Carlene's creamer recipe

DIRECTIONS:
- Blend until completely smooth. If needed, top with some SF Cool whip or Reid-whip.

NUTRITION:
100 Cal; 12g Protein; 6g Tot Fat; 12g Carb; 5g Fiber; 7g Sugar; 215mg Sodium

Pumpkin Spice Shake

PREP TIME: 5 min / **COOK TIME:** none / **YIELD:** 1 Serve
INGREDIENTS:
- 1 - 1 1/2 cups ice
- 1/4 cup pumpkin puree, unsweetened
- 1/4 cup frozen Cool Whip or no sugar added
- pinch of salt
- 1 scoop Matrix Vanilla protein powder
- 1 cup milk or soymilk
- 1/8 tsp. ginger scant 1/8 tsp. cloves OR 1/2 tsp. pumpkin pie spice instead of other separate spices
- 1/4 cup frozen Cool Whip or no sugar added
- Vanilla Ice Cream
- 2 tbsp. Splenda Granular

DIRECTIONS:
- Mix until completely smooth. If preferred, drizzle with sugar-free Cinnamon Bliss caramel drizzle.

NUTRITION:
140 Cal; 14g Protein; 15g Tot Fat; 17g Carb; 5g Fiber; 5g Sugar; 112mg Sodium

Protein Fruit Smoothie

PREP TIME: 5 min / **COOK TIME:** none / **YIELD:** 1 Serve
INGREDIENTS:
- Ice
- 1 scoop Protein Raspberry Yogurt protein powder
- 1/2 cup no sugar added vanilla yogurt
- 2-3 strawberries or 1/4 cup blueberries
- 1-inch chunk banana

DIRECTIONS:
- Blend all the ingredients in a food processor until the mixture is completely smooth.

NUTRITION:
120 Cal; 14g Protein; 6g Tot Fat; 15g Carb; 2g Fiber; 3.2g Sugar; 125mg Sodium

Hazelnut Cappuccino

PREP TIME: 5 min / **COOK TIME:** none / **YIELD:** 1 Serve
INGREDIENTS:
- Ice
- 1-2 tbsp. DaVinci of hazelnut syrup
- 1 cup cold decaf coffee
- 1 scoop Nectar Cappuccino protein powder or any brand cappuccino protein powder

DIRECTIONS:
- Mix the ingredients until the mixture is smooth and creamy.

NUTRITION:
160 Cal; 32g Protein; 17g Tot Fat; 14g Carb; 2g Fiber; 2.9g Sugar; 123mg Sodium

Cinnamon Nag

PREP TIME: 5 min / **COOK TIME:** none / **YIELD:** 1 Serve
INGREDIENTS:
- Dash nutmeg
- 1 scoop IDS Cinnamon-Vanilla protein powder or vanilla protein with 1/4 to 1/2 tsp. cinnamon
- 1-inch chunk banana
- 1-2 tbsp. DaVinci of eggnog syrup
- 1-2 cups cold water

DIRECTIONS:
- Blend all the ingredients in a food processor until the mixture is smooth and creamy.

NUTRITION:
100 Cal; 20g Protein; 3g Tot Fat; 12g Carb; 0g Fiber; 3g Sugar; 215mg Sodium

Cafe Kahlua

PREP TIME: 5 min / **COOK TIME:** none / **YIELD:** 1 Serve
INGREDIENTS:
- Ice
- 1 scoop Elite Cafe© Mocha protein powder
- 1-2 tbsp. DaVinci of Kahlua syrup
- 1-2 cups cold decaf coffee

DIRECTIONS:
- Add all in a big cup, cover with a lid and shake until well combined.

NUTRITION:

130 Cal; 20.8g Protein; 5.9g Tot Fat; 12.3g Carb; 21g Fiber; 4g Sugar; 125mg Sodium

Banana Protein Nog

PREP TIME: 5 min / **COOK TIME:** none / **YIELD:** 1 Serve
INGREDIENTS:
• 1/8 tsp. nutmeg
• One inch chunk of banana
• 1 cup skim milk
• 1/2 tsp. vanilla
• 1 scoop Matrix Simply Vanilla protein powder or any vanilla protein powder
DIRECTIONS:
• Mix all the ingredients and mix until smooth.
NUTRITION:
120 Cal; 12g Protein; 6g Tot Fat; 1.3g Carb; 4g Fiber; 4g Sugar; 121mg Sodium

Nectar Protein Cocktail

PREP TIME: 5 min / **COOK TIME:** none / **YIELD:** 1 Serve
INGREDIENTS:
• 4 scoops Nectar, fruit juice flavored whey isolate
• 1 tub Crystal Light
DIRECTIONS:
• In a plastic pitcher, combine the Crystal Light and 64 ounces of water, or to taste. Blend in 3-4 scoops of Nectar using a silicone whisk or a big spoon.
• To maintain freshness, keep refrigerated and eat within 24 hours after preparation. Because some settling occurs, stir before pouring.
NUTRITION:
120 Cal; 18g Protein; 0g Tot Fat; 0g Carb; 1g Fiber; 3g Sugar; 115mg Sodium

Chocolate Peanut Butter Smoothie

PREP TIME: 5 min / **COOK TIME:** none / **YIELD:** 1 Serve
INGREDIENTS:
• 1 scoop Protein delight, Alpine Chocolate or any chocolate protein mix
• 12 ice cubes
• 1 tsp. of peanut butter
• 2 ounces of water
DIRECTIONS:
• In a processor, combine all of the ingredients and mix until smooth.
NUTRITION:
100 Cal; 21g Protein; 2g Tot Fat; 12g Carb; 1.8g Fiber; 3g Sugar; 213mg Sodium

Banana Rum Smoothie

PREP TIME: 5 min / **COOK TIME:** none / **YIELD:** 1 Serve
INGREDIENTS:
• Da Vinci Gourmet Butter Rum SF Syrup
• Da Vinci Gourmet Banana SF Syrup
• Milk
DIRECTIONS:
• Mix all of the items in a processor with a lot of ice and IDS or Matrix vanilla protein.

NUTRITION:
240 Cal; 23g Protein; 5.1g Tot Fat; 12.3g Carb; 1.7g Fiber; 2g Sugar; 215mg Sodium

Banana Cream Pie Shake

PREP TIME: 5 min / **COOK TIME:** none / **YIELD:** 1 Serve
INGREDIENTS:
• Da Vinci Gourmet Coconut SF Syrup
• Da Vinci Gourmet Banana SF Syrup half and half
• milk
DIRECTIONS:
• Mix all of the items in a processor with a lot of ice and IDS or Matrix vanilla protein.
NUTRITION:
230 Cal; 28g Protein; 5g Tot Fat; 13g Carb; 1g Fiber; 2g Sugar; 115mg Sodium

Butter Almond Latte

PREP TIME: 5 min / **COOK TIME:** none / **YIELD:** 1 Serve
INGREDIENTS:
• Da Vinci Gourmet Butterscotch SF Syrup
• Da Vinci Gourmet Almond SF Syrup
• Espresso
• Milk
DIRECTIONS:
• In a processor with ice, combine all of the ingredients and blend to make the smoothie.
NUTRITION:
130 Cal; 13g Protein; 4g Tot Fat; 11g Carb; 1.7g Fiber; 2.9g Sugar; 211mg Sodium

Peach Almond Italian Soda

PREP TIME: 5 min / **COOK TIME:** none / **YIELD:** 1 Serve
INGREDIENTS:
• ice
• 1 oz. Half and Half
• 1/2 oz. Da Vinci Gourmet Peach SF Syrup
• 1 oz. Da Vinci Gourmet Amaretto SF Syrup
• sparkling water or plain water
DIRECTIONS:
• 3/4 fills a 16 oz. glass with ice. Fill a glass halfway with sparkling water and add the remaining ingredients. Mix thoroughly.
NUTRITION:
110 Cal; 18g Protein; 1.5g Tot Fat; 16g Carb; 3g Fiber; 6g Sugar; 213mg Sodium

Cinnamon Roll Latte

PREP TIME: 5 min / **COOK TIME:** none / **YIELD:** 2 Serves
INGREDIENTS:
• 1/2 cup vanilla Micellar Milk, vanilla ready to drink protein shakes or Carlene's creamer recipe.
• 1/2 oz. DaVinci Gourmet Cinnamon Classic Syrup
• 1 cup hot coffee
• 1/2 oz. DaVinci Gourmet Caramel Classic Syrup
DIRECTIONS:
• In a large cup, mix all of the ingredients.

NUTRITION:
220 Cal; 18g Protein; 2g Tot Fat; 7g Carb; 4g Fiber; 1g Sugar; 116mg Sodium

Cream Dream Latte
PREP TIME: 5 min / **COOK TIME:** none / **YIELD:** 2 Serves
INGREDIENTS:
• 1/2 cup vanilla Micellar Milk, vanilla ready to drink a protein shake, or Carlene's creamer recipe
• 1/2 oz. DaVinci Gourmet Irish Cream Classic Syrup
• 1 cup hot coffee
• 1/2 oz. DaVinci Gourmet Amaretto Classic Syrup
DIRECTIONS:
• In a large cup, mix all of the ingredients.
NUTRITION:
330 Cal; 18g Protein; 3g Tot Fat; 23g Carb; 3g Fiber; 5g Sugar; 115mg Sodium

Hot or Cold Chocolate Drink
PREP TIME: 5 min / **COOK TIME:** none / **YIELD:** 2 Serves
INGREDIENTS:
• 12 oz. water
• 2 packages of no sugar added hot choc.
• 3 scoops of UNFLAVORED protein
DIRECTIONS:
• In a large cup, mix all of the ingredients.
NUTRITION:
230 Cal; 28g Protein; 5g Tot Fat; 13g Carb; 1g Fiber; 2g Sugar; 115mg Sodium

Creamer Recipe
PREP TIME: 10 min / **COOK TIME:** none / **YIELD:** 2 Serves
INGREDIENTS:
• 2 packets of sweetener.
• 1 T. SF Vanilla Syrup
• 6 oz. milk of your choice
• 1 scoop vanilla or French vanilla protein mix
DIRECTIONS:
• Before combining with your coffee, combine all of the ingredients in a jar. After it's been blended, add it to your coffee or tea like any other coffee creamer you've used before RNY/Lap-Band.
NUTRITION:
130 Cal; 18g Protein; 4g Tot Fat; 10g Carb; 2g Fiber; 3g Sugar; 102mg Sodium

Hot Chocolate Drink
PREP TIME: 5 min / **COOK TIME:** none / **YIELD:** 1 Serve
INGREDIENTS:
• 6 oz. skim milk -- optional add one protein g per oz.
• 1 scoop Body Fortress Whey protein 1g of sugar chocolate (Wal-Mart good taste-cheaper)
• 1 pack of Nestles Low Carb hot chocolate
• 12 oz. mug
DIRECTIONS:

• Toss the powders into the cup. Half-fill with hot water from the tap. Stir well. Fill it up with milk the rest of the way. 1:15-1:20 minutes in the microwave (may vary). Stir once more. If desired, a squirt of Redi-Whip may be added.
NUTRITION:
231 Cal; 29g Protein; 4g Tot Fat; 23g Carb; 2g Fiber; 7g Sugar; 150mg Sodium

Jingle Java Latte
PREP TIME: 5 min / **COOK TIME:** none / **YIELD:** 1 Serve
INGREDIENTS:
• 1/2 cup vanilla Micellar Milk or vanilla ready to drink a protein shake
• 1/2 oz. DaVinci Gourmet Cinnamon Sugar-Free Syrup
• 1 cup hot coffee
• 1/2 oz. DaVinci Gourmet Amaretto Sugar-Free Syrup
DIRECTIONS:
• In a large cup, mix all of the ingredients.
NUTRITION:
130 Cal; 18g Protein; 3g Tot Fat; 23g Carb; 3g Fiber; 4g Sugar; 215mg Sodium

French Twist Mocha
PREP TIME: 5 min / **COOK TIME:** none / **YIELD:** 2 Serves
INGREDIENTS:
• 1/2 cup vanilla Micellar Milk or ready to drink a vanilla protein shake
• 1/3 oz. DaVinci Vanilla Sugar-Free Syrup
• 1 cup hot coffee
• 1/3 oz. DaVinci Butter Rum Sugar-Free Syrup
• 1/3 oz. DaVinci Chocolate Sugar-Free Syrup
DIRECTIONS:
• In a large cup, mix all of the ingredients.
NUTRITION:
230 Cal; 28g Protein; 5g Tot Fat; 13g Carb; 1g Fiber; 2g Sugar; 115mg Sodium

Cafe Caramel Mocha
PREP TIME: 5 min / **COOK TIME:** none / **YIELD:** 1 Serve
INGREDIENTS:
• 1/2 cup vanilla Micellar Milk or 1/2 cup vanilla ready to drink a protein shake
• 1 cup hot coffee
• 1/2 oz. DaVinci Caramel Sugar-Free Syrup
• 1/2 oz. DaVinci Chocolate Sugar-Free Syrup
DIRECTIONS:
• In a large cup, mix all of the ingredients.
NUTRITION:
130 Cal; 18g Protein; 3g Tot Fat; 10g Carb; 1.4g Fiber; 4g Sugar; 321mg Sodium

Chocolate Covered Caramel Mocha
PREP TIME: 5 min / **COOK TIME:** none / **YIELD:** 1 Serve
INGREDIENTS:
• 1/2 cup vanilla Micellar Milk OR ready to drink a vanilla protein shake

- 1/3 oz. DaVinci Toasted Marshmallow Sugar-Free Syrup
- 1 cup hot coffee
- 1/3 oz. DaVinci Caramel Sugar-Free Syrup
- 1/3 oz. DaVinci Chocolate Sugar-Free Syrup

DIRECTIONS:
- In a large cup, mix all of the ingredients.

NUTRITION:
232 Cal; 24g Protein; 4g Tot Fat; 14g Carb; 2g Fiber; 3g Sugar; 125mg Sodium

Creamy Fuzzy Navel

PREP TIME: 5 min / **COOK TIME:** none / **YIELD:** 1 Serve
INGREDIENTS:
- Â½ cup NSA peach or vanilla yoghurt
- Â½ cup fat-free milk
- 3-4 ice cubes
- 1 scoop Nectar Fuzzy Navel protein powder

DIRECTIONS:
- Mix until the mixture is smooth and thick.

NUTRITION:
300 Cal; 21g Protein; 2.5g Tot Fat; 9g Carb; 1.2g Fiber; 7.4g Sugar; 148mg Sodium

Pumpkin Protein Shake

PREP TIME: 5 min / **COOK TIME:** none / **YIELD:** 2 Serves
INGREDIENTS:
- 1-1 1/2 cups ice cubes
- 1/4 cup pumpkin puree
- 2 tbsp. Splenda Granular
- 1/2 tsp. pumpkin pie spice
- 1 scoop vanilla protein powder
- 1/4 cup Cool Whip or NSA Vanilla yogurt
- 1 cup skim milk or soymilk

DIRECTIONS:
- In a blender container, combine the pumpkin, milk, protein powder, spices, Splenda, cool whip or yoghurt, and a few ice cubes; process until the mixture is slushy.

NUTRITION:
230 Cal; 28g Protein; 5g Tot Fat; 13g Carb; 1g Fiber; 2g Sugar; 115mg Sodium

Boysenberry Smoothie

PREP TIME: 5 min / **COOK TIME:** none / **YIELD:** 2 Serves
INGREDIENTS:
- 1 cup ice
- 1/3 cup apple juice
- 2 cups boysenberry yogurt (low fat, if possible)
- 2 cups fresh or frozen boysenberries

DIRECTIONS:
- Mix all the ingredients. Pour in two glasses, equally divided.

NUTRITION:
310 Cal; 59g Protein; 2g Tot Fat; 12g Carb; 1g Fiber; 2g Sugar; 353mg Sodium

Buttermilk Fruit Shake

PREP TIME: 5 min
COOK TIME: none
YIELD: 1 Serve
INGREDIENTS:
- 1 tsp. vanilla or fruit flavoring sugar or sweetener to taste
- 1/2 cup frozen fruit
- 1 cup buttermilk

DIRECTIONS:
- Mix all the ingredients. Fruit should be cut into pieces and well mixed. Pour and enjoy. Strawberry, blueberry, pineapple, peaches, and other fruits work nicely.

NUTRITION:
230 Cal; 28g Protein; 5g Tot Fat; 13g Carb; 1g Fiber; 2g Sugar; 115mg Sodium

Snickers bar Mocha Protein Shake

PREP TIME: 5 min / **COOK TIME:** none / **YIELD:** 1 Serve
INGREDIENTS:
- 2 teaspoons decaffeinated instant coffee-- Omit if using Cold Decaf Coffee instead of water.
- 2 scoops Pro Complex -- Chocolate
- 1/4 cup nonfat milk -- or skim milk
- 1 tsp. butternut flavoring
- 1 tsp. caramel flavoring
- 2 tablespoons cocoa powder
- 4 ice cubes
- 1 1/2 cups water -- or cold decaf-coffee

DIRECTIONS:
- Fill a blender container halfway with water or coffee, milk, flavorings, cocoa powder, and protein powder, and mix on low until thoroughly blended. One by one, adding the ice cubes till the shake is thick and creamy.

NUTRITION:
296 Cal; 57g Protein; 2g Tot Fat; 13g Carb; 1g Fiber; 2g Sugar; 257mg Sodium

Hazelnut Mocha Cappuccino Shake

PREP TIME: 5 min / **COOK TIME:** none / **YIELD:** 1 Serve
INGREDIENTS:
- 6 ounces skim milk
- 1 scoop Pro Complex -- Vanilla
- 2 ounces Torani or DaVinci Sugar-Free Syrup-- Hazelnut
- 8 ounces cold water
- 2 teaspoons decaffeinated instant coffee
- 1 scoop Pro Complex -- Chocolate

DIRECTIONS:
- Add water to Pro Combo in a shaker or blender. Blend or shake. Mix the remaining ingredients. Blend or mix until thoroughly combined. Keep it refrigerated until you're ready to use it.

NUTRITION:
310 Cal; 59g Protein; 2g Tot Fat; 12g Carb; 1g Fiber; 2g Sugar; 353mg Sodium

Strawberry Protein Smoothie

PREP TIME: 5 min / **COOK TIME:** none / **YIELD:** 1 Serve

INGREDIENTS:
- 1 scoop vanilla protein powder
- 3 cup frozen strawberries
- 1 equal or 3 packets
- 1/4 cup skim milk or 1percent milk
- 1 cup ice cubes
- 1 carton (8 oz.) plain nonfat yogurt

DIRECTIONS:
- In a mixer container, combine equal parts yogurt and milk. Add berries, a couple at a time, through the top of the blender while it's running (opening in the lid). Blend until smooth, and then add ice cubes one by one through the lid hole. Blend until the mixture is mushy, and then serve.

NUTRITION:
150 Cal; 25g Protein; 8g Tot Fat; 15g Carb; 5g Fiber; 5g Sugar; 250mg Sodium

Protein Fruit Smoothie
PREP TIME: 5 min / **COOK TIME:** none / **YIELD:** 1 Serve
INGREDIENTS:
- Powdered milk (optional)
- 2 ice cubes
- 2 strawberries or 1/4 banana
- 1/2 cup low-fat plain
- 1 scoop of your favorite protein powder

DIRECTIONS:
- If using powdered milk, add a splash of water. It may also be substituted for yogurt. Serve by blending all of the ingredients in a mixer until the ice is crushed.

NUTRITION:
100 Cal; 20g Protein; 7g Tot Fat; 24g Carb; 5g Fiber; 5g Sugar; 300mg Sodium

Tropical Fruit Breeze Protein Shake
PREP TIME: 5 min / **COOK TIME:** none / **YIELD:** 1 Serve
INGREDIENTS:
- 1/4 cup pineapple (make sure pineapple is drained)
- 1/4 cup of frozen unsweetened peaches
- 1 serving strawberry protein powder

DIRECTIONS:
- Combine 1 serving of strawberry protein powder with 1 cup of water. Then add 1/4 cup unsweetened frozen peaches, 1/4 cup pineapple, and 3 ice cubes. 45 seconds on high speed in a blender, then serve (make sure pineapple is drained).

NUTRITION:
130 Cal; 18g Protein; 1g Tot Fat; 11g Carb; 12g Fiber; 4g Sugar; 215mg Sodium

Chapter 5: Breakfast Recipes

Cheesy Veggies Pancake

Preparation Time: 10 min. / **Cooking Time:** 15 min. / **Servings:** 2

Ingredients:
- ½ cup low-fat cottage cheese
- 1 large egg
- ⅓ cup scallion, diced
- ⅓ cup zucchini, grated
- ⅓ cup carrots, grated
- 1 tablespoon whole-wheat flour
- A pinch pepper
- A pinch sea salt
- Cooking spray

Directions:
1. Spray a pan and preheat oil.
2. When oil is hot, add the scallion and sauté for 2 minutes.
3. Stir in zucchini and carrots and cook for 5-6 minutes.
4. Meanwhile, stir together the egg, cottage cheese, flour, pepper, and salt.
5. Add the cooked ingredients to the bowl mixture, stirring until well-combined.
6. Lightly spray the pan again and spoon in the mixture to pan. Create 4 pancakes.
7. Cook on each side for 4.5 minutes. Serve and enjoy.

Nutrition: Calories: 210 - Fat: 10 g - Protein: 9 g - Carbs: 14 g

Turkey Bacon and Avocado Scramble

Preparation Time: 5 minutes / **Cooking Time:** 10 minutes / **Servings:** 1

Ingredients:
- 1 slice bacon turkey, crumbled
- ¼ avocado, diced
- 1 egg
- 1 garlic clove, finely minced
- 1 teaspoon fresh basil
- 2 cherry tomatoes, quartered
- ½ oz. low-fat mozzarella cheese, shredded
- Cooking spray

Directions:
1. Lightly spray the pan with cooking oil and heat over medium-high.
2. Sauté the garlic until the aroma is released. Stir in bacon to crisp. Remove pan contents onto a side dish and set aside.
3. Lightly whisk the egg in a mixing bowl.
4. Add tomatoes to the pan and sauté until liquid is almost gone.
5. Add egg mixture to the pan and cook until your scrambled eggs reach the desired consistency.
6. Stir in the bacon and garlic mixture, avocado and mozzarella cheese just before the eggs are cooked and stir.
7. Remove from heat, sprinkle with basil and serve.

Nutrition: Calories: 194 - Fat: 10 g - Protein: 15 g - Carbs: 7 g - Cholesterol: 25 mg - Sodium: 395 mg

Puréed Black Beans with Scrambled Eggs

Preparation Time: 10 minutes / **Cooking Time:** 15 minutes / **Servings:** 1

Ingredients:

Scrambled Eggs:
- ⅛ teaspoon sea salt
- 1 egg
- ⅛ teaspoon black pepper

Black Beans Purée:
- 3 tablespoons no-sugar added chimichurri sauce
- ½ cup no-salt added canned black beans, drained, and rinsed
- 2 tablespoons low-sodium vegetable or chicken broth
- Cooking spray
- 1 scoop protein powder (optional)

Directions:

To make Black Beans Purée:
1. Put the beans in an oil sprayed saucepan on medium heat.
2. Add the chimichurri sauce and heat for 2-3 minutes, stirring constantly.
3. Add the chicken broth and stir for 1-2 minutes.
4. Pour the contents of the saucepan into a blender. Pulse to make a smooth mixture and place it into a bowl.
5. Let it cool a bit and then mix the protein powder (if using); stir well, and keep it warm till you cook the egg.

To make Scrambled Eggs:
1. Heat an oil sprayed skillet on medium heat. Crack the egg and whisk it well.
2. Pour the egg into the skillet, sprinkle with pepper and salt, and scramble it.
3. Take it out on a plate. Top with 1 tablespoon of black beans puree. Serve and enjoy.

Nutrition: Calories: 122 - Fat: 6 g - Protein: 12 g - Carbs: 6 g - Cholesterol: 213 mg

Veggie Muffins

Preparation Time: 15 minutes / **Cooking Time:** 40 minutes/ **Servings:** 12

Ingredients:
- ½ cup red onion
- ½ cup cauliflower, chopped
- ½ cup red bell pepper, chopped
- ½ cup tomatoes, diced
- ¾ cup low-fat Cheddar cheese, shredded
- 2 cups low-fat milk
- 4 eggs
- 1 cup pancake mix
- 1 teaspoon oregano
- 1 teaspoon basil
- ½ teaspoon sea salt
- ½ teaspoon pepper
- Cooking spray

Directions:
1. Set oven to 375 °F, and lightly grease a 12 cup muffin tin with cooking spray.
2. Place tomatoes, cauliflower, pepper, onions and Cheddar into muffin cups.

3.   Add eggs and remaining ingredients in a medium bowl; whisk to combine and pour evenly on top of muffin cups.
4.   Bake in the oven for 43 minutes or until golden brown.
5.   Let cool slightly for about 5 minutes and serve.
Nutrition: Calories: 102 - Fat: 5 g - Protein: 6 g - Carbs: 3 g - Sodium: 240 mg

Steel Cut Oat Berries Pancakes

Preparation Time: 5 minutes / **Cooking Time:** 20 minutes / **Servings:** 2
Ingredients:
- ½ cup steel cut oats
- ½ cup frozen blackberries
- ½ cup frozen raspberries
- 1 ½ cup water
- 1 cup whole-wheat pastry flour
- ½ teaspoon baking powder
- ½ teaspoon baking soda
- 1 egg
- 1 cup unsweetened almond milk
- ½ cup plain low-fat Greek yogurt
- ¾ cup sugar-free maple syrup
- ⅛ teaspoon sea salt
- Cooking spray

Directions:
1.   Combine together oats, salt, and water; stir, and bring to a boil.
2.   Decrease heat to low and simmer for 10 minutes, or until oats are tender. Then, set aside.
3.   Combine all remaining ingredients, except maple syrup, in a medium bowl, and fold in oats.
4.   Lightly grease a skillet with cooking spray, and preheat over medium heat.
5.   Spoon ¼ of batter at a time and cook for about 3 minutes per side.
6.   Garnish with maple syrup.
Nutrition: Calories: 257 - Fat: 8 g - Protein: 14 g - Carbs: 39 g - Sodium: 393 mg

Blueberries and Strawberries Muesli

Preparation Time: 6 hours to chill / **Cooking Time:** 0 minutes/ **Servings:** 3
Ingredients:
- ½ cup rolled oats
- ½ cup plain low-fat Greek yogurt
- ¼ cup low-fat milk, or unsweetened almond milk
- 1 teaspoon ground cinnamon
- ¼ cup apple, chopped
- ⅛ cup fresh or frozen blueberries
- ⅛ cup fresh or frozen strawberries
- ⅛ cup almonds, chopped
- ¼ cup dried plums (optional)
- 1 scoop protein powder (optional)

Directions:
1.   Combine yogurt, milk, oats, cinnamon, and protein powder (if using) together in a bowl and mix well.
2.   Cover the bowl tightly and place in the fridge to cool for at least 6 hours.

3.   Add plums (if using), blueberries, strawberries and apples, and stir softly.
4.   Top with almonds and serve.
SUGGESTION: almonds may be too hard for the early stages of healing. If you don't tolerate almonds, or the stage of your diet doesn't call for them, simply eliminate them from the recipe.
Nutrition: Calories: 245 - Fat: 5 g - Protein: 6 g - Carbs: 32 g - Sodium: 50 mg

Peach and Raspberry Sauce Sandwich

Preparation Time: 5 minutes / **Cooking Time:** 0 minutes / **Servings:** 2
Ingredients:
- 4 slices whole-wheat bread
- 1 fresh peach, diced
- ½ cup raspberries
- 2 oz. non-fat plain Greek yogurt
- 1 teaspoon raw honey, or honey substitute
- 1 tablespoon orange juice

Directions:
1.   Add honey, orange juice, raspberries and cheese to a food processor, and pulse until fully incorporated.
2.   Spread two bread slices with the mixture and top with diced peach.
3.   Complete sandwiches with the other bread slice and enjoy.
Nutrition: Calories: 240 - Fat: 9 g - Protein: 6 g - Carbs: 26 g

Shakshuka

Preparation Time: 10 minutes / **Cooking Time:** 25 minutes / **Servings:** 2
Ingredients:
- 2 eggs
- 8 oz. no-salt added canned tomatoes, diced
- ½ red pepper, diced
- 1 tablespoon extra-virgin olive oil
- ¼ onion, minced
- ½ garlic clove, minced
- ¼ teaspoon smoked paprika
- ¼ teaspoon ground cumin
- 1 tablespoon fresh parsley, finely chopped
- Sea salt and pepper

Directions:
1.   Stir in the onions and garlic, and sauté about 5 minutes.
2.   Stir in the tomatoes and pepper, and season with the paprika and cumin.
3.   Stir and cook until the mixture begins to set and form a sauce.
4.   At this point, with the help of a spoon, create two small basins in the tomato sauce and break each egg so that it's placed in the center of each basin.
5.   Add salt and pepper and let cook for 5 to 10 minutes, depending on eggs cooking preference.
6.   Top with parsley, divide into plates, and enjoy.
Nutrition: Calories: 300 - Fat: 19 g - Protein: 13 g - Carbs: 17 g - Fiber: 4 g - Sugar: 6 g - Sodium: 655 mg

Italian Eggs in Purgatory

Preparation Time: 10 minutes / **Cooking Time:** 25 minutes / **Servings:** 4

Ingredients:
- 4 eggs
- 8 oz. no-salt added canned tomatoes, diced
- ½ white onion, diced
- ½ tablespoon fresh basil, chopped
- 2 teaspoons oregano
- 2 tablespoons extra-virgin olive oil
- A pinch sea salt
- A pinch black pepper

Directions:
1. Sauté onion until golden.
2. Stir in the tomatoes and oregano, lower the heat a little, and cook for 10-15 minutes, or until tomatoes liquids are almost evaporated.
3. Using a spoon create four wells, and crack an egg into each well. Season and cover with a lid, and cook for about 3 minutes.
4. Remove eggs from heat, scatter with basil and serve.

Nutrition: Calories: 114 - Fat: 6 g - Protein: 8 g - Carbs: 7 g

Denver Egg Muffins

Preparation Time: 10 minutes / **Cooking Time:** 25 minutes / **Servings:** 12

Ingredients:
- 4 eggs
- 6 slices extra lean fully cooked ham, roughly chopped
- ½ cup low-fat Cheddar cheese, shredded
- ½ onion, diced
- ½ green pepper, minced
- ¼ cup low-fat milk
- A pinch sea salt
- A pinch pepper
- Cooking spray

Directions:
1. Preheat the oven to 410 °F and spray a 12 muffin tin.
2. Place onion, green pepper, and ham evenly in muffin tin; add Cheddar on the top.
3. Then, take a bowl and mix eggs, milk, salt and pepper, and fill with the mixture the 12 muffin compartments.
4. Bake for 24 minutes, or until the eggs are set. Serve warm and enjoy.

Nutrition: Calories: 99 - Fat: 6 g - Protein: 8 g - Carbs: 2 g - Fiber: 1 g - Sugar: 1 g - Sodium: 296 mg

Mushroom, Lentils and Tomato Scrambled Tofu

Preparation Time: 10 minutes / **Cooking Time:** 15 minutes / **Servings:** 2

Ingredients:
- 4 oz. firm tofu
- 1 small shallot, chopped
- 4 oz. mushrooms, sliced
- 3 oz. precooked canned lentils, drained, and rinsed
- 1 small tomato, diced
- ¼ teaspoon turmeric
- 2 tablespoons extra-virgin olive oil
- A pinch sea salt
- A pinch black pepper

Directions:
1. Sauté the shallot until is golden.
2. Then, add tomato, lentils and mushrooms and cook for 3-5 minutes.
3. Stir in the tofu, scramble it, dust the turmeric, stir and cook for 5 minutes.
4. Season with salt and pepper, serve and enjoy.

Nutrition: Calories: 202 - Fat: 16 g - Protein: 13 g - Carbs: 9 g - Sodium: 140 mg

Protein Breakfast Burritos

Preparation Time: 15 minutes / **Cooking Time:** 20 minutes / **Servings:** 2

Ingredients:
- 2 precooked natural breakfast turkey sausages, crumbled
- 2 eggs
- 1 tablespoon low-fat milk
- 1 garlic clove, minced
- 1 cup fresh baby spinach
- ½ tomato, diced
- ¼ cup no-salt added canned black beans, drained, and rinsed
- 2 low-carb tortillas
- 2 tablespoons low-fat Monterey Jack cheese, shredded
- 1 tablespoon chives, finely chopped
- A pinch sea salt
- A pinch black pepper
- Cooking spray

Directions:
1. In a large oil sprayed skillet, heat the oil over medium heat.
2. Place turkey sausages and cook until golden brown. Remove from heat, set aside on a plate, and cover to keep them warm.
3. If needed, lightly spray the skillet again and add the garlic, tomato, and black beans. Cook about 5 minutes.
4. After 2 minutes stir in the spinach and continue cooking for the remaining 3 minutes, or until spinach wilts. Transfer to a plate and keep warm.
5. While the vegetables cook, in a large bowl, whisk together the eggs and milk.
6. Put the egg mixture into the skillet, season with salt and pepper, and stir until the eggs are soft and set. Remove from the heat.
7. Divide the eggs, sausages and veggies mixture evenly between the tortillas, and top with the cheese and chives.
8. Roll up tightly to close. Serve immediately.

SUGGESTION: if you don't tolerate tortillas, or the stage of your diet doesn't call for them, simply eliminate them from the recipe and enjoy the filling.

Nutrition: Calories: 354 - Fat: 19 g - Protein: 31 g - Carbs: 21 g - Fiber: 11 g - Sugar: 3 g - Sodium: 593 mg

Soft Peachy Cream of Wheat

Preparation Time: 5 minutes / **Cooking Time:** 5 minutes / **Servings:** 2

Ingredients:
- 1 ripe peach peeled, cored, and roughly chopped
- ⅓ cup cream of wheat
- 1 cup low-fat milk
- 2 tablespoons orange juice
- A pinch ground nutmeg
- A pinch ground cinnamon
- 1 teaspoon calorie-free sweetener (optional)

Directions:
1. In a blender, place the peach, orange juice, cinnamon, nutmeg and sweetener (if using), and process until creamy and well blended.
2. Bring milk to a boil
3. Lower the heat, add cream of wheat and stir constantly, cooking for 3-5 minutes until cream is set and soft.
4. Divide the cream into two bowls and top with peach blend.

Nutrition: Calories: 218 - Fat: 6 g - Protein: 7 g - Carbs: 33 g - Fiber: 3 g

Cheesy Mushrooms, Broccoli and Eggs Bake

Preparation Time: 10 minutes / **Cooking Time:** 45 minutes / **Servings:** 2

Ingredients:
- ⅓ cup fresh broccoli, chopped
- 2 medium fresh button mushrooms, sliced
- 2 eggs
- 3 tablespoons unsweetened almond milk
- 1 teaspoon onion powder
- 1 tablespoon low-fat Cheddar cheese, shredded
- 1 tablespoon low-fat cottage cheese
- A dash paprika
- A pinch sea salt
- A pinch black pepper
- Water
- Cooking spray

Directions:
1. Set the oven to 410 °F to preheat.
2. Fill a small pot with water and bring it to a boil.
3. Meanwhile, grease a saucepan with cooking oil and place over medium heat. When oil is hot, add mushrooms and cook for about 5 minutes or until golden brown. Then, remove from heat and set aside.
4. Add the broccoli in boiling water and blanch for 2-3 minutes. Drain broccoli and set aside.
5. In a large bowl, whisk the eggs and milk; then, add broccoli, mushrooms, onion powder, Cheddar cheese and cottage cheese. Season with salt, pepper and paprika, and stir until well combined.
6. Spoon the mixture evenly into the baking dish, and bake for 30-35 minutes, or until the top of the egg bake is golden brown.
7. Remove from oven and let sit for some minutes; then, serve and enjoy.

Nutrition: Calories: 139 - Fat: 10 g - Protein: 12 g - Carbs: 5 g - Sodium: 230 mg - Cholesterol: 176 mg

Puréed Black Beans and Pumpkin Soup

Preparation Time: 15 minutes / **Cooking Time:** 30 minutes / **Servings:** 2

Ingredients:
- 6 oz. no-salt added canned black beans, rinsed, and drained
- 3 oz. canned pumpkin
- ¼ cup canned tomatoes, diced
- 1 cup low-sodium chicken broth
- ½ medium onion, chopped
- ¼ tablespoon ground cumin
- 1 tablespoon extra-virgin olive oil
- 1 garlic clove, minced
- 1 tablespoon fresh parsley, chopped
- A dash black pepper
- A dash sea salt
- A pinch organic chipotle powder (optional)

Directions:
1. Place beans, tomatoes and half of the broth in a food processor and blend until creamy.
2. Pour the oil in a soup pan on low-medium heat.
3. Add the onion and sauté for 2-3 minutes; then add the garlic. Season with salt, pepper, cumin and chipotle powder (if using), and cook for 1 minute more, stirring constantly.
4. Now, stir in the remaining broth, pumpkin, and the tomatoes and black beans cream. Mix well.
5. Bring to a boil and let the mixture simmer for 25 minutes, or until thickened.
6. Then, remove from heat, and process the mixture again with an immersion blender for a smooth, soft consistency.
7. Sprinkle with parsley, serve and enjoy.

Nutrition: Calories: 246 - Fat: 10 g - Protein: 9 g - Carbs: 19 g - Fiber: 6 g - Sugar: 6 g - Sodium: 725 mg

Turmeric Leek, Broccoli and Tofu Quiche

Preparation Time: 10 minutes / **Cooking Time:** 45 minutes / **Servings:** 8

Ingredients:
- 1 pre-made pie crust
- 1 lb. firm tofu
- 1 cup broccoli, chopped
- 1 cup fresh mushrooms, chopped
- 1 cup leek, chopped
- 1 tablespoon tahini
- ½ cup soy milk
- 1 tablespoon extra-virgin olive oil
- 1 teaspoon turmeric
- ½ teaspoon sea salt
- ½ teaspoon black pepper
- A pinch nutmeg

Directions:
1. Preheat the oven at 400 °F.
2. Sauté leeks, broccoli and mushrooms for 10 minutes.

3. Combine the tofu, salt, pepper, soy milk, turmeric, nutmeg, and tahini in a food blender and process until get a soft and smooth mixture.

4. In a bowl, mix the veggies and the tofu mixture, stirring until well combined.

5. Spoon the mixture evenly into the pie crust and bake for about 30-35 minutes. Serve warm.

Nutrition: Calories: 148 - Fat: 6 g - Protein: 9 g - Carbs: 10 g - Cholesterol: 20 mg - Fiber: 3 g - Sodium: 318 mg

Cheese-Filled Tofu Acorn Squash

Preparation Time: 10 minutes / **Cooking Time:** 50 minutes / **Servings:** 2

Ingredients:
- 2 oz. firm tofu, sliced into cubes
- 1 small acorn squash, halved, and seeded
- ¼ cup low-sodium feta cheese or goat cheese, shredded
- ¼ cup fresh mushrooms, sliced
- 1 teaspoon onion, finely chopped
- ½ carrot, finely diced
- ¼ cup celery, finely diced
- 1 teaspoon parsley, chopped
- ⅛ teaspoon sea salt
- A pinch black pepper
- 2 oz. no-sugar added marinara sauce
- Cooking spray

Directions:
1. Set the oven at 400 °F to preheat.
2. Place the acorn squash pieces with cut-sides down on a lined baking dish.
3. Cook for 35 minutes. Set aside.
4. Grease a non-stick saucepan with cooking oil and heat on medium; then add the tofu. Cook until browned before stirring in the onion, carrot and celery. Cook the mixture for 2 minutes or until the onion is soft.
5. Stir in the mushrooms and cook for 3 minutes.
6. Pour in the marinara sauce, salt, and pepper, and cook, stirring, for 3 minutes more.
7. Divide portions of the mixture evenly inside the acorn squash halves. Place in the oven cooking for about 15 minutes.
8. After 15 minutes, top with the cheese and return to the oven for additional 5 minutes.
9. Remove from oven, garnish with parsley and serve.

Nutrition: Calories: 348 - Fat: 16 g - Protein: 14 g - Carbs: 42 g - Cholesterol: 42 mg - Sodium: 533 mg - Fiber: 8 g - Sugar: 6 g

Cheese Spinach Bake

Preparation Time: 10 minutes / **Cooking Time:** 25 minutes / **Servings:** 3

Ingredients:
- ½ cup Parmesan cheese, grated
- 1 cup fat-free cottage cheese
- ½ cup low-fat Monterey Jack cheese, shredded
- 10 oz. baby fresh or frozen spinach
- 1 teaspoon ground nutmeg
- 2 eggs

- Sea salt and pepper
- A pinch smoked paprika
- Cooking spray

Directions:
1. Preheat the oven to 350 °F. Lightly grease three ramekins with cooking spray.
2. Mix the eggs, season with salt and pepper, and mix.
3. Add cottage cheese, Parmesan cheese, spinach and nutmeg, and stir until well combined.
4. Divide the mixture evenly among the ramekins and top with Monterey Jack cheese.
5. Place in the oven and bake for 20-25 minutes, or until cheese on top is golden brown.
6. Remove from oven, garnish the top of ramekins with smoked paprika, and serve.

Nutrition: Calories: 285 - Fat: 17 g - Protein: 16 g - Carbs: 10 g - Sodium: 677 mg - Fiber: 2 g

Apple Cinnamon Oatmeal

Preparation Time: 10 minutes / **Cooking Time:** 10 minutes / **Servings:** 2

Ingredients:
- 1 cup rolled oats
- 2 cups water
- 1 cup apple, diced small
- ¼ teaspoon cinnamon
- ½ tablespoon calorie-free sweetener (optional)

Directions:
1. In a saucepan add oats, apple, water and cinnamon, and bring to a boil over medium heat.
2. When it's boiling decrease heat to low and cook until oats and apple become soft.
3. Remove from heat and taste: if the apples didn't sweeten the oats enough, add sweetener. Otherwise, serve and enjoy.

Nutrition: Calories: 130 - Fat: 1 g - Protein: 4 g - Carbs: 23 g - Sodium: 176 mg - Fiber: 4 g - Sugar: 6 g

Creamy 2 Cheese Grits

Preparation Time: 10 minutes / **Cooking Time:** 20-25 minutes / **Servings:** 2

Ingredients:
- ½ cup grits, uncooked
- 2 eggs, lightly beaten
- ½ cup Cheddar cheese, shredded
- 2 tablespoons Parmesan cheese, grated
- ⅛ cup fat-free half-and-half
- A pinch sea salt
- A pinch cayenne pepper

Directions:
1. Prepare the grits according to the package directions.
2. While grits cook, in a bowl, combine the beaten eggs, salt and pepper, and Cheddar.
3. When the grits are almost ready, spoon some of the hot grits into the egg mixture, and stir.
4. Add the bowl content to the cooking pan of the grits, and whisk well until the grits are smooth.
5. Add half-and-half; continue stirring until the grits reach your desired consistency.

6. Remove from heat, divide into bowls and top with Parmesan.

Nutrition: Calories: 298 - Fat: 13 g - Protein: 13 g - Carbs: 27 g

Berries Parfait and Greek Yogurt

Preparation Time: 5 minutes / **Cooking Time:** 0 minutes / **Servings:** 2

Ingredients:
- 1 cup non-fat plain Greek yogurt
- ¼ cup fresh strawberries
- ¼ cup fresh raspberries
- ¼ cup fresh cranberries
- 1 tablespoon walnuts, chopped
- 1 teaspoon agave nectar

Directions:
1. Chop the strawberries.
2. In two glasses layer yogurt, strawberries, cranberries and raspberries.
3. Top with walnuts and agave nectar

SUGGESTION: walnuts may be too hard for the early stages of healing. If you don't tolerate walnuts, or the stage of your diet doesn't call for them, simply eliminate them from the recipe.

Nutrition: Calories: 245 - Fat: 11 g - Protein: 16 g - Carbs: 25 g - Fiber: 5 g - Sugar: 21 g - Sodium: 46 g

Italian Style Tomatoes and Scrambled Eggs

Preparation Time: 5 minutes / **Cooking Time:** 45 minutes / **Servings:** 2

Ingredients:
- 3 eggs
- 8 oz. no-salt added canned tomatoes, diced
- ½ white onion, diced
- 1 tablespoon fresh basil, chopped
- 1 teaspoon dried thyme
- Sea salt and pepper
- Cooking spray

Directions:
1. In a skillet, heat spayed olive oil on medium.
2. When oil is hot, stir in the onion and sauté for about 5 minutes, or until it's golden.
3. Low the heat and add tomatoes and thyme, simmering for 30-35 minutes, until tomatoes begin to form a thickened sauce.
4. In a bowl, whisk the eggs with salt and pepper; then, add to the tomato and cook over medium heat, stirring to combine.
5. When the eggs are set and soft, remove from heat, sprinkle with basil, and serve.

Nutrition: Calories: 241 - Fat: 14 g - Protein: 13 g - Carbs: 12 g - Sodium: 148 mg

Mexican Scrambled Eggs

Preparation Time: 10 minutes / **Cooking Time:** 15 minutes / **Servings:** 2

Ingredients:
- 2 eggs, lightly beaten

- 1 tomato, diced
- ½ small red bell pepper, diced
- 2 tablespoons onion, finely chopped
- 1 cup no-salt added black beans, drained, and rinsed
- 2 tablespoons low-fat Mexican cheese, shredded
- 1 tablespoon olive oil
- ½ teaspoon cumin
- ½ teaspoon paprika
- 1 tablespoon fresh parsley, chopped
- A pinch sea salt
- A pinch black pepper

Directions:
1. Put oil over medium heat.
2. Add onion and cook until fragrant for about 2-3 minutes. Then, stir in red bell pepper and cook for 3 minutes before adding the tomato and black beans, cumin and paprika. Continue stirring and cook for 2-3 minutes more.
3. While vegetables are cooking, whisk the eggs and season with salt and pepper.
4. Add eggs to the skillet, and continue to cook, while stirring, until almost set and soft for about 2 minutes.
5. When eggs are almost done, add cheese and continue cooking for about 1 minute until the cheese melts. Sprinkle with parsley, serve and enjoy.

Nutrition: Calories: 229 - Total fat: 15 g - Protein: 14 g - Carbs: 12 g - Sodium: 149 mg

Spinach and Mushrooms Omelet

Preparation Time: 10 minutes / **Cooking Time:** 10 minutes / **Servings:** 2

Ingredients:
- ½ cup spinach, chopped
- ½ cup mushrooms, sliced
- 2 tablespoons white onion, diced
- 2 eggs
- 1 teaspoon garlic powder
- ½ teaspoon sea salt
- ¼ teaspoon ground black pepper
- Cooking spray

Directions:
1. Lightly grease a skillet with cooking spray over medium heat.
2. Cook onion for about 2-3 minutes; then add garlic powder and mushrooms, stirring constantly.
3. Cook for 3 minutes and stir in the spinach until wilts.
4. Meanwhile, whisk the eggs, seasoning with salt and pepper.
5. When the mushrooms and vegetables mixture is ready, pour eggs in the skillet and coat evenly the mixture.
6. Cook until the eggs are set, and fold the omelet in half.
7. Remove from heat, cut in half and serve.

Nutrition: Calories: 232 - Fat: 13 g - Protein: 21 g - Carbs: 3 g - Sodium: 336 mg

Almond Protein Porridge

Preparation Time: 5 minutes / **Cooking Time:** 25 minutes / **Servings:** 1

Ingredients:

- ¼ cup raw steel cut oats
- ¾ cup low-fat milk
- 1 tablespoon all-natural creamy almond butter
- 1 tablespoon no-sugar added raisins
- 1 tablespoon chia seeds
- ½ banana, sliced
- 1 scoop protein powder (optional)

Directions:

1. Bring the milk to a boil.
2. Add the oats and raisins. Low the heat and simmer for 20 minutes, stirring regularly.
3. When the oats have thickened, remove from the heat.
4. Let the mixture rest for 1 minute. Stir in protein powder (if using).
5. Top with the banana slices, almond butter and chia seeds. Enjoy warm.

Nutrition: Calories: 295 - Fat: 14 g - Protein: 10 g - Carbs: 28 g - Fiber: 7 g - Sugar: 10 g

Egg and Mashed Avocado Toast

Preparation Time: 5 minutes / **Cooking Time:** 5 minutes / **Servings:** 1

Ingredients:

- 1 slice whole-grain bread
- 1 teaspoon lemon juice
- ¼ avocado, peeled, and pitted
- 1 hard-boiled egg, cut into slices
- ½ tablespoon fresh chives, finely chopped
- Freshly ground black pepper
- A pinch sea salt

Directions:

1. Toast the bread.
2. Mash avocado with a fork, drizzle with lemon juice and spread it on the toast.
3. Place the egg slices on top. Sprinkle with chives, season with a pinch of salt and pepper, and enjoy.

SUGGESTION: If you don't tolerate bread, or the stage of your diet doesn't call for it, simply eliminate it from the recipe. You can slice the avocado instead of mashing it and enjoy it with the egg.

Nutrition: Calories: 285 - Fat: 15 g - Protein: 9 g - Carbs: 18 g - Fiber: 7 g - Sugar: 3 g - Sodium: 270 mg

Tomato, Feta and Leek Frittata

Preparation Time: 10 minutes / **Cooking Time:** 10 minutes / **Servings:** 1

Ingredients:

- ½ oz. low-salt feta cheese, crumbled
- 1 tablespoon leek, chopped
- 1 small tomato, cut into wedges
- 1 large egg
- 1 tablespoon fresh basil leaves, roughly chopped
- A pinch cayenne pepper
- Cooking spray

Directions:

1. Heat the sprayed oil in a small pan over medium heat.
2. Mix the egg and pepper. Add the basil and leek, and mix well to combine.

3. Pour the egg mixture into the pan and top with the feta and tomato.
4. Cook for 3 minutes, or until the egg is set and soft. Serve and enjoy warm

Nutrition: Calories: 194 - Fat: 11 g - Protein: 14 g - Carbs: 7 g - Fiber: 1 g - Sugar: 4 g - Sodium: 230 mg

Egg Scramble with Lox, Olives, and Avocado

Preparation Time: 10 minutes / **Cooking Time:** 5 minutes / **Servings:** 2

Ingredients:

- 2 oz. lox
- 2 eggs
- ¼ avocado, peeled, pitted, and cut into slices
- 1 tablespoon low-salt Kalamata olives, chopped
- 1 tablespoon chives, finely chopped
- 1 teaspoon orange juice
- A pinch black pepper
- Cooking spray

Directions:

1. In a lightly greased skillet over medium heat, add the eggs and scramble, cooking for about 3 minutes. Season with a pinch of black pepper.
2. Divide the eggs between the plates.
3. Top with the lox, avocado slices, Kalamata olives, and chives.
4. Season with orange juice and enjoy.

Nutrition: Calories: 240 - Fat: 12 g - Protein: 17 g - Carbs: 22 g - Fiber: 4 g - Sugar: 3 g - Sodium: 652 mg

Spinach Frittata and Bean Cream

Preparation Time: 5 minutes / **Cooking Time:** 15-20 minutes / **Servings:** 1

Ingredients:

- 1 tablespoon fat-free ricotta cheese
- ¼ cup fresh spinach
- 1 ½ teaspoons olive oil
- 1 tablespoon shallot, diced
- 1 tablespoon no-salt added canned beans, drained, and rinsed
- 1 large egg
- ½ teaspoon garlic powder
- 1 teaspoon fresh parsley, roughly chopped
- A pinch sea salt
- Freshly ground black pepper

Directions:

1. In a mixer, add the ricotta, beans, garlic powder and parsley, and blend until creamy.
2. In a small skillet over low-medium heat, heat the oil. Add the shallot and sauté for 3-5 minutes until golden brown.
3. Add the spinach to the skillet. Cook for about 3-4 minutes until spinach wilts.
4. Put the egg, salt and pepper, and whisk with a fork until smooth.
5. Pour the egg in the skillet with spinach. Cook covered for 5-6 minutes, or until the egg is firm.

6. When the egg is almost done, top the frittata with the cream of beans and cook 1-2 minutes more. Serve warm and enjoy.

Nutrition: Calories: 205 - Fat: 10 g - Protein: 12 g - Carbs: 9 g - Fiber: 1 g - Sugar: 2 g - Sodium: 192 mg

Protein Breakfast Burrito

Preparation Time: 10 minutes / **Cooking Time:** 10 minutes / **Servings:** 1

Ingredients:
- 1 slice cooked turkey bacon, chopped
- ¼ cup no-salt added canned chickpeas
- 1 tablespoon low-fat Monterey Jack cheese, shredded
- 1 large egg white
- 1 small whole-grain tortilla
- ⅛ avocado, peeled, pitted, and diced
- ¼ small red bell pepper, diced
- 2 halves sun dried tomato, chopped
- Ground black pepper
- A pinch chili powder
- Cooking spray
- 1 tablespoon red enchilada sauce, for serving (optional)

Directions:
1. In a small bowl, add the chickpeas, sun dried tomato, red bell pepper, avocado, turkey bacon, black pepper and chili powder, and mix well. Set aside.
2. In another bowl, whisk egg white and set aside.
3. Grease a skillet with cooking spray and place over medium heat.
4. Lower the heat to low-medium and add egg white. Stir every few minutes and, when egg is almost done, top with cheese and cook until cheese melts. Remove from heat and cover to keep warm.
5. Warm the tortilla; then, fill it with egg white and bowl mixture, and spoon enchilada sauce (if using).
6. Roll up the burrito and enjoy.

Nutrition: Calories: 276 - Fat: 12 g - Protein: 18 g - Carbs: 23 g - Fiber: 8 g - Sugar: 2 g - Sodium: 525 mg

Turkey Hash Mini-Cakes ✓

Preparation Time: 10 minutes / **Cooking Time:** 10-15 minutes / **Servings:** 2

Ingredients:
- 4 oz. lean ground turkey
- 1 small potato, cooked, and mashed
- ¼ yellow onion, minced
- ¼ small red bell pepper, finely diced
- 1 egg
- 2 tablespoons almond flour, for coating
- 2 teaspoon fresh parsley, minced
- A pinch ground cumin
- A pinch paprika
- A pinch sea salt
- A pinch ground pepper
- Cooking spray

Directions:
1. In a bowl, put all ingredients, except oil and flour, and mix until perfectly combined.

2. From mixture, shape two flour to coat.
3. Grease a saucepan wit medium heat.
4. When oil is hot, add and cook for about 6-7 minu
5. Then, flip the turkey other side.
6. Remove cakes from the skillet and p paper towel.
7. Put them on the plates and serve with your favu side dish.

Nutrition: Calories: 255 - Fat: 10 g - Protein: 22 g - Carbs: 15 g - Fiber: 1 g - Sodium: 644 mg

Smoothie Bowl with Greek Yogurt and Fresh Berries

Preparation Time: 5 minutes / **Cooking Time:** 0 minutes / **Servings:** 2

Ingredients:
- ½ cup low-fat plain Greek yogurt
- ½ cup unsweetened almond milk, or low-fat milk
- ¼ cup fresh strawberries
- ¼ cup fresh raspberries, sliced
- ¼ cup fresh blueberries
- 1 small ripe banana, sliced
- 2 tablespoons natural almond butter
- 1 teaspoon chia seeds
- ½ scoop protein powder (optional)

Directions:
1. In a blender, add the milk, yogurt, raspberries, blueberries, almond butter, chia seeds and protein powder (if using). Blend on high speed for 3-5 minutes, until the powder is well dissolved and ingredients are well combined.
2. Pour the smoothie into small bowls and garnish with banana and strawberries slices.

Nutrition: Calories: 287 - Fat: 7 g - Protein: 27 g - Carbs: 25 g - Fiber: 8 g - Sugar: 12 g - Sodium: 238 mg

Slow Cooker Apple-Carrot-Raisins Oatmeal

Preparation Time: 5 minutes / **Cooking Time:** 8 hours / **Servings:** 4

Ingredients:
- 1 apple, chopped
- 1 cup steel-cut oats
- 1 cup carrot, grated
- 1 cup water
- 1 teaspoon ground cinnamon
- 1 teaspoon ground nutmeg
- 2 cups low-fat milk, or unsweetened almond milk
- ¼ cup agave nectar
- 4 tablespoons no-sugar added raisins
- 2 tablespoons light powdered peanut butter
- 1 cup raspberries
- Cooking spray (olive oil or avocado oil)
- 2 scoops unflavored or vanilla protein powder (optional)

Directions:

Grease your slow cooker with cooking spray.

Add all the ingredients, except the raspberries, and mix until well combined.

Cover and cook on LOW for 8 hours (overnight), so that the oatmeal reaches a soft consistency.

4. Then, remove the lid, stir; and scoop into bowls.

5. Top with the raspberries and enjoy warm.

Nutrition: Calories: 295 - Fat: 8 g - Protein: 14 g - Carbs: 39 g - Fiber: 8 g - Sugar: 22 g - Sodium: 218 mg

Cherry-Vanilla Baked Oatmeal Muffins

Preparation Time: 10 minutes / **Cooking Time:** 20-25 minutes / **Servings:** 12

Ingredients:

- 3 cups old-fashioned oats
- 1 teaspoon ground cinnamon
- 3 tablespoons chia seeds
- 2 teaspoons baking powder
- 1 tablespoon ground flax seed
- 3 eggs
- 1 cup low-fat milk
- ½ cup light and fat-free plain kefir yogurt
- 1 teaspoon vanilla extract
- ¼ cup coconut oil, melted
- 1 cup fresh cherries, pitted, and chopped
- 1 apple, peeled, cored, and chopped
- ¾ teaspoon liquid stevia
- Cooking spray

Directions:

1. Preheat the oven to 350 °F. Lightly grease a 12 muffin tin with cooking spray.

2. In a medium bowl, stir together the oats, cinnamon, chia seeds, baking powder, and flax seed.

3. In a separate large bowl, gently whisk the eggs, milk, kefir, coconut oil, vanilla, and stevia.

4. Add the dry ingredients to the wet ones and mix to combine. Fold in the cherries and apples, and gently stir until well distributed.

5. Divide the mixture equally among the 12 muffin cups, filling them ¾ full.

6. Bake for 20-25 minutes, or until golden brown. Serve warm.

Nutrition: Calories: 208 - Fat: 9 g - Protein: 7 g - Carbs: 23 g - Fiber: 4 g - Sugar: 8 g - Sodium: 91 mg

Banana Protein Pancakes

Preparation Time: 5 minutes / **Cooking Time:** 5 minutes / **Servings:** 2

Ingredients:

- 2 eggs
- ½ ripe banana, roughly chopped
- ¼ cup low-fat plain Greek yogurt
- 2 tablespoons whole-wheat flour
- 1 ½ tablespoon coconut oil, melted
- ¼ teaspoon vanilla extract
- Cooking spray
- 1 scoop protein powder (optional)

Directions:

1. In large bowl, lightly whisk the eggs.

2. Add the yogurt, banana, vanilla extract, flour, coconut oil and protein powder (if using), and mix well.

3. Over medium heat, lightly coat a large skillet with the cooking spray.

4. Pour ¼ of batter into the skillet for each pancake.

5. Cook for 2.5 minutes, or until the surface of each pancake bubbles.

6. Turn the pancakes and cook the other side for 1-2 minutes, until golden brown.

7. Top pancakes with your favorite fresh fruits or toppings. Serve immediately.

Nutrition: Calories: 218 - Fat: 8 g - Protein: 14 g - Carbs: 16 g - Fiber: 3 g - Sugar: 7 g - Sodium: 214 mg

Pistachio Zucchini Muffins with Orange Glaze

Preparation Time: 10 minutes / **Cooking Time:** 25 minutes / **Servings:** 4

Ingredients:

- ½ cup zucchini, grated, and patted dry
- 1 egg white
- ¼ cup margarine, melted
- ½ teaspoon ground cardamom
- ¼ teaspoon ground nutmeg
- ½ teaspoon baking soda
- ¼ teaspoon vanilla extract
- ¼ cup powdered light brown sugar
- 2 tablespoons unsalted pistachios, shelled
- 6 tablespoons whole-wheat flour
- A pinch sea salt
- ¼ teaspoon ginger, grated
- ½ orange, juiced
- ¼ orange, zested
- Cooking spray

Directions:

1. Preheat the oven to 350 °F. Coat a 4 muffin tin with cooking spray.

2. In a food processor, add pistachios and process until finely chopped.

3. In a large bowl, place zucchini, margarine, vanilla, pistachios, egg white, and stir. Add in cardamom, nutmeg, zest, baking soda, salt and flour, and mix until perfectly combined.

4. Fill the muffin cups ¾ full, and bake in the oven for about 25 minutes.

5. While muffins bake, in a small bowl, combine orange juice, ginger and powdered sugar, stirring until the desired consistency is reached.

6. When muffins are ready, remove from oven and let cool for 5 minutes.

7. Top with orange glaze and enjoy.

Nutrition: Calories: 297 - Fat: 13 g - Protein: 4 g - Carbs: 35 g - Fiber: 1 g - Sugar: 24 g - Sodium: 228 mg

Pumpkin Zucchini Muffins

Preparation Time: 10 minutes / **Cooking Time:** 30 minutes / **Servings:** 12

Ingredients:

- 1 cup zucchini, shredded

- ¾ cup canned pumpkin
- 1 ⅓ cup whole-wheat pastry flour
- ⅓ tablespoon baking powder
- ⅓ teaspoon baking soda
- 2 teaspoons ground cinnamon
- 1 teaspoon ground nutmeg
- ½ cup low-fat milk
- 1 egg, lightly beaten
- ½ teaspoon vanilla extract
- ⅓ cup no-sugar added raisins
- 2 tablespoons pumpkin seeds
- ⅓ cup agave nectar

Directions:

1. Preheat the oven to 350 °F. Prepare a 12 muffin tin by coating the cups using muffins baking liners.
2. Add the flour, baking powder, baking soda, cinnamon, and nutmeg.
3. In another medium bowl, stir together the zucchini, pumpkin, milk, egg, vanilla extract, and agave nectar.
4. Add the wet ingredients to the dry and gently stir to combine. Fold in the raisins and pumpkin seeds.
5. Spoon the butter into the muffin cups and fill them about ¾ full.
6. Bake about 30 minutes, or until the muffins are done. They are ready when a toothpick inserted in the center comes out clean.
7. Let cool the muffins for 5 minutes before removing them from the tins, and serve.

Nutrition: Calories: 312 - Fat: 9 g - Protein: 8 g - Carbs: 37 g - Fiber: 3 g - Sugar: 20 g - Sodium: 411 mg

Marinated Salmon Pancake Rolls

Preparation Time: 15 minutes to marinate / **Cooking Time:** 10 minutes / **Servings:** 2

Ingredients:

- 1 egg
- ½ cup low-fat milk
- 2 teaspoons margarine, melted
- 3 oz. all-purpose flour
- ½ teaspoon baking soda
- 2 slices smoked salmon
- 1 lime, juiced
- 1 tablespoon extra-virgin olive oil
- ¼ cup low-fat cottage cheese
- 1 teaspoon dried rosemary
- ¼ teaspoon ginger, grated
- A pinch ground red pepper
- A pinch sweet paprika
- Cooking spray

Directions:

1. In a bowl, add lime juice, olive oil, ginger, paprika and red pepper, and mix well.
2. Dip salmon in the mixture, cover the bowl with plastic wrap and let marinate in the fridge for 15 minutes.
3. In the meantime, in a small bowl, add cottage cheese and stir in dried rosemary, mixing until well combined. Then, set aside.
4. Over medium heat, lightly grease a skillet with cooking spray.

5. Mix the egg and milk. Add margarine, flour and baking soda, and stir well.
6. Pour ½ of the mixture into the skillet to prepare the first pancake and cook for 2-3 minutes. Then, flip the pancake and continue cooking the other side for 1-2 minutes.
7. When pancake is done, remove from skillet and let cool for some minutes.
8. Spread the pancake with cottage cheese, top with a slice of marinated salmon and roll up the pancake and its filling.
9. Repeat for the other pancake.
10. Cut the rolled pancakes in slices and enjoy.

Nutrition: Calories: 355 - Fat: 14 g - Protein: 20 g - Carbs: 32 g - Fiber: 2 g - Sugar: 4 g - Sodium: 590 mg

✓*Turkey Frittata with Arugula and Gouda Cheese*

Preparation Time: 10 minutes / **Cooking Time:** 10 minutes / **Servings:** 2

Ingredients:

- 5 oz. extra-lean ground turkey
- 2 eggs, beaten
- 2 tablespoons fat-free milk
- 2 oz. fresh arugula, stems removed, and chopped
- ¼ onion, diced
- ½ garlic clove, minced
- 2 oz. low-fat gouda cheese, shredded
- A pinch black pepper
- A pinch sea salt
- Cooking spray

Directions:

1. Oil a skillet with the cooking spray and place it over medium-high heat.
2. Stir in the onion and sauté until golden; then, add garlic and cook for 1 minute.
3. Add the turkey and, using a wooden spoon, break it into small pieces. Cook about 5-7 minutes until golden.
4. In a medium bowl, combine together the eggs, black pepper, salt and milk.
5. Pour the eggs into the skillet. Lower the heat to medium-low and cook for 5 minutes.
6. With the help of a lid, cover the skillet and flip it so that frittata falls onto the lid. Then slide the frittata off the lid back into the pan to cook the other side.
7. Top with the cheese and when the cheese has melted, sprinkle with arugula and serve.

Nutrition: Calories: 165 - Fat: 8 g - Protein: 15 g - Carbs: 2 g - Fiber: 0 g - Sugar: 1 g - Sodium: 235 mg

Curry Lentils and Sunny-Side Up Egg with Yogurt

Preparation Time: 10 minutes / **Cooking Time:** 20 minutes / **Servings:** 2

Ingredients:

- ½ cup canned red lentils, drained, and rinsed
- 1 bay leaf
- ¼ small onion, diced
- 1 small carrot, diced
- ½ celery stalk, diced

- ½ cup tomato, diced
- 1 tablespoon extra-virgin olive oil
- 2 eggs
- ½ teaspoon curry powder
- 2 tablespoons low-fat plain Greek yogurt
- 2 teaspoons fresh parsley, finely chopped
- A pinch sea salt
- A pinch black pepper

Directions:

1. Grease a large saucepan with olive oil and place over medium heat.
2. Stir in onion, carrot, celery and bay leaf, and cook until veggies are soft.
3. Add in lentils, tomato, black pepper, salt and curry, decrease heat, and let cook for 10 minutes, stirring occasionally.
4. Remove bay leaf. Then, with the help of a spoon, form two wells in the lentils and crack the eggs in.
5. Cover with a lid and cook until the white is set but the yolks are soft and creamy.
6. Divide eggs and lentils into plates, scatter with parsley, and serve with Greek yogurt.

Nutrition: Calories: 239 - Fat: 7 g - Protein: 15 g - Carbs: 14 g - Fiber: 9 g - Sugar: 4 g - Sodium: 330 mg

Avocado Sauce Cauliflower Scrambled Burrito

Preparation Time: 15 minutes / **Cooking Time:** 20 minutes / **Servings:** 1

Ingredients:

For the Filling:
- 1 slice cooked chicken bacon
- 1 egg
- ½ cup cauliflower, chopped
- ½ cup green bell pepper, diced
- ¼ cup tomato, diced
- 1 tablespoon low-fat milk
- 1 scallion, chopped
- A pinch ground black pepper
- A pinch sea salt
- Water
- 1 low-carb whole-wheat tortilla
- Cooking spray

For the Sauce:
- ¼ avocado, peeled, pitted, and roughly chopped
- 1 ½ tablespoon plain low-fat Greek yogurt
- ½ lime, juiced
- ¼ tablespoon avocado oil
- 1 teaspoon parsley, chopped
- A pinch cayenne pepper

Directions:

1. In a blender, place the avocado, Greek yogurt, lime juice, avocado oil, cayenne pepper and parsley, and blend until perfectly smooth. If necessary, add in water to adjust consistency. Then, set aside.
2. In an oil spayed skillet over medium heat, cook chicken bacon until crisp; then, remove from the skillet and place on a paper towel lined plate. Set aside.

3. Pour water into a small pot, bring to a boil over high heat, add in cauliflower, reduce to medium, and cook for 3 minutes. Then, drain and set aside.
4. If necessary, lightly grease the skillet again. Add in the scallion and sauté until golden.
5. Place cauliflower, tomato and green bell pepper in the skillet, and stir until vegetables become tender.
6. In a bowl, whisk egg, milk, black pepper and salt.
7. Add the egg mixture into the veggies skillet, reduce the heat to medium-low and stir gently and constantly until the eggs are fluffy and set, for about 5 minutes.
8. Meanwhile, spread avocado sauce on the tortilla, and when egg and veggies mixture is done, spoon over sauce, top with chicken bacon, and roll up the burrito.

Nutrition: Calories: 330 - Fat: 17 g - Protein: 19 g - Carbs: 23 g - Fiber: 3 g - Sugar: 4 g - Sodium: 536 mg

Chicken, Broccoli, Cheese and Mushroom Casserole

Preparation Time: 15 minutes / **Cooking Time:** 50 minutes / **Servings:** 4

Ingredients:
- 1 cup cooked chicken breast, chopped
- 1 cup broccoli florets, chopped
- 4 oz. low-fat mozzarella cheese, shredded
- 3 tablespoons Parmesan cheese, grated
- ½ cup mushrooms, chopped
- 2 eggs
- ½ onion, diced
- 1 tablespoon low-fat milk
- 1 tablespoon dried thyme
- ¼ teaspoon ground black pepper
- A pinch sea salt
- Cooking spray

Directions:

1. Preheat the oven to 350 °F.
2. In a large skillet over medium heat, spray the olive oil. Stir in the onion and sauté for 1-2 minutes, or until golden.
3. Add the broccoli and cook for 5 minutes. Stir in the mushrooms and cook for an additional 3-4 minutes, or until tender.
4. In the baking dish, add chopped chicken and vegetables, and let cool.
5. Mix together the eggs, milk, black pepper, salt, thyme and mozzarella cheese.
6. Pour the egg mixture over the veggies in the baking dish and stir to combine. Top with the Parmesan cheese.
7. Bake for 35-40 minutes, or until lightly brown.
8. Remove from heat and let the casserole sit for about 5 minutes. Serve and enjoy.

Nutrition: Calories: 147 - Fat: 10 g - Protein: 12 g - Carbs: 2 g - Fiber: 1 g - Sugar: 0 g - Sodium: 193 mg

Berry-Lemon Greek Yogurt Pancakes

Preparation Time: 10 minutes / **Cooking Time:** 15 minutes / **Servings:** 2

Ingredients:
- 2 eggs
- ¾ cup low-fat plain Greek yogurt

- 3 tablespoons sugar-free maple syrup , divided
- ½ teaspoon vanilla extract
- ½ cup whole wheat flour
- ½ cup all-purpose flour
- 1 cup unsweetened almond milk
- 1 teaspoon baking powder
- ¼ teaspoon baking soda
- ¼ teaspoon ground cinnamon
- ½ lemon, zested, and juiced
- ½ cup fresh or frozen blueberries
- ½ cup fresh or frozen strawberries, sliced
- Cooking spray

Directions:

1. Mix the dry ingredients: flours, baking powder, baking soda and cinnamon.
2. In another bowl, combine wet ingredients: beat eggs, and stir in yogurt, 1 tablespoon maple syrup, almond milk, lemon zest and juice, and vanilla extract.
3. Add the wet ingredients to the dry ingredients, and stir until well mixed. Gently blend in blueberries.
4. Grease with cooking spray a non-stick skillet over medium-low heat.
5. Pour ¼ of the batter for every pancake and cook for about 3 minutes, until bubbles appear on top and the edges are golden brown.
6. Then, flip the pancake and cook for 2-3 minutes more.
7. Repeat with other ¾ of the batter.
8. Top each pancake with ½ tablespoon maple syrup, and strawberries.

Nutrition: Calories: 336 - Fat: 7 g - Protein: 17 g - Carbs: 38 g - Sugar: 16 g

Banana Strawberries Oatmeal with Almond Butter

Preparation Time: 5 minutes / **Cooking Time:** 10 minutes / **Servings:** 2

Ingredients:

- 1 cup rolled oats
- 1 cup unsweetened almond milk
- 10 fresh or frozen strawberries, cored, and sliced
- 1 banana, peeled, and mashed
- ¼ teaspoon liquid stevia
- 1 teaspoon vanilla extract
- ⅓ teaspoon ground cinnamon
- A pinch sea salt
- 6 large egg whites
- 2 tablespoons natural almond butter
- ½ cup water

Directions:

1. In a medium bowl, whisk egg whites and stevia, and set aside.
2. Over medium-high heat, in a pot, heat oats, almond milk, water, strawberries, banana, cinnamon, vanilla, and salt.
3. When boiling, lower the heat and cook stirring from time to time for about 4-5 minutes, until the blend is almost set and the most of the liquids is absorbed.
4. Add the egg whites to cooked cereal and stir quickly until consistency is set and soft.

5. Divide oatmeal in bowls, top with almond butter and enjoy.

Nutrition: Calories: 312 - Fat: 13 g - Protein: 17 g - Carbs: 45 g - Sugar: 19 g

Vanilla Cinnamon French Toast

Preparation Time: 5 minutes / **Cooking Time:** 10 minutes / **Servings:** 2

Ingredients:

- 3 egg whites, beaten
- 1 cup unsweetened almond milk
- ½ teaspoon vanilla extract
- 4 slices low-carb whole wheat bread
- ½ teaspoon ground cinnamon
- ½ teaspoon ground nutmeg
- ½ orange, zested, and juiced
- Cooking spray
- 2 teaspoons no-added sugar maple syrup (optional)
- Fresh berries of your choice (optional)

Directions:

1. In a medium bowl, mix egg whites, milk, vanilla, cinnamon, nutmeg, orange juice and orange zest, and stir until well blended.
2. Dip the bread one slice at a time in the egg blend, and let the slice soak in the mixture.
3. Over medium heat, coat a large non-stick skillet with cooking spray, and add the drenched slices of bread (if your skillet is small add one at a time and repeat with the other slices of bread).
4. Cook for about 2.5 minutes per side, or until golden brown.
5. Top with maple syrup and berries (if using).

Nutrition: Calories: 218 - Fat: 3 g - Protein: 19 g - Carbs: 34 g - Sugar: 13 g

Vegetarian Savory Bread Pudding

Preparation Time: 10 minutes / **Cooking Time:** 50 minutes / **Servings:** 4

Ingredients:

- 4 slices low-carb whole-wheat bread, diced
- 4 oz. low-fat mozzarella cheese, shredded
- 1 red bell pepper, diced
- ½ red onion, diced
- 1 cup mushrooms, diced
- 1 garlic cloves, minced
- 2 eggs
- ½ cup low-fat milk
- 1 teaspoon cumin
- ½ teaspoon cayenne pepper
- A pinch black pepper
- Cooking spray

Directions:

1. Preheat the oven to 375 °F.
2. In a medium-sized bowl, combine the bread, red bell pepper, onion, mushroom, cayenne pepper, cumin and garlic.
3. In a separate bowl, whisk the eggs, black pepper and milk until well combined.
4. Pour the egg mixture into the bread mixture and stir well.

5.   Pour the mixture into a lightly oil sprayed baking pan. Sprinkle on the shredded mozzarella.

6.   Bake at 376 °F for 45 minutes or until the eggs are set.

Nutrition: Calories: 243 - Fat: 7 g - Protein: 18 g - Carbs: 21 g - Fiber: 3 g - Sugar: 6 g

Fully Green Shakshuka with Beans

Preparation Time: 10 minutes / **Cooking Time:** 20 minutes / **Servings:** 4

Ingredients:

- 4 large eggs
- 2 garlic cloves, minced
- ½ green onion, finely chopped
- 16 canned asparagus tips, drained, and rinsed
- 4 oz. fresh baby spinach
- 4 oz. canned peas, drained, and rinsed
- ½ teaspoon ground cumin
- 1 teaspoon ground coriander
- ¼ teaspoon cayenne pepper
- 4 oz. no-salt added canned mixed beans, drained, and rinsed
- 1 tablespoon fresh parsley, chopped
- A pinch sea salt
- A pinch pepper
- Cooking spray
- 2 tablespoons soy protein powder (optional)

Directions:

1.   In oil sprayed large skillet over medium heat, cook onion and garlic for about 4-5 minutes, until soft and transparent.

2.   Add the spinach and cook for 2 minutes. Then, stir in the peas, beans and asparagus tips, and season with cayenne pepper, coriander, cumin and protein powder (if using).

3.   Stir to combine and cook for about 5-6 minutes.

4.   Break the eggs on the vegetables, season the yolks with a little pinch of salt and a little pinch of pepper, and cover with a lid.

5.   Cook for 5 minutes, or until the whites are set and the yolks are soft.

6.   Top the skillet with the chopped parsley and serve.

Nutrition: Calories: 253 - Fat: 14 g - Protein: 19 g - Carbs: 10 g - Fiber: 7 g - Sugar: 3 g

✓ *Protein-Packed Breakfast Bars*

Preparation Time: 5 minutes / **Cooking Time:** 35 minutes / **Servings:** 6

Ingredients:

- 1 cup porridge oats
- 1 tablespoon smooth nut butter
- 1 tablespoon coconut oil, melted
- 1 tablespoon agave nectar or no- sugar added maple syrup
- 1 tablespoon whey/soy vanilla protein powder
- 1 teaspoon ground cinnamon
- Cooking spray

Directions:

1.   Heat the oven to 160 °F.

2.   Grease and line the base of a 9x7 inch tin with a little cooking spray. Mix the oats and nut butter in the tin. Place in the oven for 5-10 minutes to toast.

3.   Increase oven temperature to 350 °F.

4.   Meanwhile, warm the coconut oil in a pan over low heat.

5.   Add the oat and mix, syrup, protein powder, and cinnamon to the pan. Mix everything together until all the oats are well-coated.

6.   Bake for 25 minutes, or until golden brown.

7.   Let cool in the tin and cut into 6 bars.

Nutrition: Calories: 221 - Fat: 9 g - Protein: 7 g - Carbs: 19 g - Fiber: 2 g - Sugar: 7 g

Spinach, Tomato and Cheese Soft Omelet

Preparation Time: 10 minutes / **Cooking Time:** 15 minutes / **Servings:** 2

Ingredients:

- 2 cups fresh baby spinach leaves
- ½ cup tomatoes, diced
- 2 teaspoons extra-virgin olive oil
- 3 eggs, beaten
- ¼ cup fat-free cottage cheese
- 2 tablespoons leek, chopped
- 1 tablespoon parsley, finely chopped
- A pinch ground black pepper
- A pinch sea salt
- Cooking spray

Directions:

1.   Put olive oil over medium heat, and add tomatoes and leek. Stir until vegetables become soft.

2.   Meanwhile, beat the eggs in a bowl and season with black pepper and salt.

3.   Place baby spinach in the pan with tomatoes and leek, and cook until wilted. Then, remove from heat and place in a food processor, blending until soft.

4.   Oil a skillet with cooking spray and add beaten eggs. Cook until the eggs begin to thick.

5.   Spread vegetables mixture and cottage cheese in the center of eggs and softly fold omelet in half. Let warm for 2-3 minutes more, flipping omelet halfway through.

6.   Sprinkle with parsley, divide between plates, serve and enjoy.

Nutrition: Calories: 220 - Fat: 11 g - Protein: 14 g - Carbs: 8 g - Sodium: 383 mg

Salmon and Artichokes Scrambled Eggs

Preparation Time: 10 minutes / **Cooking Time:** 15 minutes / **Servings:** 2

Ingredients:

- 2 oz. smoked salmon, chopped
- 1 artichoke heart, cleaned, stem removed and julienned
- 1 medium zucchini, thin rounds sliced
- 2 tablespoons extra-virgin olive oil
- 3 eggs
- ¼ cup light ricotta cheese
- A pinch sea salt
- A pinch black pepper

Directions:

1.   Put oil over medium heat. When oil is hot add artichoke and cook for 5 minutes.

2.   Add in zucchinis and let cook for 3 minute, or until vegetables are tender, stirring constantly.

3.   In a bowl, beat the eggs and season with salt and pepper.

4.   Turn heat on low and add eggs to the vegetables in the skillet. Stir constantly and scramble the eggs.

5.   When eggs are almost done, stir in ricotta cheese and mix all the ingredients together.

6.   Remove skillet from heat, add salmon and serve.

Nutrition: Calories: 198 - Fat: 9 g - Protein: 15 g - Carbs: 10 g - Sodium: 585 mg

Chapter 6: Soups and Salads

"Left Over "Turkey Salad
PREP TIME: 15 min **COOK TIME:** 45 min **YIELD:** 5 Serve
INGREDIENTS:
- 3 tablespoons fresh lemon juice, to taste
- 1/4 cup walnut halves (finely crush)
- 2 tablespoons extra-virgin olive oil
- 1 Bartlett pear, ripe but firm
- 1 head Boston lettuce, washed
- 1 skinless and boneless turkey breast

DIRECTIONS:
- Preheat your stove to 350 degrees Fahrenheit (175 degrees C). 2 sheets of aluminum foil (about 24 inches long). Season the turkey breast with salt and pepper and place it in the middle of one piece of foil.
- To seal the turkey in, place the second piece of foil on top and roll the edges together. Place the covered foil bag on a baking sheet and bake for 30 minutes, or until the turkey is cooked and white.
- Lightly fry the walnuts in a saucepan over medium-low heat for approximately 5 minutes while the turkey roasts. In a mixing bowl, grate the pears and add walnuts, oil, and lemon juice.
- Please remove it from the foil bag and set it aside for five minutes when the turkey is done. Fill the dressing with the juices from the foil bag. Season with salt and pepper to taste.
- Arrange the lettuce on a plate, then slice the turkey and stack the pieces on top. Serve the salad with the pear and walnut dressing while the turkey is still warm.

NUTRITION:
90 Cal; 7g Protein; 5g Tot Fat; 1g Carb; 0g Fiber; 2g Sugar; 24mg Sodium

Chestnut Chicken Salad
PREP TIME: 15 min **COOK TIME:** none **YIELD:** 5 Serve
INGREDIENTS:
- 1 cup chopped green onions
- 1 cup low-fat buttermilk
- 8 cup torn lettuce
- 2 T. soy sauce
- 2 cup shredded chicken breast
- 1 cup fat-free mayonnaise
- 1 cup sliced water chestnuts
- 1 packet (1 oz.) Hidden Valley Original Ranch Dressing Mix

DIRECTIONS:
- Combine the dressing mix, buttermilk, and mayonnaise in a mixing dish. Mix thoroughly. Cover and store in the refrigerator. To thicken, chill for 30 minutes. Add the soy sauce and mix well. Toss with the rest of the ingredients.

NUTRITION:
197 Cal; 21g Protein; 2.4g Tot Fat; 19g Carb; 3.6g Fiber; 2g Sugar; 127mg Sodium

Poached Chicken Salad
PREP TIME: 15 min **COOK TIME:** none **YIELD:** 5 Serve
INGREDIENTS:
- Tarragon
- 1 c grapes, sliced in half
- 2 celery ribs, chopped
- Chopped pecans (optional)
- 1 apple, peeled and chopped
- low-fat mayonnaise
- Salt and pepper
- 2 poached chicken breasts, skinned and chopped (See additional notes below for how to poach chicken)

DIRECTIONS:
- Mayonnaise should be used to moisten chopped chicken. Chop the almonds, apple, celery, and grapes and combine them in a bowl. Season with salt and pepper to taste.

NUTRITION:
90 Cal; 7g Protein; 5g Tot Fat; 1g Carb; 0g Fiber; 2g Sugar; 24mg Sodium

Chicken Grilled Cesar Salad
PREP TIME: 15 min **COOK TIME:** none **YIELD:** 5 Serve
INGREDIENTS:
CHICKEN:
- 1 pound Boneless Skinless Chicken Breast
- 2 tablespoons Worcestershire Sauce
- 1 clove garlic -- Crushed
- 1/4 tsp. Pepper
- 1 tsp. Ground Cumin
- Halves -- Cut into - 1-inch strips
- 1 tablespoon chili powder

DRESSING:
- 1 clove garlic -- Minced
- 3/4 cup buttermilk
- 1/2 tsp. Dry Mustard
- 1 tsp. anchovy paste
- 1 tablespoon lemon juice
- 1/4 tsp. Pepper
- 3 tablespoons fat-free parmesan cheese

SALAD:
- 3/4 cup Plain Croutons
- 2 cups Halved Cherry Tomatoes
- 12 cups Romaine Lettuce Leaves -- Sliced

DIRECTIONS:
- In a medium mixing bowl, combine all chicken ingredients; toss thoroughly, and set aside. Preheat the grill or the broiler. Cook 5 minutes on each side or until chicken is cooked through on a grill rack or broiler pan sprayed with cooking spray. In a big mixing basin, combine all of the dressing ingredients and whisk thoroughly. Combine salad ingredients, stir with dressing, and serve with grilled chicken pieces on each dish.

NUTRITION:
158 Cal; 22g Protein; 2g Tot Fat; 16g Carb; 0g Fiber; 2g Sugar; 179mg Sodium

Waldorf salad
PREP TIME: 15 min **COOK TIME:** none **YIELD:** 8 Serve
INGREDIENTS:
- 1-1/2 cup raisins
- 3 T. fat-free sour cream
- 1/2 cup miniature marshmallows

- 2 medium stalks of celery, diced
- 2 medium apples, diced
- 2 T. chopped walnuts (optional)
- 3 T. light mayonnaise (1g fat per tablespoon)

DIRECTIONS:
- Mix the mayonnaise and sour in a mixing dish. Remove from the equation. Combine the remaining ingredients in a larger mixing dish. Toss the fruit with the mayonnaise sauce. Before serving, chill the dish.

NUTRITION:
89 Cal; 1g Protein; 1.5g Tot Fat; 19g Carb; 0g Fiber; 2g Sugar; 24mg Sodium

Bahamas Shrimp Salad ✓

PREP TIME: 15 min **COOK TIME:** none **YIELD:** 5 Serve
INGREDIENTS:
- 1 tablespoon lemon juice
- 2 tablespoons fat-free French salad dressing
- 1 tablespoon chopped onion
- 3/4 cup cauliflower -- finely chopped
- 1/4 cup finely chopped celery
- 1/4 cup chopped green bell pepper
- 1 pound shrimp -- cooked
- 1/3 cup Miracle Whip® Free
- 1 cup cooked rice
- 1 tsp. salt

DIRECTIONS:
- Combine the rice and salad dressing. Stir everything together thoroughly. Shrimp should be peeled and deveined. Chop into small pieces.
- Add to the mixing bowl. In a mixing dish, combine the onion, cauliflower, celery, and bell pepper. Stir everything together well. In a mixing bowl, combine the lemon juice, Miracle Whip Free, and salt. Stir everything together well. Cover and chill until ready to serve.

NUTRITION:
110 Cal; 12g Protein; 1g Tot Fat; 11g Carb; 0g Fiber; 2g Sugar; 467mg Sodium

Southern Tuna Salad

PREP TIME: 15 min **COOK TIME:** none **YIELD:** 5 Serve
INGREDIENTS:
- 1 t. Louisiana hot sauce (optional)
- 2 T. dill pickle relish
- 2 T. fat-free mayo/or Miracle Whip Free
- 2 t. Dijon mustard
- 1 6 1/2 oz. can tuna in water/drained
- 2 eggs/hard-boiled/chopped

DIRECTIONS:
- Combine eggs and dill relish in a mixing bowl. Mix the remaining ingredients in a mixing bowl (except tuna). Mix thoroughly. After that, add the tuna. Add additional mayo if the mixture is too dry.

NUTRITION:
51 Cal; 8g Protein; 2g Tot Fat; 1g Carb; 0g Fiber; 2g Sugar; 190mg Sodium

Black Bean and Chicken Salad ✓

PREP TIME: 15 min **COOK TIME:** none **YIELD:** 5 Serve

INGREDIENTS:
- 1 T. fresh lime juice
- 1 cup cooked black beans (drained)
- 1/4 cup fat-free Italian salad dressing
- 1 T. fresh parsley
- 1/2 cup fat-free cheddar cheese (shredded)
- 6 lettuce leaves ~
- 1 med. tomato (chopped)   *+ lettuce leaf*
- 1 cup cooked chicken (cubed)
- 1 cup cooked rice (cooled)

DIRECTIONS:
- Combine the cheese, beans, rice, chicken, tomato, and parsley in a big mixing bowl. Dressing and lime juice should be poured over the salad. Toss gently. Serve on a lettuce leaf as a garnish. As desired, garnish.

NUTRITION:
142 Cal; 14g Protein; 18g Tot Fat; 1g Carb; 0g Fiber; 2g Sugar; 229mg Sodium

Cottage Cheese Salad

PREP TIME: 15 min **COOK TIME:** none **YIELD:** 2 Serve
INGREDIENTS:
- dash salt/pepper
- 1/4 cup cucumber (seeded/diced)
- 1 clove garlic (minced/small clove)
- 2 T. red bell peppers (diced)
- 1/8 cup carrot (grated)
- dash celery salt
- 1 cup fat-free cottage cheese

DIRECTIONS:
- In a small mixing dish, combine all of the ingredients. Stir. Allow 10 minutes for the flavors to meld. Refrigerate any leftover salad in a tightly covered container.

NUTRITION:
80 Cal; 15g Protein; 0.2g Tot Fat; 5g Carb; 0g Fiber; 2g Sugar; 303mg Sodium

Chicken Caesar Salad

PREP TIME: 15 min **COOK TIME:** none **YIELD:** 5 Serve
INGREDIENTS:
- 1 1/4 pounds romaine lettuce -- torn into bite-size pieces
- 3 cups roasted chicken -- shredded

DRESSING:
- 1 clove garlic -- crushed
- 3 tablespoons fresh lemon juice
- 1/4 tsp. salt
- 1 packet equal® sweetener
- 3 teaspoons Dijon mustard
- 1/4 tsp. black pepper
- 3 teaspoons Worcestershire sauce

GARNISH:
- 1/2 cup fat-free parmesan cheese
- 1 1/2 cups plain croutons

DIRECTIONS:
- To put together the salad in a big mixing basin, combine the chicken and lettuce.
To make the dressing:
- Whisk together all of the ingredients in a mixing dish.

- Toss the salad with the dressing.
- Sprinkle with croutons and cheese just before serving; mix gently to incorporate.

NUTRITION:
190 Cal; 17g Protein; 4.5g Tot Fat; 1.8g Carb; 0g Fiber; 3.2g Sugar; 354mg Sodium

Tossed Blue Cheese Salad
PREP TIME: 15 min **COOK TIME:** none **YIELD:** 4 Serve
INGREDIENTS:
- 1 tablespoon red wine vinegar
- 1 Sliced onion
- 3 tablespoons Olive oil
- Crumbled blue cheese
- Finely chopped romaine

DIRECTIONS:
- Combine the greens, onion, and cheese in a bowl with the oil and vinegar.

NUTRITION:
120 Cal; 8g Protein; 6g Tot Fat; 2g Carb; 0g Fiber; 4g Sugar; 204mg Sodium

Greek Style Egg Salad
PREP TIME: 15 min **COOK TIME:** none **YIELD:** 4 Serve
INGREDIENTS:
- 2 tablespoons crumbled Feta cheese
- 2 tablespoons finely chopped green onion
- Salt and black pepper
- 2 teaspoons milk
- 2 tablespoons reduced-fat mayonnaise
- 1/4 cup diced, seeded tomatoes
- 2 tablespoons sliced Kalamata or black olives
- 4 hard-cooked eggs, chopped

DIRECTIONS:
- Combine eggs, onion, olives, and tomatoes in a medium mixing basin. Mix in the mayonnaise, milk, and spices until everything is thoroughly combined. In a small mixing bowl, gently fold in the cheese. Cover and set aside to cool.

NUTRITION:
114 Cal; 8g Protein; 7g Tot Fat; 3g Carb; 0g Fiber; 3g Sugar; 197mg Sodium

Pasta Salad Recipe
PREP TIME: 15 min **COOK TIME:** none **YIELD:** 5 Serve
INGREDIENTS:
- 1 Pack of Pasta, you can use any kind.
- 4 or 5 Roma Tomatoes (depending on the size)
- 1 Container Feta Cheese
- 1 Red Onion, optional
- 3 Peppers. Green, Red, Yellow and Orange
- 1 English cucumber

Dressing:
- Salt to taste.
- 1/2 cup Olive Oil
- 2 tbsp. Italian Seasoning
- As much Crushed Garlic as you'd like
- 1/2 cup Balsamic Vinegar

DIRECTIONS:
- Cook the pasta. Cut everything into bite-sized pieces. After adding the spaghetti, crumble the feta cheese. Mix the dressing ingredients and put over the salad. Toss thoroughly. The following day is always better.

NUTRITION:
47 Cal; 6g Protein; 2g Tot Fat; 1.4g Carb; 0g Fiber; 0.2g Sugar; 124mg Sodium

Black Bean Salad
PREP TIME: 15 min **COOK TIME:** none **YIELD:** 1 Serve
INGREDIENTS:
- Green onion, thinly sliced
- Corn nib lets, drained
- Kidney beans, rinsed,
- Chickpeas, rinsed
- Baby zucchini, cut in semi-circles
- Black beans, rinsed

Dressing:
- Dried marjoram
- Black pepper and cayenne pepper
- Salt
- Pureed garlic
- Olive oil
- Crumbled feta
- Rice wine vinegar

DIRECTIONS:
- The quantities of all components and spices are completely up to your preference. Season while you combine, and adjust the seasonings as needed.

NUTRITION:
25 Cal; 3g Protein; 0.5g Tot Fat; 0.1g Carb; 0g Fiber; 0.2g Sugar; 213mg Sodium

Grilled Steak Salad
PREP TIME: 15 min **COOK TIME:** none **YIELD:** 4 Serve
INGREDIENTS:
- 1/2 cup Italian salad dressing on the side
- 12 OZ grilled steak (use leftovers from the night before)
- 1 cucumber, peeled and sliced
- 2 medium tomatoes cut into wedges
- 1 cup croutons
- 1 (12 oz.) bag prewashed salad greens, any variety.

DIRECTIONS:
- The steak should be cut into strips. Toss lettuce, tomato, and cucumber together. Add sliced steak and croutons on the top.

NUTRITION:
56 Cal; 5g Protein; 2g Tot Fat; 0g Carb; 0g Fiber; 0g Sugar; 87mg Sodium

Smoked Chicken Salad with Raspberry Balsamic Vinaigrette
PREP TIME: 15 min **COOK TIME:** none **YIELD:** 4 Serve
INGREDIENTS:
- 1/4 cup toasted sliced almonds
- 1/4 cup sugar-free raspberry jam

- 6 cups muscling mix (a mixture of young, crisp greens)
- 3/4 lb. boneless smoked chicken breast, cut into 3 strips
- 1/4 cup balsamic vinegar
- 2 cups fresh raspberries
- 3 tbsp. extra-virgin olive oil

DIRECTIONS:
- Combine the oil, jam, and vinegar in a sealed container. Shake vigorously after closing the cover securely. Toss the chicken with the dressing in a big mixing basin carefully. Mesclun should be used to cover a big plate or basin.
- Add the chicken mixture, raspberries, and almonds to the top. (Alternatively, serve the chicken on the mesclun with the dressing on the side or drizzled over the top, garnished with raspberries and almonds.)

NUTRITION:
110 Cal; 12g Protein; 4g Tot Fat; 1g Carb; 0g Fiber; 2g Sugar; 109mg Sodium

Garlic-Roasted Radicchio
PREP TIME: 15 min **COOK TIME:** 26 min **YIELD:** 12 Serve

INGREDIENTS:
- Grated Parmesan cheese for garnish
- 8 garlic cloves, finely chopped
- 1/2 tsp. black pepper
- 1 tablespoon chopped fresh rosemary leaves
- 1 tsp. kosher salt
- 1/4 cup balsamic vinegar
- 4 large heads radicchio, halved through the root
- 1/4 cup olive oil

DIRECTIONS:
- Combine the garlic, olive oil, rosemary, vinegar, salt, and pepper in a big mixing bowl. Toss in the radicchio, gently tossing it to coat it evenly. Marinate for 1 hour at room temperature.
- Preheat your stove to about 425 degrees Fahrenheit. In a baking sheet, place the radicchio and drizzle the marinade over it. Place in the oven and roast for 20 to 25 minutes, or until the tips of the radicchio are crisp and nearly burned.

NUTRITION:
48 Cal; 3g Protein; 2g Tot Fat; 1g Carb; 0g Fiber; 0g Sugar; 14mg Sodium

Cantaloupe and Avocado Salad
PREP TIME: 15 min **COOK TIME:** 15 min **YIELD:** 5 Serve

INGREDIENTS:
- 1 head of any loose-leaf lettuce
- 1.5 cantaloupe, seeded, peeled and cut into chunks
- 1/2 cup slivered, toasted almonds
- 2 Tbs. lemon juice
- One 14-oz. can diced hearts of palm
- 2 Tbs. melted butter (low fat)
- 2 medium-size avocados, peeled and cut into chunks

Dressing Ingredients:
- 1/2 tsp. ground ginger
- 6 Tbs. lime juice
- 1/2 tsp. white pepper

- 6 Tbs. lemon juice

DIRECTIONS:
- In a mixing dish, combine the cantaloupe, avocado, and palm hearts. Refrigerate for one hour after adding the lemon juice. In a mixing basin, whisk together the dressing ingredients.
- To toast almonds, pour two teaspoons of melted butter over them and bake for 15 minutes at 325 degrees. Line the serving dish with big, bite-size pieces of lettuce. Place the fruit in the middle. Drizzle the dressing over the fruit and top with almonds.

NUTRITION:
130 Cal; 14g Protein; 11g Tot Fat; 5g Carb; 0g Fiber; 3g Sugar; 234mg Sodium

Chicken Salad Sandwich
PREP TIME: 15 min
COOK TIME: none
YIELD: 5 Serve
INGREDIENTS:
- 1 lettuce leaf
- 1 rib of celery, chopped
- 4 tbsp. low-fat mayonnaise
- 1 apple, chopped
- 2 slices of whole wheat bread
- 1 shallot, finely chopped
- salt and pepper to taste
- Boiled chicken from soup recipe, chopped

DIRECTIONS:
- Stir together the chicken, vegetables, and mayonnaise in a medium mixing basin. On one piece of bread, spread the salad. Serve with lettuce and another piece of bread on top. (Of course, post-op patients will have to eat smaller portions!)

NUTRITION:
100 Cal; 7g Protein; 5g Tot Fat; 1g Carb; 0g Fiber; 2g Sugar; 24mg Sodium

Luncheon Salad
PREP TIME: 15 min **COOK TIME:** none **YIELD:** 4 Serve
INGREDIENTS:
- 1/4 cup(s) dill pickles
- 1 1/2 cup(s) Instant Rice
- 1/2 cup(s) chicken
- 2 egg(s), hard-cooked, finely chopped
- 1/4 cup(s) celery, diced
- 1/8 tsp. paprika
- 1/4 cup(s) onion(s), finely chopped
- 1 Tbsp. mustard
- parsley, as garnish
- 1 jar(s) pimientos, drained and chopped (4oz size)
- 1/3 cup(s) mayonnaise (low fat)
- 2 tomatoes, wedged, for garnish
- 1/2 tsp. salt

DIRECTIONS:
- Except for the tomato wedges and parsley, combine all ingredients in a mixing bowl. Chill. Serve with tomato wedges and fresh parsley on the side.

NUTRITION:

78 Cal; 10g Protein; 1.9g Tot Fat; 2g Carb; 0g Fiber; 0.6g Sugar; 65mg Sodium

Marinated Shrimp Salad

PREP TIME: 15 min **COOK TIME:** none **YIELD:** 4 Serve
INGREDIENTS:
- 1/2 lbs. grapes (red or green), seedless and halved
- 1 1/2 cup(s) Instant Rice
- 1 1/2 tsp. soy sauce
- 8 radishes, chopped
- 2 tsp. Dijon mustard romaine lettuce
- 1 clove(s) garlic, minced
- 3 red wine vinegar
- 1/4 tsp. Tabasco sauce
- 1 lb. shrimp, bay, cooked
- 1/2 tsp. parsley, (dried)
- 1/4 tsp. seasoned salt
- 6 Tbsp. vegetable oil

DIRECTIONS:
- Refrigerate for at least 1 hour after combining all ingredients except the lettuce. Serve on a lettuce bed.

NUTRITION:
65 Cal; 8g Protein; 6g Tot Fat; 1g Carb; 0g Fiber; 0.4g Sugar; 45mg Sodium

Tennessee Chicken Salad

PREP TIME: 15 min **COOK TIME:** none **YIELD:** 8 Serve
INGREDIENTS:
- 2 cups walnuts, chopped
- 4 skinless, boneless chicken breasts, poached or boiled
- 1/3 cup sweet pickle relish
- 1/8 cup Dijon mustard
- 2-1/2 cups mayonnaise (low fat)
- 1/2 cup pine nuts
- 6 hard-boiled eggs, cooled

DIRECTIONS:
- Slice the chicken into tiny pieces and finely chop the eggs. Combine the mayonnaise, mustard, relish, and nuts in a mixing bowl. Combine the chicken and egg in a mixing bowl. Refrigerate the mixture for one hour to allow the flavors to meld.

NUTRITION:
89 Cal; 9g Protein; 2g Tot Fat; 1g Carb; 0g Fiber; 2g Sugar; 46mg Sodium

Roasted Grape, Chicken, and Vegetable Salad

PREP TIME: 15 min **COOK TIME:** 15 min **YIELD:** 4 Serve
INGREDIENTS:
- 4 large lettuce cups, optional
- 2 Tbs. dry white wine
- 2 garlic cloves, quartered
- 1/2 tsp. salt
- 1 cup sliced sweet onion (see directions)
- 1-1/2 cups seedless grapes
- 1 bell pepper, cut in 1-inch squares
- 1/4 tsp. ground pepper

- 2 cups chicken or turkey breast (remove skin)
- 1 tsp. dried oregano, crumbled
- 1 (6-1/2 oz.) jar marinated artichoke hearts

DIRECTIONS:
- Drain the juice from the artichoke hearts and set aside. In a small jar or measuring cup, combine all of the liquid from the jar with the wine, oregano, salt, and pepper. Mix thoroughly. In a medium mixing dish, combine artichoke hearts and entire red or green grapes.
- 1/2-inch thick slices of sweet onion are halved. If you don't have a Vidalia or comparable sweet onion, substitute sliced red onion that has been marinated in sugar water for 20 minutes.
- Before adding to the salad, make sure it's completely dry. Toss the grape-onion-artichoke combination with bell pepper cubes and garlic slivers. Toss thoroughly with the marinade/dressing that has been made.
- In a shallow baking pan, spread the marinade-coated mixture in a single layer. Roast for 15 to 18 minutes at 425 degrees (preheated oven) or until grapes are ripe and veggies are browning on the edges. After 7 minutes, give it another stir. Toss roasted veggies and grapes with chicken or turkey. Mix thoroughly. In salad bowls or lettuce cups, serve the salad warm or at room temperature.

NUTRITION:
140 Cal; 19g Protein; 4.8g Tot Fat; 2.6g Carb; 0g Fiber; 3.3g Sugar; 284mg Sodium

Georgian Egg Salad

PREP TIME: 15 min **COOK TIME:** none **YIELD:** 4 Serve
INGREDIENTS:
- 2 tablespoons minced fresh dill
- 4 large eggs, hard-cooked
- 1/4 cup ground walnuts (optional)
- 2 tablespoons minced scallions, white part only
- 3 tbsp unsalted butter, softened to room temperature
- 1/8 tsp. salt
- 2 tablespoons minced fresh cilantro

DIRECTIONS:
- In a small dish, mash the eggs with butter. Combine the remaining ingredients in a big mixing bowl and stir thoroughly.

NUTRITION:
121 Cal; 7.1g Protein; 17.7g Tot Fat; 1.6g Carb; 0g Fiber; 2g Sugar; 97mg Sodium

Wilted Spinach Chicken Salad

PREP TIME: 15 min **COOK TIME:** none **YIELD:** 4 Serve
INGREDIENTS:
- 1 can slice, pitted ripe olives
- 4 boneless, sliced on the diagonal,
- 2 plum tomatoes, sliced in thin wedges,
- 1 10oz pkg. fresh spinach, chopped,
- 1/2 c light Italian dressing,
- 1 7oz pkg. chicken flavored rice, cooked

DIRECTIONS:
- Combine the spinach, hot cooked rice, dressing, and olives in a big mixing bowl. Stir often until the spinach starts to wilt. Stir in the tomatoes for another 2-3 minutes.

Distribute the rice mixture across four separate serving dishes. Serve with cut chicken breasts on top.
NUTRITION:
190 Cal; 13g Protein; 2g Tot Fat; 2g Carb; 0g Fiber; 1g Sugar; 106mg Sodium

Veggie Soup Base Mix
PREP TIME: 25 min **COOK TIME:** 2 hours **YIELD:** 2 Serve
INGREDIENTS:
1 medium-sized onion
2 carrots
2 cloves of garlic
1 green pepper
1 red pepper
2 tomatoes diced
1 egg
1/2 kg. Chicken along with broth
DIRECTIONS:
• Pick all the veggies listed above, slice them thin, and dehydrate. Add them to a food processor and blend them. Store the mixture in an air-tight jar. Add 2 tbsp. of the mixture per cup of boiling water or broth and tiny chicken pieces. When the mixture boils, stir in 1 beaten egg. Enjoy!
NUTRITION:
90 Cal; 7g Protein; 5g Tot Fat; 1g Carb; 0g Fiber; 2g Sugar; 24mg Sodium

Post-Op Soup
PREP TIME: 25 min **COOK TIME:** 24 hours **YIELD:** 4 Serve
INGREDIENTS:
• 4 cups your favorite broth, beef or chicken or veggie
• 2 cups bean soup mix
• 1 jalapeno finely chopped
• 2-3 bell pepper diced
• 1 tablespoon cumin
• 6 garlic cloves, well chopped
• 3 tomatoes diced or 1 cup diced sun-dried tomatoes
• 2 packages taco seasoning
• 1 large red onion
DIRECTIONS:
• Rinse the beans and soak the beans in water overnight with 1 packet of taco seasoning (do not drain). Add the remaining ingredients to the crock-pot and simmer until done.
NUTRITION:
230 Cal; 16g Protein; 6g Tot Fat; 5g Carb; 0g Fiber; 3g Sugar; 113mg Sodium

Thanksgiving Leftover Soup
PREP TIME: 25 min **COOK TIME:** 4 hours **YIELD:** 4 Serve
INGREDIENTS:
• 1/4 cup uncooked pearl barley
• whatever leftover turkey you have, shredded
• 4-6 cups premade turkey broth, depending on the size of your crock-pot or Dutch oven
• 1/2 tsp. Italian seasoning

• 1 tablespoon minced garlic
• 1 large carrot, sliced
• 1/2 cup diced onion
• Optional: 1 package frozen chopped spinach
DIRECTIONS:
• Cook onion and garlic in a skillet over medium heat (and sausage if you want). Season with a little bit of salt and pepper and a dash of Italian spice. Drain after removing the pan from the heat. In a slow cooker, combine the broth, shredded turkey, spinach, carrot, and barley. Cook for 4 hours on high, covered.
NUTRITION:
90 Cal; 7g Protein; 5g Tot Fat; 1g Carb; 0g Fiber; 2g Sugar; 24mg Sodium

Garden Gazpacho
PREP TIME: 25 min **COOK TIME:** 2 hours **YIELD:** 4 Serve
INGREDIENTS:
• Plain nonfat yogurt (optional)
• 6 large ripe tomatoes, peeled and seeded
• 1/8 tsp. black pepper
• 1/2 cup chopped seeded peeled cucumber
• 1 cup low-sodium tomato juice
• 1 clove garlic, minced
• 1 tsp. lemon juice
• 1/2 cup chopped green bell pepper
• 1/8 tsp. hot pepper sauce
• 1/2 cup coarsely chopped onion
DIRECTIONS:
• Combine the tomatoes, onion, cucumber, bell pepper, and garlic in a food processor or blender. Process until the mixture is thick and chunky, using on/off pulsing motion. Place in a medium mixing basin. Tomato juice, lemon juice, black pepper, and spicy pepper sauce should all be added at this point. Refrigerate until ready to serve. If desired, top with nonfat yogurt. As desired, garnish.
NUTRITION:
68 Cal; 3g Protein; 1g Tot Fat; 15g Carb; 4g Fiber; 2g Sugar; 25mg Sodium

Turkey-Sausage and Seafood Gumbo
PREP TIME: 25 min **COOK TIME:** 1 hour **YIELD:** 4 Serve
INGREDIENTS:
• 2.5 ounce catfish fillets, each cut into 4 pieces
• 1/4 cup all-purpose flour
• 2 teaspoons Creole or Cajun seasoning
• 1 cup chopped onion
• 1 28-ounce can diced tomatoes in juice
• 3 garlic cloves, chopped
• 3 low-fat Italian turkey sausages, casings removed
• 1 bay leaf
• 1 tsp. dried thyme
• 1 cup canned chicken broth or vegetable broth
• 1 cup chopped green bell pepper
• 8 large uncooked shrimp, peeled, deveined
• 1 tablespoon vegetable oil
DIRECTIONS:

- In the bottom of a big, heavy saucepan, sprinkle flour. Over medium-low heat, constantly whisk flour until it becomes golden brown (do not let to burn), approximately 15 minutes. In a mixing dish, place the browned flour. Heat the oil over medium heat. Put onion and bell pepper and cook for approximately 7 minutes, or until soft. Combine the garlic, thyme, and bay leaf; whisk for 1 minute.
- Combine with sausages and cook until brown, approximately 5 minutes, break up with a spoon, and add browned flour. Toss in the tomatoes and their juices, as well as the broth and Creole spice. Bring the water to a boil. cook for 20 minutes to let flavors combine. Frequently stirring Add the shrimp and catfish to the saucepan and cook for 5 minutes or until the seafood is opaque in the middle. Take out the bay leaf. Season to taste with salt and pepper.

NUTRITION:

265 Cal; 9g Protein; 7g Tot Fat; 6g Carb; 0g Fiber; 5g Sugar; 198mg Sodium

Taco Chili Soup

PREP TIME: 25 min **COOK TIME:** 1 hour **YIELD:** 7-9 Serve

INGREDIENTS:
- 1 envelope ranch salad dressing mix
- 2 lbs. ground beef or turkey
- 1 can diced tomatoes with green chilies
- 1 1/2 c water
- 1 can (15 oz.) pinto beans, rinsed and drained
- 1 can (15 1/4 ounces) whole kernel corn, drained
- 1 can (14 1/2 oz.) stewed tomatoes
- 1 can (15 3/4 ounces) mild chili beans
- 1 can (4 oz.) chopped green chilies
- 1 envelope taco seasoning

DIRECTIONS:
- Cook beef until it is no longer red in a Dutch oven, stew pot, or large kettle over medium heat; drain. Mix in taco seasoning well. Combine the remaining ingredients in a mixing bowl. Cook, stirring periodically, for 15 minutes, or until heated through.

NUTRITION:

189 Cal; 4g Protein; 5g Tot Fat; 3g Carb; 0g Fiber; 2g Sugar; 102mg Sodium

Jambalaya

PREP TIME: 30 min **COOK TIME:** 10 hours **YIELD:** 4-6 Serve

INGREDIENTS:
- 4 cups cooked brown rice
- 1 lb. boneless, skinless chicken thighs, diced
- 1/2 tsp. salt
- 1 medium onion, chopped
- 1/2 tsp. dried oregano
- 4 cloves garlic, minced
- 1 TBS dried parsley
- 1 can fat-free beef broth
- 1/3 of a can of tomato paste
- 1 1/2 tsp. dried basil
- 1 can (14 oz.) whole tomatoes, chopped
- 1 tsp. hot sauce
- 2 stalks celery, sliced

- 1 lb. shrimp, peeled
- 2 green peppers, chopped

DIRECTIONS:
- In a crock-pot, add all ingredients (excluding shrimp and rice). Cook for 8-10 hours on low. Add the uncooked shrimp and cooked rice in the final 15 minutes.

NUTRITION:

230 Cal; 12g Protein; 2g Tot Fat; 3g Carb; 0g Fiber; 2g Sugar; 235mg Sodium

Heavenly Hearty and Healthy Soup

PREP TIME: 25 min **COOK TIME:** 6 hours **YIELD:** 6 Serve

INGREDIENTS:
- 1 bay leaf
- 1 pound uncooked ground turkey
- 1/2 tsp. Splenda
- 1/2 cup thinly sliced carrots
- 1 tsp. dried oregano, crushed
- 1 14-1/2-ounce can French-cut green beans, drained
- 1-1/2 teaspoons Worcestershire sauce
- 1 tablespoon dried minced onion
- 1/2 cup chopped tomato
- 1 tsp. dried basil, crushed
- 1 cup fresh mushrooms, sliced 1/4-in. thick
- 1/2 tsp. garlic powder
- 2-1/2 cups tomato juice
- 1/4 tsp. pepper
- 1 cup chopped celery

DIRECTIONS:
- Cook the celery, turkey, and carrots in a large pan until the turkey is done; drain. Fill a 3-1/2- to 4-quart electric crockery cooker halfway with water. Tomato juice, green beans, mushrooms, tomato, dry chopped onion, Worcestershire sauce, oregano, basil, garlic powder, pepper, sugar, and bay leaf are added to the pan.
- Cook for 6 hours on low heat with the lid on. Remove the bay leaf and toss it out. Cook for 6 hours on low heat with the lid on. Remove the bay leaf and toss it out. This recipe serves 4 to 6 people.

NUTRITION:

290 Cal; 27g Protein; 15g Tot Fat; 11g Carb; 10g Fiber; 0.2g Sugar; 135mg Sodium

Fireside Beef Stew

PREP TIME: 25 min **COOK TIME:** 8-10 hours **YIELD:** 2 Serve

INGREDIENTS:
- 1 9-ounce package frozen Italian green beans
- 1.5 pounds boneless beef chuck pot roast
- 2 tablespoons cold water
- 2 small onions cut into wedges
- 1/4 tsp. ground black pepper
- 1 14-ounce can reduced-sodium beef broth
- 1 tsp. dry mustard
- 2 tablespoons Worcestershire sauce
- 1 8-ounce can tomato sauce
- 1/8 tsp. ground allspice
- 2 cloves garlic, minced

- 4 teaspoons cornstarch
- 1 pound butternut cut into 1-inch pieces (about 2-1/2 cups)

DIRECTIONS:
- Trim any excess fat from the meat. Meat should be cut into 1-inch chunks. Place the meat in a slow cooker with a capacity of 3-1/2 to 4-1/2 quarts. Combine the squash, onions, and garlic in a big mixing bowl. Combine the tomato sauce, pepper, beef broth, dry mustard, Worcestershire sauce, and allspice in a big mixing bowl.
- Cook on low heat for 8.5 hours or high heat for 4 to 5 hours, covered. Switch to a high-heat setting if you're utilizing a low-heat setting. Combine cold water and cornstarch in a small dish. In a slow cooker, combine the cornstarch mixture and green beans. Cook for 17 minutes, or until the sauce has thickened. This recipe serves 6 (1-1/3 cup) people.

NUTRITION:
212 Cal; 13g Protein; 4g Tot Fat; 2g Carb; 0g Fiber; 0g Sugar; 186mg Sodium

Chili
PREP TIME: 25 min **COOK TIME:** 2-3 hours **YIELD:** 2 Serve

INGREDIENTS:
- 2 cups water
- 1 lb. lean ground beef
- 2 teaspoons salt
- 1 medium onion, diced
- 2 teaspoons cumin
- 1 - 4 oz. can green chilies
- 15 oz. can pinto beans, with juice
- 2 - 15 ounce cans kidney beans, with juice
- 1 - 29 ounce cans tomato sauce
- 1 1/2 teaspoons pepper
- 3 medium tomatoes, chopped
- 2 teaspoons chili powder
- 1 lb. ground turkey

DIRECTIONS:
- In a large saucepot, brown the turkey and beef and break it up into tiny pea-size pieces. (At this stage, you may add the onion to infuse the meat with onion flavor.) Cook, stirring every 15 minutes or so, for 2 to 3 hours, with all other ingredients.

NUTRITION:
265 Cal; 20g Protein; 4g Tot Fat; 4g Carb; 0g Fiber; 0g Sugar; 204mg Sodium

Low Fat Chicken Cacciatore
PREP TIME: 25 min **COOK TIME:** 8 hours **YIELD:** 4 Serve

INGREDIENTS:
- 1/2 tsp. black pepper
- 2lbs uncooked boneless, skinless chicken breasts, cubed
- 1/2 tsp. garlic powder
- 1 bell pepper, chopped
- 1/2 tsp. dried oregano
- 12 oz. can low sodium diced tomatoes
- 12oz. can low sodium tomato sauce
- 6 oz. can low sodium tomato paste

- 1/2 tsp. dried basil
- 1 medium onion, chopped
- 1/2tsp salt
- 1/2 lb. fresh mushrooms

DIRECTIONS:
- Mix all ingredients and cook on low for 8 hours. Serve with whole wheat pasta.

NUTRITION:
289 Cal; 24g Protein; 0.6g Tot Fat; 1.8g Carb; 0g Fiber; 0g Sugar; 432mg Sodium

Low Carb Chili
PREP TIME: 15 min **COOK TIME:** 4-5 hours **YIELD:** 6 Serve

INGREDIENTS:
- Grated Parmesan cheese for garnish
- 1 can diced tomatoes with chilies
- 1 3/4 cups chicken stock
- 1 tsp. cumin
- 4 ribs of celery - diced fine
- Salt and pepper to taste
- 1 clove of garlic -chopped
- 1/2 cup butter
- 1/4 cup red bell pepper - diced
- 1 tablespoon chili powder (or to taste)
- 1 small bunch of scallions (five or six) chopped
- 1 cup water
- 2 pounds boneless chicken breast, cut into bite-sized pieces

DIRECTIONS:
- In the butter, sauté the scallions, celery, and bell pepper. Cook until the color of the chicken starts to change. In a heated, slow cooker, combine the chicken stock, canned tomatoes, water, garlic, cumin, and chili powder, then add the chicken and veggies. To combine, give it a quick stir. Cook on high for one hour, then reduces too low for another 4-5 hours. Serve with grated Parmesan cheese on top.

NUTRITION:
217 Cal; 13g Protein; 11g Tot Fat; 1.3g Carb; 2g Fiber; 3g Sugar; 484mg Sodium

Chicken & Mushroom Stew
PREP TIME: 15 min **COOK TIME:** 6-8 hours **YIELD:** 4 Serve

INGREDIENTS:
- 2 ribs celery, cut into small pieces
- 1/2 a soup can of water
- 1 cup baby carrots
- 1/2 tsp. salt
- 1/2 lb. fresh medium-sized white mushrooms cut up
- 1/4 tsp. black pepper
- 4 - boneless/skinless chicken breasts
- 1/2 tsp. garlic powder
- 10 3/4 oz. can 98% fat-free cream of mushroom soup

DIRECTIONS:
- In a pressure cooker, combine the soup and the water. Chicken should be cut into 2" pieces and seasoned with salt and pepper. Put everything in a slow cooker. Mushrooms, carrots, celery, and garlic powder are added to the pot. To

blend the ingredients, carefully stir them together. Cook on low for 6-8 hours, or until chicken is cooked through.

NUTRITION:
270 Cal; 21g Protein; 12g Tot Fat; 23g Carb; 4g Fiber; 3g Sugar; 342mg Sodium

Beef - Vegetable Casserole (Crock-pot)
PREP TIME: 15 min
COOK TIME: 4-5 hours
YIELD: 4 Serve
INGREDIENTS:
*   1/4-1/2 black pepper according to taste
*   1 lb. extra lean ground beef or turkey
*   1 tsp. salt
*   1/2 c celery, chopped
*   1 tablespoon flour
*   2 1/2 cups canned stewed tomatoes, slightly mashed
*   4 cups cabbage, chopped
*   1 tablespoon Splenda
*   1 medium onion, chopped

DIRECTIONS:
*   In a nonstick pan, cook the beef with the onion and celery. Pour everything into the cooker. Cover and simmer on high for 4-5 hours, layering cabbage and tomatoes, flour, salt, Splenda, and pepper on top.

NUTRITION:
267 Cal; 17g Protein; 15g Tot Fat; 11g Carb; 10g Fiber; 2g Sugar; 224mg Sodium

Pinto Bean Puree
PREP TIME: 15 min **COOK TIME:** 20 min **YIELD:** 2 Serve
INGREDIENTS:
*   Â½ cup chicken broth
*   1 medium onion, diced
*   One 15 ounce can of pinto beans, drained and rinsed
*   2 teaspoons olive oil
*   1 cup of your favorite salsa
*   2 garlic cloves, chopped

DIRECTIONS:
*   In a nonstick pan, sauté the onion and garlic until golden brown. Pulse the beans, sautéed veggies, and salsa in a food processor until chunky, and then add broth a bit at a time until the desired consistency is reached. Pour mixture into pan and simmer for 10 minutes, or until bubbling and thickened.

NUTRITION:
65 Cal; 8g Protein; 3g Tot Fat; 10g Carb; 0g Fiber; 2g Sugar; 132mg Sodium

Salmon Chowder
PREP TIME: 15 min **COOK TIME:** 20 min **YIELD:** 8 Serve
INGREDIENTS:
*   2 1/2 tablespoons flour
*   1 tablespoon butter
*   1 garlic clove, minced
*   1 cup diced onion
*   1 tablespoon olive oil
*   1 1/4 teaspoons Spice Blend (see below)
*   4 slices bacon, diced
Dash nutmeg:
*   1 cup milk

*   1/4 tsp. black pepper
*   1 cup of Half & Half
*   2 cups chicken broth
*   1 1/2 - 2 pounds fresh salmon, cooked
*   1/2 tsp. salt
Spice Blend:
*   2 teaspoons rosemary
*   2 teaspoons parsley
*   2 teaspoons thyme
*   1 tsp. dill
*   1/2 tsp. sage
*   1 tsp. marjoram
*   1 tsp. tarragon
*   2 teaspoons oregano

DIRECTIONS:
*   Spice Blend: Combine all ingredients in a glass container or zip lock bag and keep them in the refrigerator. Salmon may be baked or grilled. Into one-inch pieces, flake or rip. Remove from the equation. Melt butter and add chopped bacon. Cook until the bacon has crisped up.
*   Combine the olive oil, onion, and garlic in a mixing bowl. Cook for 9 minutes, or until the onion is tender. Cook for 1 minute after adding the flour and spices.
*   Add the broth, cream, and milk to the pot and turn the heat up to medium. Cook, stirring regularly, for 10 minutes or until the sauce has thickened. Reduce to a low heat setting and add the fish. Bring to a boil.

NUTRITION:
293 Cal; 28 g Protein; 18 g Tot Fat; 7 g Carb; 0 g Fiber; 2 g Sugar; 318 mg Sodium

✓*Taco Soup*
PREP TIME: 15 min **COOK TIME:** 2-3 hours **YIELD:** 5 Serve
INGREDIENTS:
*   2 teaspoons chili powder OR to taste
*   2 tablespoons olive oil
*   1 small can of sliced olives
*   Morningstar Crumbles
*   Two 14.5-ounce cans of peeled and diced tomatoes
*   One 16-ounce can of chili beans, undrained
*   1 can condensed tomato soup, undiluted
*   One 15-ounce can of whole kernel corn
*   One 15-ounce can of kidney beans, undrained
*   One 4.5-ounce can of diced green chilies
*   1 medium onion, chopped
*   One 1.25-ounce envelope taco seasoning
*   1 pound ground beef or turkey OR 1 pkg.
*   2 teaspoons Splenda

DIRECTIONS:
*   Brown the beef and onions in a large saucepan over medium heat. Any leftover fat should be drained as much as possible. Add the other ingredients and cook, for 2 to 3 hours, uncovered. The longer you leave it to simmer, the better it becomes!

NUTRITION:
213 Cal; 16g Protein; 8g Tot Fat; 16g Carb; 4g Fiber; 2g Sugar; 324mg Sodium

Lentil Barley Stew

PREP TIME: 15 min **COOK TIME:** 20 min **YIELD:** 10 Serve

INGREDIENTS:
- 1/4 tsp. black pepper
- One large onion, chopped
- 1/2 tsp. dried oregano
- Two celery ribs, diced
- 3/4 cup dry lentils
- One 28-ounce can of diced tomatoes, undrained
- 6 cups low-sodium vegetable broth
- 3/4 cup pearl barley
- Two carrots, sliced
- 1/2 tsp. dried rosemary, crushed
- One garlic clove, minced
- Kosher salt to taste
- 3 tablespoons olive oil

DIRECTIONS:
- Put the oil in a large soup pot over medium-low heat. In a skillet, cook celery, garlic, onion, and carrots until the onion are soft. Combine the broth, lentils, tomatoes, oregano, barley, pepper, rosemary, and salt in a big mixing bowl.
- Over moderate flame, bring to a boil. Cook, covered, for one hour, or until lentils and barley are soft. If the soup becomes too thick before it is finished, add 1/4 cup water or broth.

NUTRITION:
158 Cal; 8g Protein; 5g Tot Fat; 22g Carb; 6g Fiber; 2g Sugar; 355mg Sodium

Artichoke Feta Quiche

PREP TIME: 15 min **COOK TIME:** 26 min **YIELD:** 8 Serve

INGREDIENTS:
- 1/4 cup shredded parmesan cheese
- 1/4 cup milk
- 1 tablespoon olive oil
- 1/8 tsp. lemon pepper
- 2 garlic cloves, minced
- 1/4 tsp. oregano
- 4 eggs, beaten
- 1/8 tsp. Kosher salt
- 1 tablespoon flour
- 1/8 tsp. tarragon
- One 14-ounce can artichoke hearts, drained, chopped
- 1 tablespoon fresh parsley, minced
- 1/2 medium onion, diced
- 1/2 cup crumbled feta cheese
- Vegetable cooking spray

DIRECTIONS:
- Preheat your stove to about 350 degrees and coat a glass pie dish with veggie cooking spray. In a small nonstick pan, soften onion and garlic in olive oil.
- Cook for 1 to 2 minutes after adding the artichokes. In a big mixing basin, combine the flour, eggs, oregano, salt, lemon, parsley, pepper, tarragon, and milk. Combine the chilled vegetable mixture, feta, and parmesan cheese in a mixing bowl.

- Pour into a pie dish and bake for 20 to 25 minutes, or until the center is barely set. Serve with roasted red pepper salsa and crumbled feta cheese on top, if preferred.

NUTRITION:
112 Cal; 7g Protein; 7g Tot Fat; 6g Carb; 1g Fiber; 2g Sugar; 309mg Sodium

Creamy Black Bean Soup

PREP TIME: 15 min **COOK TIME:** 20 min **YIELD:** 2 Serve

INGREDIENTS:
- Shredded Cheddar, chopped cilantro, and sliced green onions (scallions)
- 1 tablespoon olive oil
- Kosher salt and freshly ground black pepper
- 2 garlic cloves, chopped
- 1/2 cup mild roasted tomato salsa
- 3 cups Chicken Stock or low-sodium chicken broth
- One 15-ounce can of black beans, rinsed and drained
- 1/2 cup reduced-fat sour cream
- 1 small onion, chopped

DIRECTIONS:
- Heat the oil over medium heat. Cook, occasionally stirring, until the onion and garlic are gently browned, approximately 4 minutes. Season with salt and pepper after adding the beans, stock, and salsa.
- Bring the soup to a boil, then lower to low heat and cook for 10 minutes, stirring periodically, until the flavors have melded and the soup has thickened somewhat. Puree the soup until smooth and creamy.
- Because the steam increases while pureeing hot liquids in a blender, always cover the lid with a kitchen towel, pulse the switch, and then release the steam before continuing.
- Just before serving, reheat the soup and mix in the sour cream. Make sure the seasonings are correct. Serve the soup in dishes with Cheddar, cilantro, and green onions on top. Put a bottle of spicy sauce on the table and taste it.

NUTRITION:
234 Cal; 34g Protein; 12g Tot Fat; 15g Carb; 14g Fiber; 2g Sugar; 245mg Sodium

Meatball Minestrone

PREP TIME: 15 min **COOK TIME:** 20 min **YIELD:** 4 Serve

INGREDIENTS:
- One 14-ounce can of Italian green beans, drained
- 2 tablespoons olive oil
- One 15-ounce can Cannellini or Great
- 1/2 cup diced carrots
- One 6-ounce can of tomato paste
- 2 garlic cloves, minced
- Salt and pepper
- 1 medium zucchini, sliced
- 1/4 tsp. black pepper
- 1 tablespoon Italian Seasoning herb mix
- 6 cups low-sodium beef broth
- One can of diced tomatoes, with juice
- 1 1/2 cups shredded cabbage
- 2 cups prepared meatballs (24 regular-sized)
- 3/4 cup diced celery

- Northern Beans, drained
- 1 cup diced onion
- 1/2 cup small shell pasta optional

DIRECTIONS:
- Sauté onion, garlic, carrots, celery, and zucchini in olive oil in a large saucepan over medium-low heat until onions are tender and translucent. Combine the broth, spices, tomato paste, tomatoes, and meatballs in a big mixing bowl.
- Allow it to boil over low heat until the veggies are soft. Cannellini beans, green beans, and spaghetti are added to the pot. Cook until the pasta is al dente. Serve with a sprinkling of grated parmesan cheese on top.

NUTRITION:
220 Cal; 23g Protein; 12g Tot Fat; 4g Carb; 3g Fiber; 1g Sugar; 213mg Sodium

Meatball Stew
PREP TIME: 15 min **COOK TIME:** 55 min **YIELD:** 8 Serve
INGREDIENTS:
- Kosher salt and black pepper to taste
- 1 large onion, diced
- 1 bay leaf
- 4 ribs of celery, diced
- 1 tsp. dried basil
- 1/2 cup water
- One 14.5-ounce can diced tomatoes, Undrained
- Two 14-ounce cans of reduced-sodium beef broth
- 1 tsp. dried oregano
- 2 tablespoons pearl barley
- 1/8 tsp. cumin
- 3 carrots, diced
- One 16-ounce pkg frozen pre-cooked meatballs
- 1 tablespoon olive oil

DIRECTIONS:
- Warm the olive oil. Cook onions, and then add carrots and celery. Stir in the barley and continue to cook for 1 minute. Increase the heat to medium-high. Combine the broth, water, basil, tomatoes, bay leaf, oregano, salt, cumin, and pepper in a big mixing bowl.
- Allow for 40 minutes of covered simmering. At this stage, the barley should be soft but still chewy. Continue to cook for another 15 minutes after adding the meatballs. If preferred, top with shaved Parmesan cheese.

NUTRITION:
217 Cal; 13g Protein; 11g Tot Fat; 13g Carb; 2g Fiber; 3g Sugar; 484mg Sodium

Creamy Broccoli Chowder
PREP TIME: 15 min **COOK TIME:** 26 min **YIELD:** 5 Serve
INGREDIENTS:
- 5-6 cups chopped broccoli
- 3 tablespoons butter
- 3 cups (FF) Half & Half OR milk
- 2 carrots, shredded
- 1/2 tsp. nutmeg
- 1 tsp. Kosher salt (to taste)
- 1/2 tsp. black pepper
- 5 tablespoons flour

- One 15-ounce can of chicken broth OR 2 cups homemade
- 1 sweet onion, diced
- 1 1/2 cups shredded cheddar cheese (optional)
- 3 tablespoons olive oil

DIRECTIONS:
- Heat the butter and oil in a frying pan stockpot. Add the onion and carrots and cook on low heat until the onions are tender (15 minutes). Stir in the flour and seasonings well. Combine half-and-half or milk, chicken broth, and broccoli in a mixing bowl.
- Simmer, stirring regularly, for approximately 1-1/1/2 hours over LOW heat. If using, add cheese shortly before serving. This recipe serves 10 people.

NUTRITION:
199 Cal; 4g Protein; 9g Tot Fat; 26g Carb; 1g Fiber; 5g Sugar; 249mg Sodium

Red Lentil Soup with Kale
PREP TIME: 10 min **COOK TIME:** 45 min **YIELD:** 6 Serve
INGREDIENTS:
- 2 tablespoons freshly squeezed lemon juice
- 1 tablespoon extra-virgin olive oil
- 2 large stalks of kale, stemmed, with leaves chopped (about 2 cups)
- ½ cup carrots, cut into ½-inch chunks
- 2 cups low-sodium vegetable broth
- 1 tsp. minced garlic
- 1 tsp. ground cumin
- 1 tsp. dried thyme
- 1 cup red lentils
- 2 cups water
- ½ cup celery, cut into ¼-inch chunks
- 1 bay leaf
- 1 cup chopped onion

DIRECTIONS:
- Heat the olive oil. Sauté the onion, carrots, celery, and garlic for 5 to 7 minutes, or until soft. Combine the lentils, thyme, and cumin in a big mixing bowl.
- In a large saucepan, combine the broth and water. Mix well and whisk for 1 to 2 minutes, or until all ingredients are evenly coated with spices. Bring to a low simmer, and then mix in the kale. Cover the saucepan and cook for 30 to 35 minutes after adding the bay leaf.
- Turn off the heat in the saucepan. Remove the leaf and toss it out. Add the lemon juice and mix well. Puree the soup until it reaches the desired consistency. Allow 10 minutes for the soup to cool before pureeing it in batches in a blender.
- Serve with a dollop of Greek yogurt (if using) on top of each bowl of soup.

NUTRITION:
170 Cal; 13 g Protein; 3 g Tot Fat; 24 g Carb; 3 g Fiber; 4 g Sugar; 58 mg Sodium

Cheesy Broccoli Soup
PREP TIME: 10 min **COOK TIME:** 20 min **YIELD:** 8 Serve
INGREDIENTS:
- 2 cups shredded extra-sharp Cheddar cheese
- 1 tablespoon extra-virgin olive oil
- ½ cup fat-free half-and-half

- 1 tablespoon minced garlic
- 2 cups low-sodium vegetable broth
- ¼ cup whole-wheat pastry flour
- ¼ tsp. ground nutmeg
- 2 cups nonfat or 1% milk
- 2 cups grated carrots
- 3 cups broccoli florets
- 1 medium onion, chopped

DIRECTIONS:

- Heat the olive oil. Combine the onion and garlic in a mixing bowl. Stir for 1 minute or until aromatic. Continue to stir until the carrots are soft, approximately 2 to 3 minutes.
- Combine the nutmeg and flour in a mixing bowl. Cook, stirring continuously, for another 2.5 minutes, or until browned. Whisk in the broth and then the milk until the sauce begins to thicken. Mix in the half-and-half until everything is thoroughly combined.
- Add the broccoli florets and mix well. Bring to a boil, and then turn down to low heat. Cook, occasionally stirring, for 12 minutes, or until the broccoli is cooked. Use an immersion blender to purée it to a smooth consistency if preferred, or leave it lumpy.
- Melt the Cheddar cheese in a different bowl. Set aside some cheese to use as a garnish when it's time to serve.

NUTRITION:

193 Cal; 12 g Protein; 9 g Tot Fat; 17 g Carb; 4 g Fiber; 7 g Sugar; 450 mg Sodium

Chapter 7: Side Dishes and Snacks

Spinach and Artichoke Dip

Preparation Time: 10 minutes **Cooking Time:** 15 minutes
Servings: 4-6
Ingredients:
- 4 oz. baby spinach
- 6 oz. frozen artichokes, thawed, patted dry, and coarsely chopped
- 3 oz. light cream cheese
- ¼ cup onion, finely chopped
- ¼ cup Parmesan cheese, grated
- ½ tablespoon lemon juice
- 1 garlic clove, finely grated
- ¼ teaspoon red pepper flakes
- ¼ teaspoon oregano
- 2 tablespoons extra-virgin olive oil
- ¼ teaspoon ground black pepper
- ⅛ teaspoon sea salt
- Cooking spray

Directions:
1. Wash, dry, and steam baby spinach. Set aside.
2. Preheat oven to 373 °F, and coat a baking dish with cooking spray.
3. In a medium-size non-stick saucepan, pour cooking oil and sauté onion and garlic on low-medium heat for about 5 minutes.
4. Increase heat to medium-high, put artichokes in the saucepan and cook, stirring, about 5 minutes.
5. In a food processor, put the spinach and chop it. Then add artichokes and blend them a few moments.
6. Transfer the blended artichokes and spinach into a medium-size bowl.
7. Add oregano, lemon juice, red pepper, salt, black pepper and cream cheese, and stir well.
8. Spread the mixture evenly into the baking dish and bake until it starts bubbling.
9. Now, add Parmesan cheese, and cook until cheese has melted.

Nutrition: Calories: 122 - Fat: 4 g - Carbs: 8 g - Protein: 12 g - Sodium: 280 mg

Slow Cooker Boston Beans

Preparation Time: 5 minutes **Cooking Time:** 6 hours
Servings: 6
Ingredients:
- 1 lb. white northern beans, dry
- 1 cup onion, finely chopped
- 2 garlic cloves, minced
- 4 slices extra lean bacon, chopped
- ¼ cup sugar free dark molasses
- ½ cup no-sugar added ketchup
- ¼ cup brown sugar, or sugar substitute
- 1 tablespoon Dijon mustard
- 1 tablespoon low-sodium Worcestershire sauce
- ½ smoked paprika
- ½ teaspoon sea salt
- ½ teaspoon black pepper
- 3 cups water

Directions:
1. Soak the beans in water for 9 hours. Then, drain the beans well and keep aside.
2. In a slow cooker, add the bacon and onion.
3. In a bowl, combine brown sugar, mustard, molasses, ketchup, garlic, Worcestershire sauce, salt, black pepper and paprika, and stir until well blended.
4. Place beans in the slow cooker, cover with the mixture and add water.
5. Cover the slow cooker, set the timer for 30 minutes and start cooking on HIGH.
6. Remember to check water and, if necessary, add it during cooking.

Nutrition: Calories: 234 - Fat: 6 g - Protein: 14 g - Carbs: 37 g - Sodium: 334 mg

Scalloped Potatoes

Preparation Time: 10 minutes **Cooking Time:** 1 hour
Servings: 6
Ingredients:
- 4 cups potatoes
- ½ cup onion, coarsely chopped
- 1 tablespoon parsley, chopped
- 1 ½ cup low-fat milk
- 2 teaspoons ground nutmeg
- 1 tablespoon rosemary, minced
- ¼ teaspoon ground pepper
- ¾ teaspoon sea salt
- 3 tablespoons whole-grain flour
- 3 tablespoons low-cholesterol margarine

Directions:
1. Preheat oven to 350 °F.
2. Wash, clean and finely slice the potatoes.
3. Stack the potatoes and onion layer by layer in a casserole. Drizzle flour between onion and potatoes.
4. Place milk and margarine in a medium saucepan over low-medium heat. Add parsley, pepper, nutmeg and salt.
5. Once the milk becomes hot, pour it over the potato-onion layer.
6. Cover the casserole and bake in the oven for 1 hour at 350 °F.
7. Remove the cover and bake until the top is golden brown.

Nutrition: Calories: 144 - Fat: 5 g - Protein: 5 g - Carbs: 17 g - Sodium: 580 mg

Green Beans Greek Style

Preparation Time: 5 minutes **Cooking Time:** 40 minutes
Servings: 2
Ingredients:
- 4 oz. green beans, chopped
- 4 oz. tomato, chopped
- ¼ onion, minced
- 1 teaspoon oregano
- 1 garlic clove, minced
- A dash parsley
- A dash ground black pepper
- Cooking spray

Directions:

1. Place a large saucepan coated with cooking spray over medium heat.
2. Stir in the onion and sauté 2-3 minutes. Then, add garlic, oregano, black pepper and tomato, and bring to a boil.
3. Add green beans and stir until the ingredients are well blended.
4. Lower the heat, cover the pan, and cook for 35-40 minutes, or until green beans become tender.
5. Sprinkle with parsley and serve as a side dish.
Nutrition: Calories: 234 - Fat: 22 g - Carbs: 15 g - Protein: 4 g - Sodium: 349 mg

Marinated Mushrooms
Preparation Time: 2 hours to marinate **Cooking Time:** 7 minutes **Servings:** 4
Ingredients:
- 1 lb. mushrooms, sliced
- 1 lemon, juiced
- 2 tablespoons whole-grain mustard
- ½ teaspoon Tabasco sauce
- 1 teaspoon parsley flakes
- 1 garlic clove, minced
- ¼ teaspoon sea salt
- A pinch black pepper
- Cooking spray

Directions:
1. In a skillet, add garlic and sauté for 1-2 minutes.
2. Cook mushrooms for 5-7 minutes, or until the excess water from the mushrooms has evaporated. Set aside and let cool.
3. Meanwhile, in a medium bowl, mix all the remaining ingredients until well combined.
4. Stir in the cooled mushrooms, cover with kitchen foil and place in the fridge for 2 hours.
5. Remove from fridge and serve.
Nutrition: Calories: 132 - Fat: 6 g - Carbs: 6 g - Protein: 3 g - Sodium: 135 mg

Cauliflower Purée
Preparation Time: 5 minutes **Cooking Time:** 15-20 minutes **Servings:** 1
Ingredients:
- 4 oz. frozen cauliflower or fresh cauliflower, coarsely chopped
- ¼ cup low-sodium vegetable broth
- A pinch sea salt
- A pinch black pepper
- A pinch nutmeg
- 6 cups water

Directions:
1. In a small saucepan pour water, add cauliflower, black pepper and salt, and cook for about 15 minutes. Cauliflower should become soft.
2. After cooking, drain cauliflower from excess water and pat it dry with paper towel.
3. Mash the cooked cauliflower. Add the broth and nutmeg into the mashed cauliflower, stir, and cook until broth is absorbed. Serve hot.

Nutrition: Calories: 165 - Fat: 4 g - Carbs: 23 g - Protein: 6 g - Sodium: 318 mg

Minty Summer Squash and Mushrooms Mix
Preparation Time: 10 minutes **Cooking Time:** 15 minutes **Servings:** 1
Ingredients:
- ½ cup yellow summer squash
- 4 tablespoons low-sodium vegetable broth
- ¼ onion, sliced
- ½ cup mushrooms, thinly sliced
- 1 teaspoon fresh mint, finely chopped
- ¼ teaspoon chili powder
- A pinch sea salt
- ¼ teaspoon black pepper
- Cooking spray

Directions:
1. In a lightly greased skillet over medium heat, add onion and chili powder, and sauté for 2-3 minutes.
2. Stir in yellow summer squash, cook for 5 minutes and add mushrooms.
3. Cook for about 2 minutes and pour in the broth. Lower the heat and simmer until the broth is absorbed.
4. Season with salt and pepper, stir for 1 minute and remove from heat.
5. Sprinkle with fresh mint and serve.
Nutrition: Calories: 212 - Fat: 4 g - Carbs: 18 g - Protein: 8 g - Sodium: 234 mg

Puréed Classic Egg Salad
Preparation Time: 5 minutes **Cooking Time:** 0 minutes **Servings:** 2
Ingredients:
- 2 eggs, hard-boiled
- 1 tablespoon low-fat mayonnaise
- 1 tablespoon low-fat plain Greek yogurt
- ¼ teaspoon black pepper
- 1 teaspoon paprika
- 1 teaspoon fresh parsley, roughly chopped

Directions:
1. Roughly cut the boiled eggs. Put the chops of eggs into a food-mixer and blend them.
2. Add black pepper, paprika, parsley, mayonnaise, and Greek yogurt as the seasonings to the eggs.
3. Mix finely as far as the egg salad becomes smooth.
Nutrition: Calories: 154 - Fat: 12 g - Carbs: 6 g - Protein: 10 g - Sodium: 128 mg

Maple-Mashed Sweet Potatoes
Preparation Time: 5 minutes **Cooking Time:** 10 minutes **Servings:** 2
Ingredients:
- ½ lb. sweet potatoes
- ½ cup carrot, thinly sliced
- 1 tablespoon no-added sugar maple syrup
- ⅛ teaspoon nutmeg
- ⅛ teaspoon fresh ground pepper
- 2 cups water

- A pinch sea salt

Directions:

1. Wash and clean sweet potatoes. Peel and cut into small chunks.
2. In a pot, pour water and bring to boil. Then, add carrot and sweet potatoes.
3. Reduce heat and continue cooking for about 10 minutes, until the carrots and sweet potatoes become soft.
4. Drain the vegetables using a colander and put them into a bowl. Mash the vegetables until become smooth.
5. Sprinkle ground pepper and nutmeg, and stir.
6. Drizzle maple syrup, stir, and serve.

Nutrition: Calories: 183 - Fat: 4 g - Carbs: 23 g - Protein: 4 g - Sodium: 190 mg

Basil-2 Cheeses Chips

Preparation Time: 15 minutes to cool **Cooking Time:** 5 minutes **Servings:** 2

Ingredients:

- ¼ cup Parmesan cheese, shredded
- ¼ cup low-fat sharp Cheddar cheese, shredded
- ¼ teaspoon garlic powder
- 1 teaspoon dried sage
- A dash ground black pepper
- A dash sea salt

Directions:

1. Preheat the oven to 400 °F. Coat a baking dish with parchment paper.
2. In a bowl, stir in the Parmesan cheese, Cheddar cheese, garlic powder, basil, black pepper and salt, and mix well.
3. Scoop one spoonful at a time of the mixture onto the baking dish and try to form 12 chips using all of the mixture.
4. Bake for 5 minutes, or until the chips begin to turn golden on the edges.
5. Remove from the oven. Serve and enjoy.

Nutrition: Calories: 110 - Fat: 6 g - Protein: 6 g - Carbs: 3 g - Sodium: 349 mg

Thyme-Radish Chips

Preparation Time: 5 minutes **Cooking Time:** 30 minutes **Servings:** 2

Ingredients:

- 1 cup radishes, thinly sliced
- 1 teaspoon thyme, minced
- 1 tablespoon extra-virgin olive oil
- ¼ teaspoon sea salt
- A dash freshly ground black pepper

Directions:

1. Preheat the oven to 375 °F. Line a baking sheet with parchment paper.
2. Place the radishes into a small bowl and coat with the oil.
3. In a small bowl, mix the thyme, salt, and pepper.
4. Place the radish slices onto the baking sheet, and sprinkle the thyme mixture.
5. Bake for about 15 minutes, turn the chips, and bake for 15 minutes more until crispy and golden brown. Serve and enjoy.

Nutrition: Calories: 107 - Fat: 8 g - Protein: 3 g - Carbs: 4 g - Fiber: 1 g - Sodium: 337 mg

Rosemary Cheese Biscuits

Preparation Time: 5 minutes **Cooking Time:** 15 minutes **Servings:** 4

Ingredients:

- 1 cup almond flour
- ¼ cup Parmesan cheese, shredded
- ¼ cup low-fat Cheddar cheese, shredded
- 2 teaspoons baking powder
- 2 teaspoons garlic powder
- 1 teaspoon rosemary, minced
- ½ teaspoon sea salt
- 2 large eggs

Directions:

1. Preheat the oven to 350 °F.
2. Mix the almond flour, Parmesan cheese, Cheddar cheese, baking powder, garlic powder, rosemary and salt, and stir until well blended. Then, add the eggs and continue stirring to get a homogeneous mixture.
3. Scoop one spoonful at a time of the mixture onto the baking dish and try to form 8 circles using all of the mixture.
4. Bake in the oven for 17 minutes, or until biscuits are golden brown. Serve warm.

Nutrition: Calories: 282 - Fat: 25 g - Protein: 13 g - Carbs: 7 g - Fiber: 4g - Sugar: 1 g - Sodium: 473 mg

Kohlrabi Chips

Preparation Time: 10 minutes **Cooking Time:** 20 minutes **Servings:** 4

Ingredients:

- 1 lb. kohlrabi, peeled, and thinly sliced
- 1 teaspoon paprika
- 1 tablespoon olive oil
- A pinch sea salt
- A pinch black pepper

Directions:

1. Preheat the air fryer to 323 °F.
2. Add all ingredients into the bowl and toss to coat.
3. Transfer kohlrabi into the air fryer basket and cook for 20 minutes. Toss halfway through. Serve and enjoy.

Nutrition: Calories: 89 - Fat: 2 g - Protein: 6 g - Carbs: 14 g - Sugar: 4 g - Sodium: 230 mg

Daikon Chips

Preparation Time: 10 minutes **Cooking Time:** 16 minutes **Servings:** 4

Ingredients:

- 15 oz. daikon, slice into chips
- 1 tablespoon olive oil
- ½ teaspoon chili powder
- ½ teaspoon turmeric
- ½ teaspoon pepper
- A pinch sea salt

Directions:

1. Preheat the air fryer to 373 °F.
2. Add all ingredients into a bowl and toss to coat.

3.	Transfer sliced daikon into the air fryer basket and cook for 16 minutes. Toss halfway through. Serve and enjoy.
Nutrition: Calories: 125 - Fat: 9 g - Protein: 2 g - Carbs: 15 g - Fiber: 4 g - Sodium: 84 mg

Parmesan Herb Muffins
Preparation Time: 5 minutes **Cooking Time:** 15 minutes
Servings: 4
Ingredients:
- 1 large egg
- ¼ cup Parmesan cheese, shredded
- 1 teaspoon Italian seasoning
- ⅓ cup low-fat milk
- ½ tablespoon nutritional yeast flakes
- ½ cup almond flour
- 1 teaspoon baking powder
- ¼ teaspoon sea salt
- Cooking spray

Directions:
1.	Preheat the oven to 350 °F. Line a 4 muffin tin with cooking spray.
2.	In a large bowl, mix the flour, Parmesan cheese, nutritional yeast, Italian seasoning, and baking powder.
3.	In another bowl, mix egg, milk and salt until well combined.
4.	Stir in wet ingredients with dry ingredients.
5.	Fill muffin cups ¾ full with the mixture.
6.	Bake until golden brown.
Nutrition: Calories: 152 - Fat: 12 g - Protein: 10 g - Carbs: 7 g - Fiber: 3 g - Sugar: 3 g - Sodium: 232 mg

2 Cheese Cauliflower Patties
Preparation Time: 10 minutes **Cooking Time:** 15 minutes
Servings: 4
Ingredients:
- 1 cup cauliflower rice
- ½ cup almond flour
- ½ cup low-fat mozzarella cheese, shredded
- ½ cup Parmesan cheese, grated
- 1 large egg
- 1 teaspoon garlic powder
- 1 tablespoon chives, finely chopped
- 1 tablespoon cornstarch
- ¼ teaspoon ground black pepper
- ¼ teaspoon sea salt

Directions:
1.	Preheat the oven to 400 °F.
2.	Mix the cauliflower rice, almond flour, mozzarella cheese, Parmesan cheese, garlic powder, chives, egg, cornstarch, black pepper and salt, and stir until well mixed.
3.	Using all the mixture, create about 16 small slightly flatten patties and place onto the baking dish.
4.	Bake until crispy and golden brown. Serve and enjoy.
Nutrition: Calories: 163 - Fat: 11 g - Protein: 10 g - Carbs: 5 g - Fiber: 1 g - Sugar: 1 g - Sodium: 287 mg

Mozzarella Mushroom Caps
Preparation Time: 5 minutes **Cooking Time:** 20 minutes
Servings: 4

Ingredients:
- 12 white mushroom caps
- 4 oz. fresh low-fat mozzarella, shredded
- ¼ cup Parmesan cheese, grated
- ½ onion, diced
- 2 tablespoons almond flour
- 1 tablespoon margarine, melted
- ½ teaspoon garlic powder
- 1 tablespoon parsley, chopped
- A dash sea salt
- Cooking spray

Directions:
1.	Preheat the oven to 350 °F. Line a baking dish with parchment paper.
2.	Clean the mushrooms and remove the cap from each one. Place the mushrooms onto the lined baking dish.
3.	Spray a skillet with oil over medium heat. While oil is heating, chop the mushrooms stems.
4.	In the skillet, add the onion and sauté for 2-3 minutes.
5.	Stir in chopped mushrooms stems and parsley, and cook for 6-7 minutes, or until golden brown. Then, remove from heat.
6.	In a bowl, mix the almond flour, margarine, garlic powder and salt.
7.	Fill each mushroom cap with 1 tablespoon mozzarella, mushrooms stems, flour and margarine mixture, and top with Parmesan cheese.
8.	Bake for about 20 minutes or until the cheese has melted.
Nutrition: Calories: 120 - Fat: 7 g - Protein: 8 g - Carbs: 4 g - Fiber: 1 g - Sugar: 1 g - Sodium: 171 mg

3-Cheese Bake
Preparation Time: 10 minutes **Cooking Time:** 25 minutes **Servings:** 2
Ingredients:
- 4 oz. low-fat ricotta cheese
- ¼ cup Parmesan cheese, grated
- ¼ cup low-fat mozzarella cheese, shredded
- 1 large egg, beaten
- 1 teaspoon Italian seasoning
- Salt and pepper, as required
- ¼ cup no-sugar added marinara sauce

Directions:
1.	Preheat the oven to 350 °F.
2.	In a bowl, add the ricotta cheese, Parmesan cheese, egg, Italian seasoning, salt, and black pepper and mix well.
3.	Place the mixture into a baking dish and top each with 1 tablespoon of marinara sauce, followed by the mozzarella cheese.
4.	Bake for about 20-25 minutes. Serve warm.
Nutrition: Calories: 86 - Fat: 5 g - Protein: 7 g - Carbs: 4 g - Fiber: 1 g - Sugar: 2 g

Crusted Mozzarella Sticks
Preparation Time: 2 hours to freeze **Cooking Time:** 6 minutes **Servings:** 2
Ingredients:

- ⅓ cup low-carb breadcrumbs
- 6 tablespoons almond flour
- ½ teaspoon Italian seasoning
- ⅛ teaspoon garlic powder
- ¼ teaspoon sea salt
- 1 large eggs
- 4 low-fat mozzarella sticks
- Cooking spray

Directions:

1. Prepare three bowls. In the first, mix almond flour and garlic powder. In the second, whisk the egg and salt. In the third, stir breadcrumbs and Italian seasoning.

2. Cut the mozzarella sticks in half and coat each mozzarella stick in flour mixture, dip in the egg, and then coat well in the breadcrumbs mixture. Pay attention to carefully coat each mozzarella piece with the batter.

3. Place mozzarella on a large plate, cover with plastic wrap and freeze for about 2 hours.

4. Preheat the oven to 402 °F, and line a baking tin with parchment paper.

5. Place the mozzarella pieces on the baking sheet, and lightly grease with cooking spray.

6. Bake for 5-6 minutes, until the crust turn golden. Serve with your favorite sauce and enjoy.

Nutrition: Calories: 176 - Fat: 12 g - Protein: 12 g - Carbs: 3 g - Fiber: 1 g - Sugar: 1 g - Sodium: 330 mg

Light Almond Cookies

Preparation Time: 10 minutes **Cooking Time:** 8 minutes **Servings:** 4

Ingredients:

- 8 tablespoons almond flour
- 1 tablespoon margarine
- 1 egg
- 1 teaspoon baking powder
- 1 teaspoon light brown sugar
- 1 teaspoon ground cinnamon
- 2 teaspoons vanilla extract
- ⅓ teaspoon almond extract
- ½ teaspoon stevia, or no-calorie sweetener
- ¼ teaspoon sea salt

Directions:

1. Preheat the oven to 348 °F and coat a baking dish with parchment paper.

2. In a bowl, combine the almond flour, margarine, egg, vanilla extract, almond extract, baking powder, sugar, cinnamon, stevia, and salt. Stir until well incorporated.

3. Scoop the mixture onto the baking dish to form 8 cookies.

4. Bake for 7 minutes, or until cookies are golden brown. Let cool and serve.

Nutrition: Calories: 109 - Fat: 8 g - Protein: 4 g - Carbs: 7 g - Fiber: 1 g - Sugar: 3 g - Sodium: 260 mg

Raspberry Gelatin Tea

Preparation Time: 5 minutes **Cooking Time:** 5 minutes **Servings:** 1

Ingredients:

- ½ cup frozen raspberries, chopped
- ¼ teaspoon stevia, or low-calorie sweetener
- 2 fresh mint leaves, finely chopped
- ½ cup hot water
- 2 tablespoons low-calorie plain gelatin powder

Directions:

1. In a small saucepan, stir in the raspberries over medium heat for 2 minutes, add stevia, and cook for 1 minute. Remove from the heat and set aside.

2. Pour the hot water into a mug. Stir in the gelatin powder and add in the raspberries and mint, stirring constantly.

3. In a mixer, process the mixture until foamy, pour into a mug, let cool and enjoy immediately.

Nutrition: Calories: 93 - Fat: 0 g - Protein: 9 g - Carbs: 8 g - Fiber: 1 g - Sugar: 4 g - Sodium: 54 mg

Cinnamon Vanilla Coconut Milk

Preparation Time: 1 hour to chill **Cooking Time:** 5 minutes **Servings:** 1

Ingredients:

- ½ cup light unsweetened coconut milk
- 2 teaspoons vanilla extract
- 1 teaspoon stevia, or low-calorie sweetener
- ¼ teaspoon cinnamon
- 1 teaspoon lemon zest
- 2 mint leaves, finely chopped
- 1 tablespoon low-calorie plain gelatin powder

Directions:

1. Put the coconut milk for 1-2 minutes. Sprinkle in the vanilla extract, mint and stevia and stir to dissolve.

2. Add the gelatin while stirring constantly to dissolve the gelatin completely. Remove from the heat.

3. In a mixer, transfer the mixture and blend for a few seconds until frothy, and pour into a small mug.

4. Put in the fridge for 1 hour. Serve and enjoy.

Nutrition: Calories: 139 - Fat: 8 g - Protein: 5 g - Carbs: 6 g - Fiber: 0 g - Sugar: 4 g - Sodium: 71 mg

Yogurt, Chocolate and Chia Pudding

Preparation Time: 8 hours to chill **Cooking Time:** 0 minutes **Servings:** 2

Ingredients:

- ½ cup unsweetened almond milk
- ½ cup non-fat plain Greek yogurt
- 2 tablespoons chia seeds
- 1 teaspoon unsweetened cocoa powder
- ¼ teaspoon ground cinnamon
- ⅛ teaspoon vanilla extract
- ½ teaspoon stevia, or no-calorie sweetener
- 1 tablespoon vanilla whey protein (optional)

Directions:

1. In small bowl, combine the almond milk, yogurt, chia seeds, cocoa powder, stevia, vanilla extract, cinnamon, and whey protein (if using).

2. Cover and let sit in refrigerator overnight, or at least 4-5 hours, stirring after 1 hour that has been put in the refrigerator.

Nutrition: Calories: 209 - Fat: 10 g - Protein: 16 g - Carbs: 21 g - Fiber: 9 g - Sugar: 8 g - Sodium: 98 mg

Vanilla Frozen Yogurt

Preparation Time: 8 hours to freeze **Cooking Time:** 0 minutes **Servings:** 4

Ingredients:

- 2 cups non-fat plain Greek yogurt
- 2 tablespoons vanilla whey protein powder
- 1 teaspoon vanilla extract
- 2 teaspoons stevia, or no-calorie sweetener
- 1 tablespoon lemon juice
- ¼ teaspoon cardamom powder

Directions:

1. In a bowl, combine yogurt, protein powder, lemon juice, cardamom powder, vanilla extract, and stevia.
2. Cover and freeze overnight, or for at least 8 hours.
3. Place in the refrigerator about 1 hour before serving. Serve and enjoy.

Nutrition: Calories: 185 - Fat: 1 g - Protein: 14 g - Carbs: 22 g - Fiber: 1 g - Sugar: 10 g - Sodium: 96 mg

Italian Salad Bites

Preparation Time: 10 minutes **Cooking Time:** 15 minutes **Servings:** 6

Ingredients:

For the Bites:

- 24 cherry tomatoes
- 12 low-fat mozzarella balls
- 12 fresh basil leaves

For the Balsamic Glaze:

- ½ cup balsamic vinegar
- 2 tablespoons extra-virgin olive oil
- 1 garlic clove, minced
- 1 teaspoon dried thyme
- ¼ teaspoon black pepper

Directions:

To Make the Bites:

1. Using 12 toothpicks assemble each with 1 cherry tomato, 1 mozzarella ball, 1 basil leaf, and another tomato. Place on a serving platter.

To Make the Glaze:

1. bring the balsamic vinegar to a simmer. Cook for 15 minutes, or until syrupy. Set aside to cool and thicken.
2. In a small bowl, whisk 1 tablespoon olive oil, garlic, black pepper, thyme, and cooled vinegar.
3. Drizzle the remaining olive oil and balsamic glaze over the skewers. Serve and enjoy.

Nutrition: Calories: 72 - Fat: 3 g - Protein: 3 g - Carbs: 3 g - Sugar: 2 g - Sodium: 101 mg

Greek Salad

Preparation Time: 15 minutes **Cooking Time:** 0 minutes **Servings:** 4

Ingredients:

- 1 medium English cucumber, chopped
- 1 cup cherry tomatoes, halved
- 1 red bell pepper, seeded, and diced
- ½ red onion, diced
- ½ cup low-salt Kalamata olives, pitted, and roughly chopped
- 1 cup feta cheese, crumbled
- ¼ cup fresh mint, chopped
- ¼ cup dried oregano
- 1 tablespoon lemon juice
- ½ cup balsamic dressing

Directions:

1. toss the cucumber, tomatoes, bell pepper, onion, mint, oregano, olives, and cheese with the balsamic dressing and lemon juice, and serve.

Nutrition: Calories: 213 - Fat: 13 g - Protein: 6 g - Carbs: 15 g - Fiber: 3 g - Sugar: 9 g - Sodium: 343 mg

Eggs and Veggie Cauliflower Rice

Preparation Time: 15 minutes **Cooking Time:** 15 minutes **Servings:** 4

Ingredients:

- 1 teaspoon + 1 tablespoon sesame oil
- 2 large eggs, beaten
- 4 cups cauliflower rice (or 1 head cauliflower florets riced in a food processor)
- ½ cup red bell pepper, diced
- ½ cup low-salt canned peas
- 1 garlic clove, minced
- 2 tablespoons low-sodium soy sauce
- 1 scallion, diced

Directions:

1. heat 1 teaspoon of sesame oil. Add the eggs, and stir until they are cooked. Set aside.
2. In the same skillet over medium heat, heat the remaining tablespoon of oil.
3. Add the cauliflower rice, bell pepper, peas, garlic, soy sauce, scallion, and eggs.
4. Cook, stirring, until well combined and the cauliflower is soft, for about 4 minutes.

Nutrition: Calories: 121 - Fat: 7 g - Protein: 6 g - Carbs: 9 g - Fiber: 3 g - Sugar: 3 g - Sodium: 357 mg

Healthy Roasted Vegetables

Preparation Time: 10 minutes **Cooking Time:** 30 minutes **Servings:** 4

Ingredients:

- 1 small onion, halved, and sliced
- 2 carrots, peeled, and sliced
- 1 small zucchini, sliced into rounds
- 2 tomatoes, thickly sliced
- 1 medium bell pepper, cut into strips
- 2 tablespoons extra-virgin olive oil
- 1 tablespoon dried oregano
- A pinch sea salt
- Freshly ground black pepper

Directions:

1. Preheat the oven to 400 °F.
2. Using a large baking sheet, arrange the vegetables without overlapping.
3. Pour the olive oil over the vegetables evenly, and gently toss to coat, using either a spoon or your hands. Add salt, oregano and pepper.
4. Roast for 20-30 minutes, or until soft, stirring halfway through.

Nutrition: Calories: 155 - Fat: 5 g - Protein: 4 g - Carbs: 15 g - Fiber: 5 g - Sugar: 6 g - Sodium: 92 mg

Asian Cabbage Salad ✓

Preparation Time: 10 minutes **Cooking Time:** 0 minutes
Servings: 6
Ingredients:
- 1 (14 oz.) package coleslaw
- 1 large carrot, grated
- ¼ cup scallions, diced
- 1 red bell pepper, thinly sliced
- ¼ cup fresh cilantro, chopped
- ½ tablespoon grated fresh ginger
- ¼ cup peanuts, chopped
- 1 teaspoon sesame seeds
- 1 teaspoon sunflower seeds
- ⅓ cup spicy peanut dressing

Directions:
1. In a large bowl, combine coleslaw, bell pepper, carrot, scallions, cilantro, ginger, sesame seeds, sunflower seeds, and peanuts.
2. Toss with the dressing and serve.
SUGGESTION: peanuts may be too hard for the early stages of healing. If you don't tolerate peanuts, or the stage of your diet doesn't call for them, simply eliminate them from the recipe.
Nutrition: Calories: 128 - Fat: 6 g - Protein: 6 g - Carbs: 14 g - Fiber: 6 g - Sugar: 8 g - Sodium: 194 mg

Southwest Deviled Eggs

Preparation Time: 10 minutes **Cooking Time:** 0 minutes
Servings: 2
Ingredients:
- 2 large hard-boiled eggs
- 1 tablespoon low-fat plain Greek yogurt
- ¼ teaspoon Dijon mustard
- 2 teaspoons chives, finely chopped
- ¼ teaspoon taco seasoning

Directions:
1. Peel the eggs, and halve them lengthwise. Remove the yolks, and transfer them to a small bowl, setting the whites aside.
2. In a bowl, add the yogurt, mustard, yolks and taco seasoning, and mix together.
3. Spoon the mixture into the egg white halves, top with chives, and serve.
Nutrition: Calories: 123 - Fat: 9 g - Protein: 7 g - Carbs: 1 g - Fiber: 0 g - Sugar: 1 g - Sodium: 149 mg

Turkey Cajun Roll-Ups ✓

Preparation Time: 5 minutes **Cooking Time:** 0 minutes
Servings: 2
Ingredients:
- 2 slices deli turkey
- 2 teaspoons whole-grain mustard
- 2 slices low-fat Monterey Jack cheese
- ¼ steak tomato, seeded, and diced
- ⅛ red onion, thinly sliced
- 1 cup lettuce, shredded
- ¼ red bell pepper, thinly sliced
- ¼ avocado, diced
- 1 teaspoon Cajun seasoning

Directions:
1. combine mustard and Cajun seasoning.
2. On a cutting board, lay out deli turkey and spread with the mixture.
3. Top with cheese, tomato, red onion, bell pepper, lettuce and avocado.
4. Wrap the deli turkey tightly and pin with a toothpick.
Nutrition: Calories: 152 - Total fat: 9 g - Protein: 10 g - Carbs: 6 g - Fiber: 2 g - Sugar: 1 g - Sodium: 488 mg

Parmesan Chips ✓

Preparation Time: 10 minutes **Cooking Time:** 10 minutes **Servings:** 6
Ingredients:
- 12 tablespoons Parmesan cheese, grated
- 1 teaspoon sunflower seeds
- 1 teaspoon flax seeds
- 1 teaspoon paprika
- 1 teaspoon onion flakes

Directions:
1. Preheat the oven to 400 °F.
2. In a small bowl, mix the sunflower seeds, flax seeds, paprika, and onion flakes together.
3. Line a sheet pan with parchment paper. With a tablespoon, place the Parmesan onto the sheet pan and flatten it.
4. Sprinkle with seeds and onion mixture.
5. Bake for 6-8 minutes, or until golden and crisp, and serve.
Nutrition: Calories: 26 - Fat: 2 g - Protein: 3 g - Carbs: 0.5 g - Fiber: 0 g - Sugar: 0 g - Sodium: 97 mg

Edamame Hummus

Preparation Time: 10 minutes **Cooking Time:** 10 minutes
Servings: 2
Ingredients:
- 1 ½ cup frozen edamame, thawed, rinsed, and drained
- ¼ cup tahini
- 2 tablespoons sesame oil
- 2 garlic cloves, peeled
- ½ teaspoon fresh parsley, chopped
- 1 lemon, juiced
- A pinch sea salt
- A pinch ground black pepper
- Water

Directions:
1. Combine the edamame, tahini, sesame oil, garlic, parsley, salt, pepper and lemon juice. Process until smooth.
2. If necessary, add a tablespoon of water at a time to dilute and achieve the desired consistency and continue processing.
3. Transfer to a bowl, and serve.
Nutrition: Calories: 125 - Fat: 8 g - Protein: 4 g - Carbs: 6 g - Fiber: 2 g - Sugar: 1 g - Sodium: 120 mg

Spicy Roasted Chickpeas

Preparation Time: 5 minutes **Cooking Time:** 1 hour
Servings: 4
Ingredients:

- 1 can garbanzo beans, rinsed and drained
- ½ tablespoon chili powder
- ½ tablespoon ground cumin
- 1 teaspoon ground cayenne powder
- 1 teaspoon garlic powder
- 1 teaspoon paprika
- ½ teaspoon sea salt
- 1 tablespoon extra-virgin olive oil

Directions:

1. Preheat the oven to 300 °F. Coat a baking dish with aluminum foil.
2. In a large bowl, mix the garbanzos, chili powder, cumin, cayenne, garlic powder, paprika, salt, and olive oil, and stir until well combined.
3. Place on the baking sheet. Bake for 30 minutes, and stir gently.
4. Bake for 20-30 minutes more, until hard and crunchy, and serve.

Nutrition: Calories: 124 - Fat: 3 g - Protein: 7 g - Carbs: 19 g - Fiber: 6 g - Sugar: 4 g - Sodium: 451 mg

Mashed Beans and Cauliflower

Preparation Time: 10 minutes **Cooking Time:** 5 minutes
Servings: 2
Ingredients:

- ½ large head cauliflower
- 2 oz. canned cannellini beans, drained, and rinsed
- ¼ cup water
- ⅓ cup low-fat buttermilk
- ½ tablespoon garlic, minced
- ½ tablespoon extra-virgin olive oil
- ½ tablespoon fresh rosemary
- A pinch sea salt
- A pinch black pepper

Directions:

1. Break the cauliflower into small florets.
2. Place in a large microwave-safe bowl with the water. Cover and microwave for about 5 minutes, or until the cauliflower is soft. Drain the water from the bowl.
3. In a blender or food processor, purée the buttermilk, cauliflower, beans, garlic, rosemary, salt, pepper, and olive oil on medium speed until the cauliflower is smooth and creamy. Serve immediately.

Nutrition: Calories: 63 - Fat: 2 g - Protein: 4 g - Carbs: 8 g - Fiber: 3 g - Sugar: 3 g - Sodium: 74mg

Chicken and Pickle Roll-Ups

Preparation Time: 20 minutes **Cooking Time:** 0 minutes
Servings: 4
Ingredients:

- 8 slices deli chicken breast, thinly sliced
- 8 oz. low-fat cottage cheese
- 1 teaspoon dried dill
- 1 teaspoon onion powder
- 1 teaspoon fresh rosemary, finely chopped
- 8 whole kosher dill pickle spears
- A pinch ground black pepper

Directions:

1. Mix together cottage cheese, dill, rosemary, onion and black pepper.
2. On a cutting board, lay the chicken slices and spread on the cheese mixture.
3. Place a pickle on an end of the chicken slices and roll.
4. Slice each pickle roll-up and skew each with a toothpick.

Nutrition: Calories: 186 - Fat: 9 g - Protein: 9 g - Carbs: 4 g - Fiber: 0 g - Sugar: 2 g - Sodium: 540 mg

Baked Zucchini Fries

Preparation Time: 15 minutes **Cooking Time:** 30 minutes **Servings:** 2
Ingredients:

- 2 small zucchinis
- 1 large eggs
- 4 tablespoons whole-wheat breadcrumbs
- 2 tablespoons Parmesan cheese, shredded
- 1 teaspoon garlic powder
- 1 teaspoon onion powder
- 1 teaspoon paprika
- 1 teaspoon dried rosemary
- A pinch sea salt

Directions:

1. Preheat the oven to 425 °F. Coat a baking sheet with aluminum foil.
2. Halve each zucchini lengthwise and continue slicing each piece into fries until you have about 8 strips per zucchini.
3. Season zucchini with salt, let sit for 15 minutes, and pat dry with paper towel.
4. lightly whisk the eggs.
5. In a medium bowl, mix the breadcrumbs, Parmesan cheese, garlic powder, paprika, rosemary, and onion powder.
6. Dip each zucchini into the egg; then roll it in the breadcrumb mixture. Place on the prepared baking sheet.
7. Bake in the oven for 30 minutes, stirring the fries halfway through, until zucchini are brown and crispy. Serve with a dipping sauce and enjoy.

Nutrition: Calories: 89 - Fat: 3 g - Protein: 6 g - Carbs: 11 g - Fiber: 1 g - Sugar: 3 g - Sodium: 179 mg

Eggplant Pizzas

Preparation Time: 15 minutes **Cooking Time:** 30 minutes **Servings:** 2
Ingredients:

- 1 eggplant, cut into ½ inch slices
- 1 tablespoon sea salt
- 1 tablespoon extra-virgin olive oil
- 2 teaspoons garlic, minced
- ½ teaspoon dried oregano
- ½ teaspoon dried thyme
- 1 cup no-sugar added marinara sauce
- 1 cup fresh basil leaves, roughly chopped
- 1 cup low-fat mozzarella cheese, shredded
- ¼ cup Parmesan cheese, shredded

- 2 tablespoons no-salt added Kalamata olives, pitted, and chopped

Directions:

1. Preheat the oven to 425 °F. Line a baking dish with aluminum foil.
2. Sprinkle eggplant slices with the salt. Let them rest for 10-15 minutes to release the water of the eggplant. Then, pat dry, and remove the salt.
3. Mix together the olive oil, garlic, thyme and oregano.
4. Place the eggplant slices on the baking sheet. Lightly coat each side of the eggplant with the olive oil mixture, and bake for 15 minutes.
5. Top each eggplant slice with 1 tablespoon of marinara sauce, 1 tablespoon of mozzarella cheese, Kalamata olives and ½ tablespoon of Parmesan cheese.
6. Bake the pizzas for 10 minutes more or until the cheese has melted.
7. Sprinkle with basil, serve immediately and enjoy.

Nutrition: Calories: 99 - Total fat: 6 g - Protein: 5 g - Carbs: 7 g - Fiber: 2 g - Sugar: 4 g - Sodium: 500 mg

Tomato, Basil, Cucumber and Feta Salad

Preparation Time: 30 minutes to chill **Cooking Time:** 0 minutes **Servings:** 4

Ingredients:

- 1 large cucumber, seeded, and sliced
- 4 medium tomatoes, diced
- 1 medium red onion, thinly sliced
- ½ cup fresh basil, chopped
- 3 tablespoons red wine vinegar
- 1 tablespoon extra-virgin olive oil
- ½ teaspoon Dijon mustard
- ½ cup low-salt feta cheese, diced
- ½ teaspoon freshly ground black pepper

Directions:

1. Mix together the cucumber, tomatoes, red onion, feta and basil.
2. whisk together the vinegar, olive oil, mustard, and pepper.
3. Put the dressing over the vegetables, and gently stir until well combined.
4. Cover and chill for at least 30 minutes before serve.

Nutrition: Calories: 82 - Fat: 4 g - Protein: 3 g - Carbs: 9 g - Fiber: 3 g - Sugar: 6 g - Sodium: 45 mg

Roasted Root Vegetables

Preparation Time: 15 minutes **Cooking Time:** 45 minutes **Servings:** 4

Ingredients:

- 1 red beet, peeled, and roughly chopped
- 1 fennel, peeled, and roughly chopped
- 1 carrot, peeled, and roughly chopped
- ½ celeriac, peeled, and roughly chopped
- 1 red onion, quartered
- 2 tablespoons extra-virgin olive oil
- 2 teaspoons garlic, minced
- 2 teaspoons dried thyme
- 1 teaspoon dried sage
- Cooking spray

Directions:

1. Preheat the oven to 425 °F.
2. Arrange the vegetables on the baking sheet without overlapping, and sprinkle them with the olive oil, garlic, sage and thyme. Mix the vegetables to coat them with the oil and seasonings.
3. Roast for 45 minutes, stirring the vegetables every 15 minutes, until all the vegetables are tender. Serve immediately.

Nutrition: Calories: 108 - Fat: 4 g - Protein: 3 g - Carbs: 25 g - Fiber: 10 g - Sugar: 7 g - Sodium: 90 mg

Cauliflower Rice

Preparation Time: 5 minutes **Cooking Time:** 5 minutes **Servings:** 2

Ingredients:

- ½ cauliflower head, stems and leaves removed
- ½ lime, juiced
- A pinch ground white pepper
- Cooking spray

Directions:

1. Roughly chop the cauliflower.
2. The cauliflower until it breaks down into pieces the size of rice. Otherwise, you can use a box grater.
3. Transfer the cauliflower to a paper towel and pat it dry.
4. Place a small skillet over medium heat and grease with cooking spray.
5. add the cauliflower, lime juice and white pepper. Sauté for 5-6 minutes, or until tender.

Nutrition: Calories: 112 - Fat: 2 g - Protein: 2 g - Carbs: 7 g - Fiber: 2 g - Sugar: 2 g - Sodium: 115 mg

Tomato and Mozzarella Skewers

Preparation Time: 20 minutes **Cooking Time:** 0 minutes **Servings:** 2

Ingredients:

- 5 grape tomatoes, halved
- 5 fresh basil leaves
- 5 small balls low-fat fresh mozzarella cheese
- ⅛ cup balsamic vinegar
- 1 tablespoon extra-virgin olive oil
- 2 teaspoons dried oregano
- 1 teaspoon dried marjoram
- A pinch sea salt
- A pinch pepper

Directions:

1. Into a toothpick, stick half a tomato, a basil leaf, a ball of mozzarella, and another half a tomato, and repeat with the remaining ingredients.
2. In a small bowl, mix vinegar, oregano, marjoram, salt, pepper and oil together.
3. Place skewers on a serving plate and sprinkle with the seasoning mixture.

Nutrition: Calories: 218 - Fat: 16 g - Protein: 9 g - Carbs: 6 g - Cholesterol: 36 mg - Sodium: 157 mg

Baked Homemade Potato Chips ✓

Preparation Time: 30 minutes **Cooking Time:** 12 minutes **Servings:** 2

Ingredients:

- 1 unpeeled medium potato
- ¼ teaspoon sea salt
- ¼ teaspoon garlic powder
- ¼ teaspoon dried rosemary
- ¼ teaspoon pepper
- Cold water
- Cooking spray

Directions:

1. Preheat the oven to 450 °F.
2. Slice the potatoes into very thinly slices.
3. Place potatoes in a bowl; fill with cold water, add salt and let soak for 30 minutes.
4. Dry the potatoes with paper towels.
5. In a small bowl, stir in the garlic powder, rosemary and pepper. Set aside.
6. Coat a baking dish with cooking spray and place the potatoes without overlapping. Lightly spray potatoes slices with cooking oil.
7. Bake for 10-12 minutes, or until golden and crunchy.
8. Let cool and enjoy.

Nutrition: Calories: 156 - Fat: 8 g - Protein: 3 g - Carbs: 20 g - Cholesterol: 0 g - Sodium: 603 mg

Baked Brie with Apricot

Preparation Time: 20 minutes **Cooking Time:** 12 minutes **Servings:** 4

Ingredients:

- 4 oz. light Brie cheese
- ¼ cup dried apricots, chopped
- 1 tablespoon brown sugar, or sugar substitute
- 1 tablespoon water
- 1 teaspoon lemon juice
- A dash sea salt
- ½ teaspoon fresh rosemary, minced
- 1 tablespoon almonds, chopped

Directions:

1. Heat the oven to 400 °F.
2. mix the apricots, brown sugar, water, lemon juice and salt, and bring to a boil.
3. Cook until slightly thickened, add the rosemary, stir, and remove from heat.
4. From the top of the cheese, cut the rind off. Put the cheese in an oven-proof, non-greased serving dish.
5. Top the cheese with the apricot mix and almonds. Bake until the cheese is softened, for about 10-12 minutes. Serve and enjoy.

Nutrition: Calories: 117 - Fat: 7 g - Protein: 6 g - Carbs: 7 g - Sugar: 5 g - Sodium: 198 mg

Chocolate Energy Protein Bites

Preparation Time: 10 minutes **Cooking Time:** 0 minutes **Servings:** 6

Ingredients:

- ¾ cup old-fashioned rolled oats
- ½ cup natural peanut butter
- ⅛ cup raw honey, or honey substitute
- 1 scoop chocolate protein powder
- 2 tablespoons chia seeds
- 1 tablespoon dark chocolate chips

Directions:

1. In a bowl, place the oats, peanut butter, honey, chia seeds, chocolate chips and protein powder and stir to combine.
2. From the mixture, shape 12 small balls.
3. Store in the fridge and keep cold before serve.

Nutrition: Calories: 129 - Fat: 6 g - Protein: 7 g - Carbs: 9 g - Fiber: 1 g - Sugar: 5 g

Hummus

Preparation time: 10 minutes **Cooking Time:** 0 minutes **Servings:** 4

Ingredients:

- 1 can chickpeas, drained, and rinsed
- ½ tablespoon tahini
- ½ lemon, juiced
- 1 teaspoon lemon zest, grated
- 1 teaspoon sea salt
- ¼ teaspoon red pepper flakes, crushed
- ½ teaspoon cumin
- 1 tablespoon olive oil
- 1 garlic clove
- 2 tablespoons water
- 1 tablespoon fresh parsley, chopped
- 2 teaspoons poppy seeds

Directions:

1. Pulse all the ingredients.
2. Add water and blend, continuing until desired consistency is reached.
3. Place in a bowl, top with poppy seeds and keep cool in the fridge.

Nutrition: Calories: 104 - Fat: 5 g - Protein: 6 g - Carbs: 14 g - Fiber: 1 g - Sugar: 2 g

Seasoned Cheese Chips ✓

Preparation Time: 5 minutes **Cooking Time:** 12 minutes **Servings:** 2

Ingredients:

- 10 tablespoons low-fat Monterey Jack cheese, shredded
- A pinch garlic powder
- A pinch cayenne pepper
- 2 tablespoons fresh basil, finely chopped

Directions:

1. Heat the oven to 350 °F. Line a baking sheet with parchment paper.
2. Scoop one tablespoon of cheese and drop on the baking sheet.
3. Flatten the cheese into circle and add a pinch of garlic powder, cayenne pepper and basil.
4. Repeat using all of the cheese.
5. Place sheet in oven and cook for about 10-12 minutes, or until golden brown. Let cool and serve.

Nutrition: Calories: 211 - Fat: 14 g - Protein: 12 g - Carbs: 2 g - Sodium: 365 mg

Cabbage and Plums Salad

Preparation Time: 10 minutes **Cooking Time:** 0 minutes
Servings: 6
Ingredients:
- 1 (14 oz.) package coleslaw
- 1 red bell pepper, thinly sliced
- 1 large carrot, grated
- ¼ cup leek, diced
- ½ cup bean sprouts
- ¼ cup fresh cilantro, chopped
- ¼ cup mint leaves
- 4 dried plums, chopped
- 4 tablespoon extra-virgin olive oil
- 1 tablespoon balsamic vinegar
- A pinch black pepper

Directions:
1. mix olive oil, balsamic vinegar and black pepper, and mix well until combined.
2. In a large bowl, combine coleslaw, bell pepper, carrot, leek, cilantro, mint, bean sprouts and plums.
3. Toss with the dressing and serve.

Nutrition: Calories: 213 - Fat: 8 g - Protein: 10 g - Carbs: 18 g - Fiber: 5 g - Sugar: 8 g - Sodium: 398 mg

Cinnamon Fried Bananas

Preparation time: 5 minutes **Cooking Time:** 10 minutes
Servings: 1
Ingredients:
- 1 cup low-carb breadcrumbs
- ½ teaspoon cinnamon
- ½ cup almond flour
- 2 egg whites, beaten
- 1 ripe banana
- 2 tablespoons coconut oil
- ½ tablespoon lemon juice
- ¼ teaspoon nutmeg, grated

Directions:
1. Preheat air fryer oven to 280 °F.
2. Place a skillet over medium heat.
3. Heat coconut oil and add breadcrumbs, lemon juice, nutmeg and cinnamon, and cook around 3 minutes until golden, remove from heat, and pour into a bowl.
4. Peel and cut the banana into rounds, ⅓-½ inch thick. Roll each slice of banana into flour, egg whites, and crumb mixture.
5. Place the banana slices into the air fryer oven, and cook for 10 minutes, turn them halfway through.

Nutrition: Calories 210 - Fat: 8 g - Protein 4 g - Carbs: 19 g - Fiber: 3 g - Sugar: 13 g

Melting Tuna and Cheese Toasties

Preparation Time: 10 minutes **Cooking Time:** 15 minutes
Servings: 2
Ingredients:
- 6 oz. canned line-caught tuna in water
- 1 teaspoon lemon juice
- ½ tablespoon olive oil
- ¼ cooked yellow corn
- 4 slices whole-meal bread
- ½ cup low-fat Cheddar cheese
- 2 teaspoons chives, finely chopped
- 2 tablespoons plain fat-free Greek yogurt
- 2 teaspoons Dijon mustard
- A pinch sea salt
- A pinch black pepper

Directions:
1. Preheat your broiler/grill on its highest setting.
2. In a bowl, combine the lemon juice, oil, salt, pepper, chives, yogurt, mustard and corn.
3. Drain the tuna and place into the bowl. Stir to combine, breaking up the tuna flakes.
4. Toast the bread and spread the tuna mixture on two slices of bread.
5. Top with the cheese and grill until the cheese is bubbling.
6. Cover the toast with the other slice of bread, cut in half, and enjoy.

Nutrition: Calories: 270 - Fat: 7 g - Protein: 28 g - Carbs: 19 g - Fiber: 3 g - Sugar: 4 g - Sodium: 590 mg

Smoked Tofu Quesadillas

Preparation Time: 10 minutes **Cooking Time:** 10 minutes **Servings:** 6
Ingredients:
- 1 lb. extra firm tofu, sliced
- 6 low-carb whole-grain tortillas
- 2 tablespoons coconut oil
- 6 slices low-fat Cheddar cheese
- 2 tablespoons sun-dried tomatoes
- 1 small red onion, chopped
- 1 ½ teaspoon smoked paprika
- 1 tablespoon cilantro
- 6 tablespoons low-fat plain Greek yogurt
- Cooking spray

Directions:
1. Put a large skillet over medium-high heat.
2. Fill the tortillas in half with tofu, tomato, onion, cheese, oil, and top with paprika and coconut oil. Fold and close the tortillas.
3. Cook in the skillet for 5 minutes per side and remove from heat.
4. Top with yogurt and enjoy.

Nutrition: Calories: 236 - Fat: 8 g - Protein: 11 g - Carbs: 23 g - Fiber: 4 g - Sugar: 3 g - Sodium: 504 mg

Chapter 8: Dressings, Sauces, and Seasonings

Greek Salad Dressing

Serves: 1 cup **Total time:** 10 minutes
Ingredients:

- 1/3 cup extra virgin olive oil
- Juice of 1 lemon
- 4 teaspoons minced garlic
- 1 tablespoon dried oregano
- 1 teaspoon dried basil
- ½ teaspoon freshly ground black pepper.
- ½ teaspoon Dijon mustard
- ½ cup vinegar

Preparation:
In a medium bowl, whisk together olive oil, lemon juice, garlic, oregano, basil, pepper, and mustard. Whisk in vinegar until well emulsified. Serve immediately. Refrigerate any leftovers in an airtight container. When ready to use, let the dressing sit for 10 to 15 minutes at room temperature before serving if the oil is solidified. Give it a whisk or shake before dressing your salad.
Nutrition information per serving: Calories: 89 kcal, Protein: 0g, Total Carbs: 1g, Dietary Fibers: 0g, Total Fat: 9g

Creamy Peppercorn Ranch Dressing ✓

Serves: 1 cup **Total time:** 10 minutes
Ingredients:

- ¾ cup low-fat plain Greek yogurt
- 1/3 cup grated Parmigiano-Reggiano Cheese.
- ¼ cup low-fat buttermilk
- Juice of 1 lemon
- Two teaspoons of freshly ground black pepper.
- ½ teaspoon onion flakes
- ¼ teaspoon salt

Preparation:
In a blender or food processor, puree the yogurt, cheese, buttermilk, lemon juice, pepper, onion flakes, and salt on medium-high speed until the dressing is completely smooth and creamy.
Nutrition information per serving: Calories: 35 kcal, Protein: 4g, Total Carbs: 2g, Dietary Fibers: 0g, Total Fat: 1g

Seafood Sauce

Serves: 2 cups **Total time:** 10 minutes
Ingredients:

- 1 ½ cups catsup (free of high-fructose corn syrup)
- 2 tablespoons grated horseradish
- Juice of 1 lemon
- 1 tablespoon Worcestershire sauce
- 1 teaspoon chili powder
- ¼ teaspoon freshly ground black pepper.

Preparation:
In a small bowl, combine the catsup, grated horseradish, lemon juices, Worcestershire sauce, chili powder, and black pepper. Refrigerate and cover for at least 30 minutes or overnight to let the flavors meld. Serve with shrimp cocktail, oysters, grilled scallops, or other seafood.

Nutrition information per serving: Calories: 56 kcal, Protein: 0g, Total Carbs: 14g, Dietary Fibers: 0g, Total Fat: 0g

Homemade Enchilada Sauce

Serves: 2 cups **Total time:** 15 minutes
Ingredients:

- 1 tablespoon extra-virgin olive oil
- ¼ cup chopped onion.
- 1 teaspoon minced garlic
- 2 tablespoons whole wheat pastry flour
- 1 tablespoon chili powder
- ½ teaspoon dried oregano
- ½ teaspoon smoked paprika 1 teaspoon ground cumin.
- 1 cup low sodium vegetable or chicken broth
- ½ cup water
- 1 medium tomato seeded and chopped.

Preparation:
Place a small saucepan on the stove over medium heat. Add the oil, onion, and garlic. Sauté for 1 to 2 minutes or until tender. Add the flour. Continue stirring until the onion and garlic are evenly coated. Mix in the chili powder, oregano, paprika, and cumin. Gradually whisk in the broth and water, constantly whisking to prevent lumps from forming. Add the tomatoes. Cook for 8 to 10 minutes, stirring frequently or until the mixture has thickened. Use an immersion blender to puree the tomato chunks until smooth. Alternatively, transfer the sauce to a blender and puree until smooth. Serve immediately or refrigerate in an airtight container for up to 1 week. You can also freeze and use it at a later date.
Nutrition information per serving: Calories: 37 kcal, Protein: 0g, Total Carbs: 7g, Dietary Fibers: 2g, Total Fat: 0g

Mango Salsa

Serves: 2 cups **Total time:** 15 minutes
Ingredients:

- 1 large mango peeled and diced.
- ¼ cup fresh cilantro, finely chopped.
- Juice of 2 limes
- 1 jalapeno pepper, stemmed, seeded, and diced.
- ¼ large red onion, finely diced (about ¼ cup)

Preparation:
In a medium bowl, mix the mango, cilantro, lime juice, jalapeno pepper, and red onion. Enjoy immediately or refrigerate in an airtight container for up to 3 days.
Nutrition information per serving: Calories: 27 kcal, Protein: 0g, Total Carbs: 7g, Dietary Fibers: 1g, Total Fat: 0g

Basil Pesto

Serves: 5 tablespoons **Total time:** 5 minutes
Ingredients:

- 1 cup fresh basil leaves
- ¼ cup Parmigiano-Reggiano Cheese
- 2 ½ tablespoons extra virgin olive oil
- 2 tablespoons pine-nuts
- 2 tablespoons water

Preparation:

Place all ingredients in a food processor or blender. Pulse until smooth. Serve immediately or keep in an airtight container before serving.

Nutrition information per serving: Calories: 99 kcal, Protein: 2g, Total Carbs: 1g, Dietary Fibers: 0g, Total Fat: 10g

Marinara Sauce with Italian herbs

Serves: 3 cups **Total time:** 40 minutes

Ingredients:

- 1 teaspoon extra-virgin olive oil
- 2 teaspoons minced garlic
- ½ large yellow onion, finely diced.
- 1 medium red bell pepper, washed, seeded, and finely diced.
- 10 to 12 fresh whole tomatoes chopped or 1 (28-ounce) can crushed tomatoes.
- 1 teaspoon dried oregano
- ¼ teaspoon red pepper flakes
- 1 teaspoon dried basil
- 2 bay leaves

Preparation:

Place a saucepan over medium heat. Heat the olive oil and garlic for 1 minute. Add the onion and red bell pepper. Cook for 1 to 2 minutes, stirring frequently or until tender. Add the tomatoes, oregano, red pepper flakes, and basil. Gently stir to combine. Add bay leaves. Cover and reduce the heat to medium-low. Let simmer for 30 minutes. Remove the cover and discard bay leaves. Use an immersion blender to puree the marinara to your desired consistency. Alternatively, transfer the sauce to blender and pulse to achieve the preferred consistency.

Nutrition information per serving: Calories: 37 kcal, Protein: 0g, Total Carbs: 7g, Dietary Fibers: 2g, Total Fat: 0g

Baba Ghanoush Dip

Serves: 4 **Total time:** 45 minutes

Ingredients:

- 1 medium eggplant (about 1 lb.), halved.
- 1 tsp. olive oil
- 2 tbsp. lightly roasted tahini
- 1/2 tsp. cumin
- Juice of 1/2 lemon
- 1/2 tsp. cayenne pepper
- 1 clove garlic, minced.
- 1 tbsp. fresh parsley, chopped.

Preparation:

Prick the eggplant in several places with a fork and lay it on an oven tray. Broil the eggplants on the top oven rack under medium-low heat for 45 minutes, turning every 10 minutes or so, until the eggplant is charred all over. Remove from the oven and cover very loosely with foil to allow to sweat. When cool, remove the skin and transfer the pulp to a blender or food processor. Add all remaining ingredients except the fresh parsley and blend until very smooth. Transfer to a serving bowl and sprinkle with the parsley.

Nutrition information per serving: Calories: 87 kcal, Protein: 1g, Total Carbs: 8g, Dietary Fibers: 4g, Total Fat: 5g

Homemade BBQ Sauce

Serves: 2 **Total time:** 10 minutes

Ingredients:

- 1 1/2 cup reduced-sodium tomato paste.
- 1/4 cup apple cider vinegar
- 1 tbsp. finely chopped onions
- 1 tsp. minced garlic
- Freshly ground black pepper
- A dash of hot sauce
- 1 tbsp. stevia

Preparation:

Combine the tomato paste and apple cider vinegar in a bowl. Heat a small saucepan over low heat, and gradually add the tomato paste mixture a tablespoon to simmer until the sauce starts to thicken. Add the onions, garlic, pepper, sauce to the pot, and simmer for 2 minutes. Stir in the stevia and remove from the heat.

Nutrition information per serving: Calories: 37 kcal, Protein: 1g, Total Carbs: 9g, Dietary Fibers: 2g, Total Fat: 0g

Mixed Bean Salsa

Serves: 2 **Total time:** 35 minutes

Ingredients:

- 3 tbsp. canned mixed beans
- 1 beef tomato finely diced.
- 1/4 red onion finely diced.
- 1/2 tbsp. olive oil
- 1 tsp. red wine vinegar
- Juice of 1/2 lemon
- Freshly ground black pepper

Preparation:

Combine all the ingredients in a serving bowl, and chill for at least 30 minutes before serving.

Nutrition information per serving: Calories: 82 kcal, Protein: 3g, Total Carbs: 8g, Dietary Fibers: 2g, Total Fat: 4g

Spicy Lentils

Serves: 2 **Total time:** 1hr. 5 minutes

Ingredients:

- 1/2 cup lentils
- 1/2 cup water
- 1/4 cup onion, chopped.
- 1 tsp. cumin
- 1 tsp. curry powder

Preparation:

Combine all the ingredients in a nonstick pot and bring to a boil. Reduce the heat to a simmer and leave to cook, covered, for an hour until the lentils are softened.

Nutrition information per serving: Calories: 52 kcal, Protein: 3g, Total Carbs: 9g, Dietary Fibers: 1g, Total Fat: 0g

Parsley Hummus

Serves: 2 **Total time:** 5 minutes

Ingredients:

- 1/4 cup reduced-sodium canned chickpeas, juice reserved.
- Juice of a lemon
- Freshly ground black pepper
- 1 clove garlic, crushed.
- 1/4 cup fresh parsley, chopped.
- 2 tbsp. low-fat Greek yogurt

Preparation:

Combine all the ingredients in a food processor and blend until it reaches your desired consistency (use the reserved juice from the chickpeas or use olive oil to adjust the hummus's consistency.)

Nutrition information per serving: Calories: 58 kcal, Protein: 3g, Total Carbs: 10g, Dietary Fibers: 2g, Total Fat: 1g

White Cheese Sauce

Serves: 5 **Total time:** 15 minutes
Ingredients:
* 1 tbsp. low-fat butter
* 1/4 cup low carb all-purpose flour
* 3/4 cup skim milk
* 4 oz. low-fat soft cheese
* 1/4 tsp. white pepper

Preparation:

Melt the butter over low heat in a nonstick frying pan. Add the flour to the butter, stirring consistently to get a paste. Slowly add in the skim milk and cream cheese, and stir continuously until the sauce thickens. Season with the white pepper, and use with the desired recipe.

Nutrition information per serving: Calories: 85 kcal, Protein: 7g, Total Carbs: 6g, Dietary Fibers: 1g, Total Fat: 4g

Cheesy Vegetable Dip

PREP TIME: 10 min **COOK TIME:** none **YIELD:** 22 Serves
INGREDIENTS:
* Wheat Thins reduced-fat baked snack crackers
* 1/4 cup sliced green onions
* 1 small tomato, chopped (about 3/4 cup)
* 1 medium zucchini, shredded (about 1 cup)
* 1/4 cup Kraft Special Collection Balsamic Vinaigrette Dressing
* 1/4 tsp. Italian seasoning
* 1 container (16 oz.) Breakstone as or Knudsen low fat cottage cheese

DIRECTIONS:
* In a mixer or food blender bowl, combine the cottage cheese and the dressing. Blend until completely smooth. Fill a serving dish halfway with the sauce.
* Cover and set aside the green onions, tomato, zucchini, and spice. Refrigerate for a few hours or until completely cold. Serve with bread as a dip.

NUTRITION:

23 Cal; 4g Protein; 0.5g Tot Fat; 7g Carb; 4.2g Fiber; 2.2g Sugar; 168mg Sodium

Sugar-Free BBQ Sauce

PREP TIME: 15 min **COOK TIME:** 30 min **YIELD:** 10 Serves
INGREDIENTS:
* Hot sauce to taste
* 2 strips of thick bacon, chopped fine
* 1 tbsp. Worcestershire sauce
* 1/4 cup low carb (sugar-free) catsup
* 1 can (12 oz.) diet (sugar-free) cola - Splendor-sweetened preferred
* 1 small can (6 oz.) tomato paste

* 3 tbsp. mustard
* 1 clove garlic, minced or 1/4 tsp. garlic powder
* 1 pinch ground cloves
* 1 small onion, minced

DIRECTIONS:
* In a pot, fry the bacon - a 2-quart pan works nicely. Cook, occasionally stirring, until the onion is tender, about 3-5 minutes. If you're using fresh garlic, add it now and stir for about half a minute.
* Add the other ingredients, as well as approximately a half cup of water. Stir everything together well. Cook for 20-30 minutes on low heat. It will simmer down a little, and the flavors will meld together.
* Season to taste with vinegar, artificial sweetener (liquid preferable), or hot sauce to get the desired balance. (Adding additional sweetness will cool it down if it's too warm.)

NUTRITION:

97 Cal; 31g Protein; 2.5g Tot Fat; 9g Carb; 5.2g Fiber; 8.2g Sugar; 368mg Sodium

Layered Mexican Dip

PREP TIME: 25 min **COOK TIME:** 26 min **YIELD:** 24 Serves
INGREDIENTS:
* 1/2 cup low-fat sour cream
* 6 oz. lean ground turkey
* 1/4 cup chopped green onions
* 1/2 cup chopped onion
* 1/2 cup Shredded low-fat Cheddar cheese
* 1/2 cup shredded reduced-fat Monterey Jack cheese
* 1 (4 oz.) can chopped green chilies, undrained
* 1/2 cup Picante sauce
* 1 (16 oz.) can pinto beans, drained & mashed
* 1 tbsp. sliced ripe olives
* 6 oz. lean ground pork

DIRECTIONS:
* In a big nonstick pan, sauté the pork, turkey, and onion over medium heat, turning to crumble the meat. Using paper towels absorb any excess liquid. Remove from the equation. Consume with tortilla chips or Melba pieces that haven't been salted.

NUTRITION:

93 Cal; 5.1g Protein; 3.5g Tot Fat; 12g Carb; 5.2g Fiber; 6.2g Sugar; 222mg Sodium

Cinnamon Applesauce

PREP TIME: 15 min **COOK TIME:** 30 min **YIELD:** 4 cups
INGREDIENTS:
* Splenda granular to taste
* 2 whole cinnamon sticks
* 6 large apples

DIRECTIONS:
* Cut each apple into 4 quarters, peel and remove the outer from each quarter, put prepped apple in a covered pot. Add 1/4 cup of water and the cinnamon sticks to the apples.
* Cover pan, bring to a boil, then reduce to a low heat and cook apples for 30 minutes, or until very soft. Remove from the heat, drop cinnamon sticks, and mash apples with a

potato masher or a wooden spoon until smooth. 1/2 cup should be added. Splenda with more sweeteners to taste.

NUTRITION:
31 Cal; 0.1g Protein; 0g Tot Fat; 8g Carb; 6.2g Fiber; 6.2g Sugar; 268mg Sodium

Italian Herb-Roasted Chicken in Tomato-Basil Sauce

PREP TIME: 15 min **COOK TIME:** 30 min **YIELD:** 4 Serve
INGREDIENTS:
- 1/8 tsp. freshly ground black pepper
- 1 (2 1/2 to 3-pound) broiler-fryer chicken
- 2 tablespoons snipped fresh basil
- 2 teaspoons dried Italian seasoning, crushed
- 1 large tomato, peeled, seeded and chopped
- 1/4 tsp. garlic salt
- 1 tablespoon cornstarch
- 1 clove garlic, minced
- 1/4 cup chopped onion
- 1 (5 1/2 or 6-ounce) can tomato juice (3/4 cup)
- 1/4 tsp. onion salt
- 1 tablespoon red wine vinegar
- 2 teaspoons dried parsley flakes
- 1/4 tsp. salt
- 2 tablespoons olive oil
- 2 packets Splenda

DIRECTIONS:
- Rinse and pat dry the chicken. Twist wing tips under and pull neck skin to behind. 1 tablespoon olive oil, brushed on the exterior of the chicken Combine the Italian seasoning, parsley, garlic, and onion salts; season the chicken inside and out with the spice combination. Legs should be tied together. In a shallow roasting pan, place the chicken breast side up on a rack. In a small roasting pan, roast uncovered. Roast for 1 1/4 to 1 1/2 hours, uncovered, at 375°F (190°F).
- Before cutting, cover and set aside for 15 minutes, make the sauce. In the remaining 1 tablespoon olive oil, cook the onion and garlic until the onion is soft. Combine the cornstarch, tomato juice, tomato, vinegar, basil, salt, and pepper in a mixing bowl. Cook, constantly stirring, until the sauce has thickened and is bubbling. Cook and stir for another 2 minutes. Remove the pan from the heat and whisk in the Splenda. Serve the sauce with the chicken. If preferred, serve over rice.

NUTRITION:
172 Cal; 8 g Protein; 6 g Tot Fat; 9 g Carb; 0 g Fiber; 1 g Sugar; 101 mg Sodium

Steamed Fish with Yogurt Dill Sauce

PREP TIME: 15 min **COOK TIME:** 30 min **YIELD:** 4 Serve
INGREDIENTS:
- 1/2 cup fat-free, reduced-sodium chicken broth
- 1 Tbsp. finely chopped fresh chives
- 1 scallion, finely chopped (green part included)
- 1 Tbsp. fresh dill, divided
- 2 red bell peppers, thinly sliced
- 1/3 cup of low-fat, plain yogurt
- Salt and freshly ground pepper
- 2 orange or yellow bell peppers, thinly sliced
- 1-1/2 lb. firm-fleshed fish fillet, cut into 4 pieces
- 1 large lemon, thinly sliced
- 1 tsp. finely chopped fresh basil
- 4 sprigs of fresh dill for garnish (optional)
- 2 Tbsp. extra virgin olive oil

DIRECTIONS:
- Combine the oil, chives, basil, and half of the dill in a small bowl. Sprinkle salt and pepper on both sides of the fish after rubbing the mixture in. Remove from the equation. Set aside the leftover dill with the yogurt sauce. Arrange bell peppers and scallions equally down the bottom of a deep-rimmed serving dish big enough to contain the fish and liquid. Arrange the fish on top.
- Serve the fish with lemon slices on top. Pour in the broth. Place in microwave and cook on high for 3 minutes, or until salmon flakes easily with a fork. Remove the dish from the microwave and top with the remaining dill. Serve with a dill yogurt sauce.

NUTRITION:
242 Cal; 32 g Protein; 12 g Tot Fat; 13 g Carb; 0 g Fiber; 2 g Sugar; 241 mg Sodium

Beef Kabobs with Peanut Dipping Sauce

PREP TIME: 15 min **COOK TIME:** 30 min **YIELD:** 4 Serve
INGREDIENTS:
- 1 red bell pepper, cut into squares
- 2 tbsp. granulated brown sugar substitute
- 1/4 tsp. ground red pepper
- 4 cloves garlic, pressed
- 3 tbsp. lime juice
- 3/4 cup water
- 1/2 cup creamy unsweetened natural peanut butter
- 1 tbsp. finely chopped ginger
- 1 1/2 lb. sirloin steak, 1 1/2â## thick, cut into 1-inch pieces
- 1 green bell pepper, cut into squares
- 2 tbsp. sugar substitute
- 1 large onion, cut into wedges
- 1/2 cup light soy sauce

DIRECTIONS:
- Combine half of the soy sauce, 1 tbsp. brown sugar replacement, 1 tbsp. sugar substitute, and 2 crushed garlic cloves in a shallow dish. Stir in the meat to coat it. Allow for 20 minutes of resting time, stirring once.
- Meanwhile, mix the water, peanut butter, ginger, lime juice, crushed red pepper, the other half of the soy sauce, 1 tbsp. brown sugar replacement, 1 tbsp. sugar substitute, and the leftover garlic cloves in a large saucepan over high flame. Cook, stirring continuously until the mixture boils. Remove the pan from the heat.
- Using cooking spray, coat a grill rack. Preheat the grill to a high temperature. Using 4 metal skewers, thread the steak, peppers, and onion. Cook for 10 minutes on the grill rack, rotating periodically, or until the steak is no longer pink and a thermometer placed in the thickest part registers 160 degrees and the juices flow clear.

NUTRITION:
233 Cal; 21 g Protein; 7 g Tot Fat; 3 g Carb; 0 g Fiber; 1 g Sugar; 161 mg Sodium

Turkey Tacos with Avocado-Corn Salsa

PREP TIME: 15 min **COOK TIME:** 10 min **YIELD:** 12 Serve

INGREDIENTS:
- 3/4 cup water
- 1 firm, ripe avocado, peeled, pitted, and chopped
- 1 pkg (1.25 oz.) reduced-sodium taco seasoning mix
- 1 cup cherry tomatoes, halved
- 1 pkg (12 counts) corn taco shells
- 1 tbsp. lime juice
- 12 oz. cooked boneless, skinless, turkey breast, sliced into thin strips
- 1 cup can sweet corn kernels, rinsed and drained

DIRECTIONS:
- In a medium bowl, combine the avocado, corn, tomatoes, and lime juice. Set aside the salsa. In the oven, warm the shells. Combine spices, turkey, and water in a medium skillet. Bring to a boil, lower to low heat and continue to cook for 5 minutes, stirring regularly. Fill shells halfway with turkey mixture, then top with salsa.

NUTRITION:
234 Cal; 22 g Protein; 9 g Tot Fat; 11 g Carb; 0 g Fiber; 0 g Sugar; 221 mg Sodium

South Beach Barbecue Sauce

PREP TIME: 15 min **COOK TIME:** none **YIELD:** 1 cup

INGREDIENTS:
- 1/8 tsp. garlic powder
- 1 can (8 ounces) tomato sauce
- 2 teaspoons chopped parsley
- 1 tsp. mustard powder
- 1 tsp. Worcestershire sauce
- 1/4 tsp. salt
- 1/8 tsp. ground black pepper
- 2 tablespoons white vinegar

DIRECTIONS:
- Mix the pepper, vinegar, tomato sauce, mustard powder, Worcestershire sauce, salt, parsley, and garlic powder in a zip lock bag.

NUTRITION:
21 Cal; 0.5g Protein; 0g Tot Fat; 1g Carb; 0.5g Fiber; 0g Sugar; 290mg Sodium

Roma Tomatoes Salsa

PREP TIME: 15 min **COOK TIME:** none **YIELD:** 5 Serve

INGREDIENTS:
- juice of 2 limes freshly squeezed
- 1 big yellow or white onion
- Half salt to taste
- 2 jalapenos finely minced
- 1/2 of a bunch of cilantro
- 5 Roma tomatoes

DIRECTIONS:
- Mix thoroughly. There will be a lot of chopping...roll up the cilantro and cut it up small...it will be simpler this way.

NUTRITION:
60 Cal; 14g Protein; 5g Tot Fat; 1g Carb; 0g Fiber; 2g Sugar; 45mg Sodium

Jalapeno Salsa

PREP TIME: 15 min **COOK TIME:** none **YIELD:** 5 Serve

INGREDIENTS:
- Sweetener to taste, i.e., Splenda, stevia, honey, NutraSweet, whatever you choose to use.
- salt to taste
- 1/2 red onion diced
- 1/2 bunch of cilantro leaves cut up
- 4 peaches peeled and diced
- 1/2 jalapeno finely diced
- juice from 4 limes
- cereals from two cooked cobs of corn
- cracked black pepper to taste
- 1 orange pepper diced
- 1 red pepper diced

DIRECTIONS:
- Add all the ingredients listed above to a bowl, mix well and enjoy!

NUTRITION:
60 Cal; 14g Protein; 5g Tot Fat; 1g Carb; 0g Fiber; 2g Sugar; 45mg Sodium

White Chicken Chili

PREP TIME: 15 min **COOK TIME:** 35 min **YIELD:** 12 Serve

INGREDIENTS:
- Kosher salt and freshly ground black pepper
- 1 medium onion, chopped
- 1 tsp. chili powder
- 2 tablespoon olive oil
- Two 14.5-ounce cans of chicken broth
- 2 tablespoons flour
- One 4.5-ounce can dice green chilies
- 1 cup corn
- 4 cups diced, cooked chicken or turkey
- 1 tsp. cumin
- Two 15-ounce cans of Cannellini or white beans, drained
- 1/2 tsp. oregano
- 2 garlic cloves, minced

DIRECTIONS:
- In a large saucepan, sauté onion and garlic in olive oil over medium-high heat until the onion is soft. Set aside one can of drained beans to puree. Cook for one minute after adding the flour to the onion mixture. Combine the chicken, corn, chilies, broth, cumin, chili powder, oregano, beans, and one cup of water in a big mixing bowl. Salt & pepper to taste. Reduce heat to low and cook for 30 minutes.

NUTRITION:
357 Cal; 26 g Protein; 20 g Tot Fat; 13 g Carb; 3 g fiber

Party Curried Chicken Rice

PREP TIME: 15 min **COOK TIME:** 30 min **YIELD:** 4 Serve

INGREDIENTS:
- 1c.toasted flaked almonds
- 1c green apples <skins on>
- 2c.chopped cooked chicken
- 1/4c. Chopped 1/2c.diced green peppers
- 1c. plain no-fat yogurt

- 1/2c. diced green peppers
- 1c. sliced celery
- 1/4c. chopped onion
- 1c. diced carrots
- 1c. golden and dark raisins
- 1 pkg. long-grain and wild rice

DRESSING:
- 1/4 ground black pepper
- 1 c plain yogurt
- 2 tsp. curry powder
- 2 tsp. Splenda
- 1/2 tsp. cumin (optional)
- 1/2 cup light mayo

DIRECTIONS:
- Cook rice according to per package directions (cool). Combine the rice and salad ingredients in a big mixing basin. Combine the dressing ingredients in a small bowl. Toss in the rice mixture. Mix thoroughly. Place in the refrigerator until ready to serve. Garnish with apple slices and watercress sprigs.

NUTRITION:
182 Cal; 6 g Protein; 3 g Tot Fat; 4 g Carb; 0 g Fiber; 0.5 g Sugar; 32 mg Sodium

Pasta with Chickpea Sauce
Preparation Time: 10 minutes **Cooking Time:** 10 minutes **Servings:** 4
Ingredients:
- ½ cup no-salt added cooked chickpeas
- 2 cups hot cooked spelt pasta
- ½ cup onion, chopped
- 2 tablespoons basil, chopped
- 1 ½ tablespoon olive oil
- ⅓ cup spring water
- ½ teaspoon sea salt
- ¼ teaspoon cayenne pepper

Directions:
1. Take a medium skillet pan, place it over medium heat, add oil and when hot, add onion, and cook for 4-5 minutes until golden brown.
2. Spoon the onion mixture into a food processor, add chickpeas, salt, cayenne pepper, and water and then pulse until smooth.
3. Place pasta into a large bowl, add blended chickpea sauce, toss until mixed, and then garnish with basil.
Nutrition: Calories: 327 - Fat: 9 g - Protein: 12 g - Carbs: 46 g - Fiber: 5 g - Sodium: 516 mg

Lemon Avocado Salad Dressing
Preparation Time: 5 minutes **Cooking Time:** 0 minutes **Servings:** 4
Ingredients:
- 1 medium ripe avocado, peeled, and mashed
- 2 tablespoons olive oil
- 1 garlic clove, minced
- ⅓ teaspoon salt
- ½ teaspoon black pepper
- ¼ cup water
- 2 tablespoons low-fat sour cream

- 2 tablespoons lemon juice
- 1 tablespoon fresh dill, minced or 1 teaspoon dill weed
- ½ fresh parsley, finely chopped
- ½ teaspoon raw honey, or honey substitute

Directions:
1. In a blender, combine all the ingredients, cover and process until well blended.
Nutrition: Calories: 158 - Fat: 16 g - Protein: 1 g - Carbs: 4 g - Fiber: 2 g - Sodium: 261 mg

Creamy Avocado Cilantro Lime Dressing
Preparation Time: 5 minutes **Cooking Time:** 0 minutes
Servings: 8
Ingredients:
- 1 avocado
- ¼ cup olive oil
- ¼ teaspoon sea salt
- ½ cup cilantro, chopped
- ¼ cup low-fat plain goat yogurt
- ½ lime, juiced
- 1 teaspoon lime zest
- 1 garlic clove, peeled
- ½ jalapeño, chopped
- ¼ teaspoon pepper
- ½ teaspoon cumin

Directions:
1. Place all the ingredients in a food processor or mixer and mix it until well balanced.
Nutrition: Calories: 95 - Fat: 11 g - Protein: 1 g - Carbs: 3 g - Fiber: 1 g - Sodium: 74 mg

Creamy Avocado Dressing
Preparation Time: 5 minutes **Cooking Time:** 0 minutes
Servings: 4
Ingredients:
- 1 large avocado
- 1 garlic clove, peeled
- ½ tablespoon fresh lime
- 3 tablespoons avocado oil
- ½ tablespoon coriander
- ½ tablespoon dill
- ¼ teaspoon kosher salt
- ¼ teaspoon ground black pepper
- Water, as needed

Directions:
1. Put the peeled garlic clove, lime juice, avocado, coriander, dill, avocado oil, salt, and pepper into a mixer.
2. Process until smooth. If necessary, add a little water at a time until the desired creaminess is achieved.
Nutrition: Calories: 88 - Fat: 9 g - Carbs: 3.5 g - Protein: 1 g - Fiber: 1 g - Sodium: 61 mg

Southwestern Avocado Salad Dressing
Preparation Time: 1 hour to chill **Cooking Time:** 0 minutes **Servings:** 8
Ingredients:
- 1 ripe avocado, pitted, and peeled
- 1 cup low-fat buttermilk

- ½ teaspoon garlic powder
- ½ teaspoon chipotle chili powder
- ½ teaspoon black pepper
- ¼ cup cilantro
- ½ lime, juiced
- A pinch sea salt
- 1 teaspoon ranch seasoning powder, homemade or store-bought

Directions:

1. Place all the ingredients together into a mixer. Blend in until creamy and smooth.
2. Refrigerate for 1 hour and serve.

Nutrition: Calories: 69 - Fat: 5 g - Protein: 1 g - Carbs: 5 g - Fiber: 1 g - Sodium: 219 mg

Mango Salsa

Preparation Time: 15 minutes **Cooking Time:** 0 minutes **Servings:** 6-8

Ingredients:

- 1 avocado, peeled, pitted, and cubed
- 2 tablespoons fresh key lime juice
- 1 mango, peeled, pitted, and cubed
- 1 cup cherry tomatoes, quartered
- 1 tablespoon fresh cilantro, chopped
- A pinch sea salt
- A pinch black pepper

Directions:

1. In a bowl, add avocado cubes and lime juice and mix well.
2. In the same bowl, add remaining ingredients and stir to combine. Serve immediately.

Nutrition: Calories 145 - Fat: 9 g - Protein: 2 g - Carbs: 12 g - Fiber: 4 g - Sodium: 344 mg

Zoodles with Basil and Avocado Sauce

Preparation Time: 10 **minutes Cooking Time:** 0 minutes **Servings:** 6

Ingredients:

- 2 zucchinis, spiralized into noodles
- 2 avocados, peeled, and pitted
- ½ cup walnuts
- 2 cups basil leaves
- 24 cherry tomatoes, sliced
- ⅓ teaspoon sea salt
- 4 tablespoons key lime juice
- ½ cup spring water

Directions:

1. Prepare the sauce placing all the ingredients, except for zucchini noodles and tomatoes, in a food processor and then pulse until smooth.
2. Take a large bowl, place zucchini noodles in it, add tomato slices, pour in the prepared sauce and toss until coated.

Nutrition: Calories: 258 - Fat: 15 g - Protein: 8 g - Carbs: 24 g - Fiber: 8 g - Sodium: 312 mg

Roasted Tomato Sauce

Preparation Time: 15 minutes **Cooking Time:** 30 minutes **Servings:** 24

Ingredients:

- 18 Roma tomatoes
- ½ red bell pepper
- ½ sweet onion
- ½ red onion
- 1 medium shallot
- ⅛ cup grapeseed oil
- 1 tablespoon agave
- 3 teaspoons sea salt
- 3 teaspoons basil
- 2 teaspoons oregano
- 2 teaspoons onion powder
- ⅛ teaspoon cayenne powder

Directions:

1. Preheat your oven to 400 °F.
2. Chop the vegetables in half and place them in a bowl.
3. In a little bowl, mix grapeseed oil and a teaspoon of both basil and sea salt.
4. Sprinkle the chopped vegetables with the mixture until they are fully coated.
5. Place all the vegetables on a cookie sheet. Bake in the oven for 30 minutes. Then, let cool a little.
6. Place the roasted vegetables and the remaining ingredients into a blender and mix on high speed. Get an excellent sauce to season your favorite dishes.

Nutrition: Calories: 60 - Fat: 3 g - Protein: 2 g - Carbs: 8 g - Fiber: 3 g - Sodium: 254 mg

Avocado Mayo

Preparation Time: 5 minutes **Cooking Time:** 0 minutes **Servings:** 4

Ingredients:

- 1 avocado
- ½ lime, juiced
- ¼ cup cilantro
- ⅓ teaspoon sea salt
- ½ tablespoon onion powder
- 2 tablespoon extra-virgin olive oil
- A pinch cayenne powder

Directions:

1. Remove the pit of the avocado and scoop the insides into a blender.
2. Add the rest of the ingredients and blend at high speed.

Nutrition: Calories: 45 - Fat: 5 g - Protein: 1 g - Carbs: 3 g - Fiber: 1 g - Sodium: 75 mg

Applesauce

Preparation Time: 5 minutes **Cooking Time:** 0 minutes **Servings:** 6-8

Ingredients:

- 3 cups apples, peeled, and chopped
- 3 tablespoons agave
- ⅛ teaspoon cloves
- 1 teaspoon lime juice
- 1 tablespoon fresh mint, chopped
- ½ cup strawberries
- ⅛ teaspoon sea salt
- 1 tablespoon spring water

Directions:

1. In a blender, place sliced apples, mint, cloves, salt, lime juice, and agave.
2. Pulse until a creamy mixture is reached.
3. Add the strawberries and blend through just until combined.
4. If it doesn't mix well, add 1 tablespoon of spring water.

Nutrition: Calories: 129 - Fat: 1 g - Protein: 1 g - Carbs: 28 g - Fiber 4 g - Sugar: 21 g

Beef Roasted in Applesauce

Preparation Time: 10 minutes **Cooking Time:** 45 minutes **Servings:** 14-16

Ingredients:

- 3 lb. center cut beef roast
- ½ cup carrots, chopped
- ½ cup apple cider vinegar
- ½ teaspoon smoked paprika
- 4 apples, chopped
- 1 yellow onion, chopped
- 4 garlic cloves, pressed
- 17 oz. low-sodium beef stock
- ½ teaspoon chicken salt
- A pinch black pepper

Directions:

1. Preheat the air fryer to 360 °F.
2. In a bowl, add paprika, black pepper, and chicken salt, and stir. Rub the beef with the mixture and transfer to a pan that will fit into the air fryer.
3. Add the remaining ingredients and cook for 45 minutes. Enjoy and serve.

Nutrition: Calories: 304 - Fat: 15 g - Protein: 32 g - Carbs: 12 g - Sodium: 312 mg

Beet and Arugula Salad with Parsley Dressing

Preparation Time: 10 minutes **Cooking Time:** 15 minutes **Servings:** 4

Ingredients:

- 4 beets
- 1 garlic clove, minced
- 2 tablespoons balsamic vinegar
- 2 tablespoons low-salt capers
- 1 bunch parsley, chopped
- 1 tablespoon olive oil
- 1 bunch arugula, roughly chopped
- A pinch black pepper
- A pinch sea salt

Directions:

1. Place beets on the air fryer grill pan. Set the air fryer grill to AIR FRY function.
2. Set timer and temperature to 15 minutes and 360 °F.
3. In a small bowl, mix black pepper, garlic, capers, salt, parsley, and olive oil. Mix well.
4. Remove beets from the air fryer grill and place them on a flat surface to cool.
5. Peel and cut them into cubes, then put in a salad bowl. Add the arugula.

6. Season with vinegar and parsley mixture, and mix well. Serve and enjoy.

Nutrition: Calories: 155 - Fat: 6 g - Protein: 5 g - Carbs: 14 g - Fiber: 5 g - Sugar: 12 g - Sodium: 232 mg

Short Ribs and Beer Sauce

Preparation Time: 15 minutes **Cooking Time:** 45 minutes **Servings:** 6

Ingredients:

- 4 lbs. short ribs, cut into small pieces
- 1 dried Portobello mushroom
- 1 yellow onion, chopped
- 1 cup low-sodium chicken stock
- 6 thyme sprigs, chopped
- ¼ cup tomato paste
- 1 bay leaf
- 1 cup dark beer
- 1 tablespoon olive oil
- A pinch sea salt
- A pinch pepper

Directions:

1. Preheat the air fryer to 350 °F.
2. In a pan that fits into your air fryer, heat oil over medium heat, add onion, stock, tomato paste, beer, mushroom, bay leaf, and thyme. Simmer for 3-5 minutes.
3. Add the rib and transfer to the air fryer; cook for 40 minutes.
4. Remove from air fryer, discard bay leaf, and serve.

Nutrition: Calories: 380 - Fat: 17 g - Protein: 43 g - Carbs: 17 g - Sodium: 452 mg

Short Ribs and Special Sauce

Preparation Time: 10 minutes **Cooking Time:** 40 minutes **Servings:** 3

Ingredients:

- 2 lbs. short ribs
- ¼ cup low-sodium soy sauce
- 2 garlic cloves, pressed
- ¼ cup water
- 1 tablespoon sesame oil
- ⅛ cup rice wine
- 2 ginger slices
- ⅛ cup no-sugar added pear juice
- 1 teaspoon vegetable oil
- 1 green onion, chopped

Directions:

1. Preheat the air fryer to 350 °F.
2. Heat oil in a pan over medium heat, add in green onion, garlic and ginger. Stir and cook for 2-3 minutes.
3. Add the ribs and remaining ingredients, transfer to the air fryer and cook for 35 minutes. Serve and enjoy.

Nutrition: Calories: 328 - Fat: 22 g - Protein: 20 g - Carbs: 9 g - Sodium: 388 mg

Beef Patty in Mushroom Sauce

Preparation Time: 15 minutes **Cooking Time:** 15 minutes **Servings:** 8

Ingredients:

- 2 lbs. ground beef

- ¾ cup almond flour
- 1 tablespoon onion flakes
- ½ teaspoon garlic powder
- ¼ cup low-sodium beef stock
- 1 tablespoon parsley, chopped
- 1 tablespoon low-sodium soy sauce
- 2 cups mushroom, sliced
- 2 tablespoons light unsalted butter, or margarine
- 1 cup yellow onion, chopped
- ¼ cup low-fat sour cream
- A pinch sea salt
- A pinch black pepper
- Cooking spray

Directions:
1. Preheat the air fryer to 350 °F.
2. In a bowl, mix beef, black pepper, salt, garlic powder, ¼ cup beef stock, parsley, onion flakes, and flour. Stir and shape eight patties.
3. Place them into the greased air fryer basket and cook for 14 minutes.
4. While the patties cook, heat butter in a pan on medium heat, add the mushroom and cook for 4 minutes with constant stirring.
5. Add onion and cook for another 4 minutes.
6. Add soy sauce and sour cream, and simmer over low heat until the sauce thickens. Remove from heat.
7. Serve patties with mushroom sauce.

Nutrition: Calories: 275 - Fat: 15 g - Protein: 29 g - Carbs: 12 g - Sodium: 326 mg

Beef Brisket and Onion Sauce

Preparation Time: 15 minutes **Cooking Time:** 2 hours
Servings: 8
Ingredients:
- 2 lbs. beef brisket
- ½ lb. yellow onion, chopped
- ½ lb. sweet onion, sliced
- ¼ lb. celery, chopped
- ½ lb. carrots, chopped
- 2 cups water
- ¼ cup vegetable oil
- 1 ½ teaspoon fresh rosemary, chopped
- A pinch sea salt
- A pinch black pepper

Directions:
1. Preheat the air fryer to 300 °F.
2. Put water in a pan that fits into the air fryer.
3. Add yellow onions, half celery, half carrots, salt, and pepper. Stir and allow to cook over medium-high heat, for about 15 minutes.
4. Lower the heat, add the beef brisket, stir, and cook for 15 minutes more.
5. Put the pan into the air fryer and cook for 1 hour and 30 minutes.
6. Meanwhile, place a pan over medium-high heat, add vegetable oil, and heat until shimmering. Add sweet onion and sauté for 10 minutes.
7. Add the remaining celery and carrots, and cook for 10 minutes.

8. When beef brisket is tender, remove from air fryer.
9. Cut and serve the beef brisket with the onion sauce. Sprinkle with rosemary and enjoy.

Nutrition: Calories: 294 - Fat: 18 g - Protein: 32 g - Carbs: 12 g - Sodium: 378 mg

Turkey Wraps with Thai Sauce

Preparation Time: 15 minutes **Cooking Time:** 16 minutes
Servings: 8
Ingredients:
For the Turkey Breasts:
- 2 lbs. grilled turkey breasts
- A pinch sea salt
- A pinch black pepper
- Cooking spray

For the Wraps:
- 8 large lettuce leaves, stems removed
- 1 medium avocado, sliced
- ½ cucumber, thinly sliced
- 1 cup mango, diced
- 8 teaspoons no-sugar added raisins
- 24 mint leaves

For the Sauce:
- 2 tablespoons all-natural peanut butter
- 2 tablespoons light coconut cream
- 2 tablespoons low-sodium soy sauce
- ¼ cup fresh lime juice
- 1 teaspoon sesame oil
- 1 tablespoon apple cider vinegar
- 1 tablespoon tahini
- 1 garlic clove, crushed
- 1 tablespoon fresh ginger, grated
- ½ teaspoon chili flakes
- ½ teaspoon ground coriander
- ¼ teaspoon black pepper

Directions:
To Make the Turkey Breasts:
1. Set your air fryer to 350 °F.
2. Lightly grease the basket of the air fryer with cooking spray.
3. Season the turkey with salt and pepper, and air fry it for 8 minutes on each side.
4. Remove it from air fryer and let cool slightly.
5. Then, dice it up.
To Make the Wraps:
1. Divide wraps ingredients (fruits, veggies and diced turkey) evenly among the eight lettuce leaves.
2. Roll up the wraps and stick a toothpick in each one.
To Make the Sauce:
1. In a blender, combine all the sauce ingredients and mix until creamy.
2. Divide and serve with the wraps.

Nutrition: Calories: 371 - Fat: 28 g - Protein: 25 g - Carbs: 14 g - Sodium: 376 mg

Cod Steaks and Plum Sauce

Preparation Time: 15 minutes **Cooking Time:** 20 minutes **Servings:** 3
Ingredients:

- 3 cod steaks
- 1 tablespoon plum sauce
- ½ teaspoon garlic powder
- ½ teaspoon ginger powder
- ¼ teaspoon turmeric powder
- 1 tablespoon water
- A pinch black pepper
- A pinch sea salt
- Cooking spray

Directions:
1. Lightly grease cod steaks with cooking spray.
2. Add black pepper, ginger powder, salt, turmeric powder, and garlic powder. Allow the coated cod steaks to rest for 10 minutes.
3. Place the coated cod steaks in the air fryer grill. Set the function to AIR FRYER/GRILL.
4. Grill for about 20 minutes at 360 °F, flipping halfway through.
5. When codfish is almost ready, in a pan, heat plum sauce with water over medium heat for 2 minutes.
6. Divide the sauce among the cod steaks and serve immediately.

Nutrition: Calories: 293 - Fat: 13 g - Protein: 30 g - Carbs: 27 g - Sodium: 328 mg

Steamed Salmon and Yogurt Sauce

Preparation Time: 5 minutes **Cooking Time:** 10 minutes **Servings:** 2
Ingredients:
- 6 oz. fresh salmon
- 1 cup water
- 1 teaspoon vegetable oil
- ½ cup plain low-fat Greek yogurt
- ½ cup low-fat sour cream
- 1 tablespoon dill, finely chopped (keep a bit for garnishing)
- 1 teaspoon cilantro, finely chopped
- A pinch sea salt
- A pinch white pepper

Directions:
1. Pour the water into the tray of the air fryer oven and start heating to 285 °F.
2. Brush oil over fish and season with salt and white pepper.
3. Now put it into the air fryer oven for 10 minutes.
4. In the meantime, mix yogurt, cream, dill and cilantro.
5. When fish is done, serve with the sauce and garnish with sprigs of dill.

Nutrition: Calories: 285 - Fat: 17 g - Protein: 21 g - Carbs: 10 - Sodium: 332 mg

Salmon and Coconut Sauce

Preparation Time: 10 minutes **Cooking Time:** 20 minutes **Servings:** 4
Ingredients:
- 1 lb. salmon fillets, boneless
- ⅓ cup low-fat heavy cream, or heavy cream substitute
- ¼ cup lime juice

- ½ cup coconut, shredded
- ¼ cup light coconut cream
- 1 teaspoon lime zest, grated
- 1 teaspoon dried oregano
- A pinch sea salt
- A pinch black pepper

Directions:
1. Take a bowl and mix all the ingredients, except salmon.
2. Arrange the fish in a pan that fits your air fryer, drizzle the coconut sauce all over.
3. Put the pan in the air fryer and cook at 360 °F for 20 minutes.
4. Divide among plates and serve.

Nutrition: Calories: 294 - Fat: 17 g - Protein: 29 g - Carbs: 6 g - Fiber: 2 g - Sodium: 90 mg

Salmon and Chives Sauce

Preparation Time: 10 minutes **Cooking Time:** 20 minutes **Servings:** 4
Ingredients:
- 1 lb. salmon fillets, boneless
- ¼ garlic cloves, minced
- ¼ cup ghee, melted
- ½ cup low-fat heavy cream, or heavy cream substitute
- 2 tablespoons chives, chopped
- 1 teaspoon lemon juice
- 1 teaspoon dill, chopped
- A pinch sea salt
- A pinch ground red pepper

Directions:
1. Take a bowl and mix all the ingredients, except salmon and red pepper.
2. Arrange the salmon in a pan that fits the air fryer, drizzle the sauce all over.
3. Introduce the pan in the air fryer and cook at 360 °F for 20 minutes.
4. Divide among plates, season with red pepper and serve.

Nutrition: Calories: 298 - Fat: 14 g - Protein: 32 g - Carbs: 8 g - Fiber: 2 g - Sodium: 347 mg

Lobster Tails with White Wine Sauce

Preparation Time: 10 minutes **Cooking Time:** 14 minutes **Servings:** 4
Ingredients:
- 4 small lobster tails, shell cut from the top
- ½ onion, quartered
- ½ cup light unsalted butter, or margarine
- ⅓ cup white wine
- ¼ cup raw honey, or honey substitute
- 3 garlic cloves, crushed
- 1 tablespoon lemon juice
- 2 tablespoons fresh parsley, chopped
- 1 teaspoon dried sage
- A pinch white pepper

Directions:

1.	Place the lobster tails in the air fryer oven baking tray.

2.	Whisk the rest of the ingredients, except parsley, in a bowl and pour over the lobster tails.

3.	Press POWER button of air fry oven and turn the dial to select the BROIL mode.

4.	Press TIME button and again turn the dial to set the cooking time to 14 minutes.

5.	Now push TEMPERATURE button and rotate the dial to set the temperature at 350 °F.

6.	Once preheated, place the lobster baking tray in the oven and close its lid.

7.	Remove from the air fryer, sprinkle with parsley and serve warm.

Nutrition: Calories: 284 - Fat: 15 g - Protein: 21 g - Carbs: 16 g - Sodium: 687 mg

Chicken Wings with Alfredo Sauce

Preparation Time: 5 minutes **Cooking Time:** 30 minutes
Servings: 2-3
Ingredients:
•	1 ½ lb. chicken wings, pat-dried
•	½ cup light Alfredo sauce
•	A pinch sea salt
•	A pinch black pepper
•	A pinch sweet paprika
•	Cooking spray

Directions:
1.	Season the wings with salt, paprika and pepper. Arrange them in the greased air fryer basket, making sure they do not touch each other.

2.	Air fry them for 12 minutes at 380 °F until no longer pink in the center. Then, flip them, and cook for another 12 minutes.

3.	Now, increase the heat to 400 °F and cook for 5 minutes more.

4.	Plate the wings and drizzle with Alfredo sauce to serve.

Nutrition: Calories: 150 - Fat: 5 g - Protein: 14 g - Carbs: 7 g

Zucchini Strips with Marinara Dip

Preparation Time: 1 hour **Cooking Time:** 30 minutes
Servings: 4
Ingredients:
•	2 zucchinis, sliced into strips
•	1 ½ cup all-purpose flour
•	2 eggs, beaten
•	2 cups low-carb breadcrumbs
•	2 teaspoons onion powder
•	1 tablespoon garlic powder
•	¼ cup Parmesan cheese, grated
•	½ cup marinara sauce
•	A pinch sea salt
•	Cooking spray

Directions:
1.	Season zucchini with salt. Let sit for 15 minutes. Pat dry with paper towels.

2.	Add flour to a bowl. Add eggs to another bowl. Mix remaining ingredients, except marinara sauce in a third bowl.

3.	Dip zucchini strips in the first, second and third bowl. Cover with foil and freeze for 45 minutes.

4.	Lightly grease the air fryer basket. Select AIR FRY function. Preheat to 360 °F for 3 minutes.

5.	Add zucchini strips to the crisper plate, and cook for 20 minutes.

6.	Flip and cook for another 10 minutes. Serve with marinara dip.

Nutrition: Calories: 166 - Fat: 35 g - Protein: 9 g - Carbs: 22 g - Sodium: 299 mg

Chapter 9: Poultry and Meat Recipes

Artichoke and Spinach Chicken Rolls

Prep time: 10 min | **Cook time:** 25 minutes | **Serves** 4

½ teaspoon extra-virgin olive oil

4 cups baby spinach

4 (4-ounce / 113-g) boneless, skinless chicken breasts

½ cup ricotta cheese

1 (6-ounce / 170-g) jar marinated artichoke hearts, drained

Salt and pepper, to taste

¼ cup white wine

Nonstick cooking spray

1. Preheat the oven to 378°F.
2. warm the olive oil. Sauté the baby spinach.
3. While the spinach cooks, pound the chicken breasts with a rolling pin until you're left with thin cutlets.
4. pulse the ricotta cheese and artichoke hearts, then transfer the mixture to a bowl.
5. Remove the cooked spinach from the skillet and add it to the cheese mixture. Stir to combine.
6. Put the chicken on a flat surface, then spoon the cheese mixture on top of each cutlet. Roll the chicken to enclose the filling and place seam-side down in the casserole dish. Repeat until all the chicken is rolled.
7. Lightly coat the top of each chicken roll with cooking spray and season with salt and pepper.
8. Pour the white wine into the casserole dish so that it coats the bottom, then cover the dish with aluminum foil. Bake until the chicken is fully cooked and juices run clear. Serve hot.

Per Serving

calories: 215 | total carbs: 6.0g | protein: 28.0g | total fat: 8.0g | sugar: 1.0g | fiber: 1.0g | sodium: 389mg

Avocado Turkey Blt

Prep time: 15 min | **Cook time:** 15 minutes | **Serves** 4

8 slices turkey bacon

1 head iceberg lettuce

1 medium avocado, peeled, pitted, and mashed

Freshly ground black pepper, to taste

1 pound (454 g) deli-sliced turkey

1 large tomato, thinly sliced

1. Preheat the oven to 400°F (205°C).
2. Put the turkey bacon on a baking sheet and cook for about 10 minutes, then flip and cook about 5 more minutes, or until crispy. Remove and set aside to cool.
3. While the turkey bacon cooks, slicing the root end off the head of lettuce and separating the leaves.
4. To assemble each wrap, stack 2 lettuce leaves on top of one another, spread a thin layer of avocado on top, then season with freshly ground pepper.
5. Layer 2 or 3 slices of turkey, 2 slices of tomato, and 1 slice of crispy turkey bacon, then roll the lettuce wraps and serve immediately.

Per Serving

calories: 291 | total carbs: 18.0g | protein: 28.0g | total fat: 13.0g | sugar: 10.0g | fiber: 5.0g | sodium: 1342mg

BBQ Chicken with Avocado

Prep time: 5 min | **Cook time:** 25 minutes | **Serves** 4

½ cup low-sugar barbecue sauce

2 tablespoons water

Nonstick cooking spray

1 pound (454 g) boneless, skinless chicken breasts

1 medium avocado, peeled and pitted

¼ cup apple cider vinegar

1 (14-ounce / 397-g) bag coleslaw mix

1. Preheat the oven to 375°F.
2. combine the barbecue sauce and water.
3. Spray a baking dish, then add the chicken.
4. Using a brush to coat the chicken with the barbecue sauce.
5. Cover the dish with aluminum foil and bake for 20 to 25 minutes, until cooked through.
6. While the chicken is cooking, mash together the avocado and vinegar, then add the mixture to the coleslaw mix. Toss well to combine and set aside.
7. When the chicken has an internal temperature of 165°F (74°C), remove from the oven. Serve the chicken on a bed of coleslaw.

Per Serving

calories: 221 | total carbs: 13.0g | protein: 25.0g | total fat: 9.0g | sugar: 6.0g | fiber: 5.0g | sodium: 591mg

Chicken and Water Chestnut Wraps

Prep time: 10 min| **Cook time:** 15 minutes | **Serves** 4

1 tablespoon sesame oil

1 pound (454 g) lean ground chicken

1 head butter lettuce

1 (8-ounce / 227-g) can water chestnuts, drained and roughly chopped

¼ cup hoisin sauce

1. In a large skillet over medium heat, warm the sesame oil, then add the chicken.
2. prepare the lettuce by removing the leaves from the head and setting them aside.
3. Add the water chestnuts to the chicken and stir to combine. Add the hoisin sauce and break up the chicken into smaller pieces.
4. Cook for about 15 minutes, or until the internal temperature of the chicken reaches at least 165°F (74°C).
5. When the chicken is finished cooking, fill each lettuce wrap with the chicken mixture, fold like tacos, and serve.

Per Serving

calories: 263 | total carbs: 14.0g | protein: 23.0g | total fat: 13.0g | sugar: 12.0g | fiber: 2.0g | sodium: 399mg

Cucumber Turkey Rolls

Prep time: 10 min | **Cook time:** 0 minutes | **Serves** 4

8 Kirby cucumbers

1 large carrot, peeled

1 pound (454 g) deli-sliced turkey

8 ounces (227 g) thinly sliced Cheddar cheese

½ cup grainy mustard

Freshly ground black pepper, to taste

1. Halve each cucumber lengthwise and set aside.

2. peel the carrot into thin and pliable ribbons and set aside.

3. On 2 slices of turkey, place ½ slice of cheese, topped with mustard, a sprinkle of pepper, and a few carrot strips.

4. Put 1 cucumber half on top and roll the turkey around the cucumber. Plate the roll seam-side down or use a toothpick to secure the seam.

5. Repeat until all cucumbers are used. Serve cold.

Per Serving

calories: 392 | total carbs: 14.0g | protein: 35.0g | total fat: 23.0g | sugar: 8.0g | fiber: 2.0g | sodium: 1421mg

Mexican Salsa Chicken

Prep time: 5 minutes | **Cook time:** 45 minutes | **Serves** 4

1 (12-ounce / 340-g) jar salsa

1 pound (454 g) boneless, skinless chicken breast, pounded until about ½-inch thick

1 (12-ounce / 340-g) can fat-free refried beans

1 medium white onion, sliced

Salt and pepper, to taste

¾ cup shredded Cheddar cheese

Nonstick cooking spray

1. Preheat the oven to 350°F

2. Coat a casserole dish with cooking spray and spread half of the salsa on the bottom of the pan. Put the chicken on the salsa and spread the refried beans atop the chicken. Add a layer of onion, followed by the remaining salsa, then season with salt and pepper.

3. Evenly sprinkle the cheese over the top and cover with aluminum foil. Bake for 35 minutes, or until the chicken is cooked through and juices run clear.

4. Remove the foil and bake for another 10 minutes, until the cheese is just golden brown. Serve hot.

Per Serving

calories: 313 | total carbs: 24.0g | protein: 34.0g | total fat: 10.0g | sugar: 5.0g | fiber: 8.0g | sodium: 1135mg

Salsa Verde Chicken Bowl

Prep time: 5 minutes | **Cook time:** 20 minutes | **Serves** 4

3 (6-ounce / 170-g) boneless, skinless chicken breasts, each cut into 4 pieces

4 cups water, plus 2 tablespoons

1 (1-pound / 454-g) package frozen cauliflower rice

1 tablespoon extra-virgin olive oil

1 (12-ounce / 340-g) jar tomatillo salsa

1 avocado, peeled, pitted, and diced

1 limes, quartered, for serving

1. add the chicken with 4 cups water and bring to a boil. When the water is just boiling, reduce the heat to medium-low, cover with a lid, and cook for about 10 minutes, or until the chicken is fully cooked and no longer pink.

2. While the chicken cooks, in a nonstick pan over medium heat, add the cauliflower rice, olive oil, and the remaining 2 tablespoons of water. Stir to combine and cook for about 5 minutes, until the rice is just softened or the water has evaporated.

3. Once the chicken is cooked, drain the water and let the chicken cool slightly.

4. Put the chicken in a blender or food processor and pulse to shred it into small pieces. Alternatively, you can shred the chicken by hand with two forks.

5. In the same pan used to cook the chicken, over medium heat, add the shredded chicken and salsa and mix to combine. Cook until the mixture is hot.

6. Plate the dish with the cauliflower rice first, topped with the shredded chicken, avocado, and 1 or 2 quarters of lime.

Per Serving

calories: 292 | total carbs: 15.0g | protein: 29.0g | total fat: 13.0g | sugar: 6.0g | fiber: 9.0g | sodium: 724mg

Turkey and Spinach Burgers

Prep time: 5 minutes | **Cook time:** 25 minutes | **Serves** 4

1 small white onion, diced

⅓ cup crumbled feta

2 tablespoons chopped fresh dill

3 teaspoons extra-virgin olive oil, divided

Salt and pepper, to taste

3 cups baby spinach

1 pound (454 g) lean ground turkey

Nonstick cooking spray

1. Preheat the oven to 375°F.

2. In a large bowl, mix the onion, feta, dill, and 1 teaspoon olive oil. Season the mixture with salt and pepper and stir to combine.

3. In a medium skillet over low heat, warm the remaining 2 teaspoons olive oil. Sauté the spinach for about 5 minutes, or until just wilted. Set aside to cool.

4. Chop the spinach roughly and add to the onion mixture. Stir to combine.

5. Add the ground turkey and mix until just combined. Do not overmix. Using clean hands, form the mixture into 4 burgers.

6. Put the burgers on the prepared baking sheet and bake for about 10 minutes, then flip and bake another 10 minutes, until fully cooked and the internal temperature reaches 165°F (74°C). Serve hot.

Per Serving

calories: 197 | total carbs: 3.0g | protein: 29.0g | total fat: 8.0g | sugar: 2.0g | fiber: 1.0g | sodium: 235mg

Veg and Chicken Meatballs

Prep time: 5 minutes | **Cook time:** 25 minutes | **Serves** 4

1 medium zucchini, shredded

1 large carrot, shredded

¼ cup honey mustard

4 garlic cloves, minced

Salt and pepper, to taste

1 pound (454 g) lean ground chicken

Nonstick cooking spray

1. Preheat the oven to 375°F.

2. In a colander, drain the shredded zucchini and carrot and press out any residual liquid.

3. In a large bowl, combine the drained zucchini and carrot mixture with the honey mustard and garlic. Season with salt and pepper and stir to combine.

4. Add the chicken to the vegetable mixture and mix to combine, being careful not to overmix. Using an ice cream

scoop, portion out 2-inch meatballs onto the prepared baking sheet.

5.   Bake for 20 to 25 minutes, flipping 15 minutes into cooking, until the meatballs are fully cooked and their internal temperature has reached 165°F (74°C).

6.   Serve immediately.

Per Serving

calories: 254 | total carbs: 22.0g | protein: 23.0g | total fat: 9.0g | sugar: 19.0g | fiber: 1.0g | sodium: 154mg

Apple Braised Pork

Prep time: 10 minutes | **Cook time:** 30 minutes | **Serves** 4

1 pound (454 g) pork tenderloin
2 garlic cloves, minced
¼ teaspoon ground nutmeg
1 tablespoon ground fresh grated ginger
1 large onion, cut into ½-inch wedges
2 medium Granny Smith apples, peeled, cored, and cut into ½-inch wedges
2 packets Splenda
½ teaspoon ground cinnamon
½ cup water
Cooking spray

1.   Preheat the oven to 350°F.Spritz a baking pan with cooking spray. Put pork tenderloin in the baking pan.

2.   In a small bowl, combine garlic, nutmeg, and ginger and rub onto pork.

3.   Surround tenderloin with alternating wedges of onion and apple. Spray onion and apple wedges with cooking spray, sprinkle with sweetener and cinnamon, and pour water over onions and apples.

4.   Cover with foil for 22 minutes. Remove foil and bake for 10 minutes more.

5.   Slice meat thinly and serve.

Per Serving

calories: 233 | total carbs: 17.0g | protein: 24.0g | total fat: 7.0g | sugar: 14.0g | fiber: 3.0g | sodium: 56mg

Beef and mushroom Stroganoff

Prep time: 10 minutes | **Cook time:** 1 hour 30 minutes | **Serves** 4

2 garlic cloves, minced
1 pound (454 g) lean eye round, cut into 1-inch cubes
1 (6-ounce / 170-g) can tomato sauce
½ cup dry red wine
1 cup sliced fresh mushrooms
1 bay leaf
½ cup fat-free sour cream
Salt and ground black pepper, to taste
Butter-flavored cooking spray

1.   Coat bottom of large nonstick lidded skillet with cooking spray and heat over medium-high heat until hot. Sauté garlic for 1 minute until soft. Add meat and brown, stirring, for 3 minutes.

2.   Add tomato sauce, wine, mushrooms, and bay leaf and lower heat. Simmer, covered, over low heat for 1½ hours.

3.   Turn off heat and stir in sour cream. Add salt and pepper. Serve immediately.

Per Serving

calories: 229 | total carbs: 10.0g | protein: 27.0g | total fat: 4.0g | sugar: 9.0g | fiber: 1.0g | sodium: 254mg

Beef Brisket Roast

Prep time: 15 minutes | **Cook time:** 2 hours 10 minutes | **Serves** 8

2 tablespoons olive oil
2 pounds (907 g) lean beef brisket
1½ cups coarsely chopped onion
2 garlic cloves, minced
2 tablespoons sweet paprika
1 (14.5-ounce / 411-g) can low-sodium beef broth
1 cup strong brewed coffee
1 cup water
2 tablespoons concentrated beef broth
2 bay leaves
1 ounce (28 g) dried mushrooms
1½ cups coarsely chopped carrot
¾ pound (340 g) green beans, ends trimmed
Salt and ground black pepper, to taste

1.   In a nonstick Dutch oven, heat the olive oil over medium-high heat until hot but not smoking. Put meat in Dutch oven and brown on both sides, about 5 minutes. Remove meat from pot and pour off accumulated fat.

2.   Put onion, garlic, and paprika in pot, stir, cover, and cook over medium heat for 5 to 7 minutes, or until onion is softened.

3.   Add meat back to pot on top of onion mixture and pour in beef broth, coffee, and water. Stir in concentrated beef broth, and bring to a boil. Then, add bay leaves, mushrooms, and carrot, lower heat to a simmer, cover, and cook for 1½ hours.

4.   Remove meat from pot and slice thinly on diagonal.

5.   Add meat back to pot, place green beans on top, cover, and cook for another 30 minutes. Add salt and pepper to taste.

Per Serving

calories: 231 | total carbs: 11.0g | protein: 27.0g | total fat: 9.0g | sugar: 8.0g | fiber: 3.0g | sodium: 681mg

Creamy Horseradish London Broil

Prep time: 6 minutes | **Cook time:** 10 minutes | **Serves** 4

1 pound (454 g) lean London broil (top round or flank steak)
1½ teaspoons garlic powder
1 tablespoon lemon pepper
½ cup fat-free sour cream
1 tablespoon concentrated beef broth
2 tablespoons prepared horseradish

1.   Preheat broiler and arrange rack to top position.

2.   With a sharp knife, score top of London broil to keep it from curling. Sprinkle with garlic powder and lemon-pepper.

3.   Put in a nonstick broiling pan and broil for 4 minutes on each side for medium rare.

4.   While steak is broiling, combine sour cream, concentrated beef broth, and horseradish in a small bowl.

5.   Slice the steak thinly on diagonal, pour the sauce over it, and serve.

Per Serving

calories: 182 | total carbs: 8.0g | protein: 28.0g | total fat: 5.0g | sugar: 8.0g | fiber: 0g | sodium: 723mg

Hearty Beef Bordelaise
Prep time: 15 minutes | **Cook time:** 2 hours 15 minutes | **Serves** 4
1 tablespoon olive oil
1 pound (454 g) lean beef round, trimmed and cut into 1-inch cubes
1½ cups chopped onion
2 large garlic cloves, chopped
½ cup dry red wine
½ cup fat-free, low-sodium beef broth
1 cup chopped tomato
1 (6-ounce / 170-g) can tomato juice
1 piece orange peel
1 teaspoon Worcestershire sauce
1 teaspoon chopped fresh rosemary, or ½ teaspoon dried
½ pound (227 g) peeled baby carrots
1. In a heavy pot, heat the olive oil over medium-high heat until hot but not smoking. Brown beef on all sides and transfer to a bowl.
2. Discard any fat accumulated in pot. Add onion and garlic and cook over medium heat, stirring, for 2 minutes, or until golden.
3. Add wine, broth, tomato, tomato juice, orange peel, Worcestershire, and rosemary to pot and bring to a boil. Add back to pot beef and any meat juices that have accumulated.
4. Cover and lower heat; simmer for 30 minutes.
5. Stir in carrots, cover, and simmer for 1½ hours.
6. Uncover, increase heat to medium-high, and cook for 15 minutes, or until liquid in pot reduces and is slightly thickened.
Per Serving
calories: 244 | total carbs: 16.0g | protein: 27.0g | total fat: 4.0g | sugar: 13.0g | fiber: 3.0g | sodium: 133mg

Madeira Pork Tenderloin
Prep time: 10 minutes | **Cook time:** 18 minutes | **Serves** 4
1 tablespoon olive oil
1 pound (454 g) pork tenderloin
¾ cup thinly sliced shallots
¾ cup Madeira wine
¼ teaspoon vanilla extract
2 tablespoons balsamic vinegar
Brown-sugar artificial sweetener (1 teaspoon equivalent)
Salt and ground black pepper, to taste
1. Slice the tenderloin into ½-inch slices.
2. heat the olive oil and sauté the pork over medium heat for 4 minutes, turning once. Remove from pan and keep warm.
3. Add shallots to pan and sauté for 3 minutes.
4. Add wine and vanilla to pan, stirring to scrape up any browned bits. Lower heat and simmer until liquid is reduced slightly.
5. Stir in balsamic vinegar and sweetener, return pork and any accumulated juices to pan, and turn once to coat. Add salt and pepper to taste.
Per Serving

calories: 259 | total carbs: 12.0g | protein: 24.0g | total fat: 7.0g | sugar: 14.0g | fiber: 0g | sodium: 176mg

Pork Medallions with Mushrooms
Prep time: 10 minutes | **Cook time:** 8 minutes | **Serves** 4
1 pound (454 g) pork tenderloin, sliced into ½-inch slices
1 tablespoon olive oil
½ cup thinly sliced shallots
1 cup thinly sliced fresh mushrooms
½ cup dry white wine
2 tablespoons concentrated chicken broth
¼ teaspoon dried thyme
2 teaspoons whole-grain mustard
¼ cup fat-free sour cream
Salt and ground black pepper, to taste
1. heat the olive oil over medium-high heat until hot but not smoking. Brown pork on both sides, then lower heat and sauté for 3 minutes, until cooked through. Remove the pork from pan.
2. Re-spray the pan and sauté shallots and mushrooms, stirring until lightly browned.
3. Stir in wine, scraping up any browned bits. Add concentrated chicken broth and thyme and simmer for 2 minutes.
4. Stir in mustard and sour cream and simmer for 1 to 2 minutes. Add pork and any accumulated meat juices and turn pork to coat. Add salt and pepper to taste.
Per Serving
calories: 232 | total carbs: 8.0g | protein: 25.0g | total fat: 8.0g | sugar: 8.0g | fiber: 0g | sodium: 521mg

Pork Tenderloin Asian Style
Prep time: 10 minutes | **Cook time:** 35 minutes | **Serves** 4
2 pounds (907 g) pork tenderloin
2 tablespoons Worcestershire sauce
⅓ cup soy sauce (light)
4 cloves garlic, minced
2 tablespoons rice vinegar
2 tablespoons lemon juice
1 tablespoon ginger
⅓ cup brown sugar
1 tablespoon dry mustard
1½ teaspoons ground black pepper
1. Combine all the ingredients in a resealable plastic bag. Toss to coat the pork tenderloin well. Refrigerate overnight.
2. Preheat the oven to 375°F (190°C).
3. Remove the pork from the marinade and transfer to a baking pan. Pour the marinade over.
4. Arrange the pan in the oven and bake for 35 minutes or until the pork is well browned. Flip the pork halfway through.
5. Serve warm.
Per Serving
calories: 399 | total carbs: 27.7g | protein: 49.6g | total fat: 9.0g | sugar: 23.1g | fiber: 1.0g | sodium: 574mg

Ritzy Beef and Veg Stir-fry
Prep time: 20 minutes | **Cook time:** 15 minutes | **Serves** 4

⅓ cup low-sodium soy sauce
2 tablespoons rice vinegar
¼ cup dry sherry
1 teaspoon minced fresh ginger
1 teaspoon sesame oil
2 packets Splenda
Cooking spray
1 pound (454 g) lean beef, sliced thinly
1 large sweet onion, peeled, cut in half, and sliced into ¼-inch slices
1 clove garlic, minced
2 scallions or green onions sliced into ¼-inch slices
1 red, yellow, or orange bell pepper, deseeded and cut into ¼-inch slices
4 large white mushrooms, sliced
1 medium zucchini, cut into ¼ inch rounds
½ pound (227 g) snow peas, stringed, cut in half diagonally
½ head bok choy, rinsed, sliced on the diagonal into ½-inch slices

1. To make sauce: In a saucepan, combine all sauce ingredients and bring to a simmer.
2. Spray cooking spray in a skillet, then heat over medium-high heat until it shimmers. Add sliced beef and stir-fry for 2 minutes, or until barely browned. Remove beef from pan and keep warm.
3. Wipe pan, re-spray, and heat until shimmering. Add onion and garlic and cook, stirring, for about 4 minutes, or until translucent, but do not brown.
4. Stir in scallions, peppers, mushrooms, and zucchini. Add sauce and cook, stirring, for 3 to 4 minutes.
5. Stir in peas and bok choy, cover, and steam for 2 minutes.
6. Stir beef back into pan and cook for 2 minutes, or until heated through.

Per Serving

calories: 334 | total carbs: 23.0g | protein: 27.0g | total fat: 12.0g | sugar: 19.0g | fiber: 4.0g | sodium: 899mg

Chicken Soup

Preparation Time: 30 minutesCooking Time: 6 hoursServings: 4
Ingredients:
- ½ lb. chicken tenderloins
- 1 cup black beans salsa
- ½ teaspoon sea salt
- 1 teaspoon Mexican spice
- ½ teaspoon ground cumin
- 3 cups water
- 1 cup frozen corn
- 2 oz. green chilies
- 5 oz. tomatoes, diced
- 1 tablespoon fresh coriander
- 5 oz. black beans
- ½ teaspoon black pepper
- Low-fat cheese and lime juice, for garnishing (optional)

Directions:
1. Rinse the chicken tenderloins. Sprinkle with pepper before putting them in the slow cooker.

2. Add in the salsa, the spices, 2 cups water, and half of the other ingredients. Then cook for 4 hours on low heat.
3. Take out and shred the chicken. Put it back in the slow cooker. Add 1 cup water, additional beans, corn, tomatoes, coriander, and chilies. Cook for 2 hours more.
4. Garnish with cheese and coriander leaves. Add lime juice and serve.

Nutrition: Calories: 236 - Fat: 3 g - Protein: 22 g - Carbs: 20 g - Sodium: 560 mg

Mexican Chicken Chili

Preparation Time: 10 minutes Cooking Time: 40 minutes
Servings: 4
Ingredients:
- 1 lb. skinless, boneless chicken breasts, diced
- 1 cup carrots, diced
- 1 tablespoon cumin
- ½ cup Pepper Jack cheese, shredded
- 8 oz. no-salt added canned beans, drained, and rinsed
- ¼ cup low-fat cream cheese
- ½ cup low-sodium chicken broth
- 1 teaspoon oregano
- 1 tablespoon chili powder
- ⅓ cup jarred jalapeño slices, diced
- 1 tablespoon extra-virgin olive oil

Directions:
1. Add olive oil to a pan and place on medium heat.
2. Add in the diced chicken along with the diced jalapeños. Cook until chicken turns opaque.
3. Add oregano, chili powder, and cumin to the chicken and jalapeños. Stir everything together until well combined.
4. Mix in the carrots and chicken broth. Stir to combine and bring to a boil. Once boiling, turn heat down to low and cover.
5. Let simmer the mixture for 20 minutes until the carrots are soft.
6. Add in beans, Pepper Jack and cream cheese. Stir until mixed and cheese is melted.
7. Simmer for 5 minutes more.
8. Divide evenly into bowls. Serve and enjoy.

Nutrition: Calories: 331 - Fat: 7 g - Protein: 19 g - Carbs: 26 g - Sodium: 632 mg

Herbed Turkey Purée

Preparation Time: 5 minutes **Cooking Time:** 0 minutes
Servings: 2
Ingredients:
- 4 oz. cooked turkey breast slices
- 2 tablespoons no-sugar added tomato sauce
- ½ teaspoon dried basil
- ½ teaspoon dried marjoram
- A pinch chili powder
- 1 teaspoon sunflower seeds oil

Directions:
1. Place the turkey slices in a food processor and pulse until soft.
2. Add all the other ingredients and continue mixing until a puréed consistency is reached.

Nutrition: Calories: 112 - Fat: 6 g - Protein: 15 g - Carbs: 5 g - Fiber: 1 g - Sodium: 366 mg

Greek Yogurt Chicken
Preparation Time: 10 minutes **Cooking Time:** 45 minutes **Servings:** 2
Ingredients:
- 2 skinless, boneless chicken breasts
- ½ teaspoon garlic powder
- ¼ teaspoon pepper
- ½ teaspoon dried thyme
- ½ teaspoon dried rosemary
- ¼ cup Parmesan cheese, grated
- ½ cup low-fat plain Greek yogurt
- Cooking spray

Directions:
1. Set your oven to 375 °F.
2. Mix the garlic powder, pepper, thyme, rosemary, cheese, and Greek yogurt.
3. Lay a baking sheet with aluminum foil and grease it with cooking spray.
4. Spread the Greek yogurt mixture over the chicken breasts and lay them on the prepared baking sheet.
5. Transfer to the oven and cook for 45 minutes.
Nutrition: Calories: 246 - Fat: 4 g - Protein: 40 g - Carbs: 3 g - Sodium: 232 mg

Herbed Turkey Breast
Preparation Time: 10 minutes **Cooking Time:** 1 ½-2 hours **Servings:** 12
Ingredients:
- 1 (5 ½-6 lbs.) bone-in turkey breast
- ½ cup margarine, cubed
- ¼ cup lemon juice
- 2 tablespoons reduced-sodium soy sauce
- 2 tablespoons green onions, finely chopped
- 1 tablespoon rubbed sage
- 1 teaspoon dried thyme
- 1 teaspoon dried marjoram
- ¼ teaspoon pepper

Directions:
1. Mix all ingredients, except turkey, in a small saucepan.
2. Bring them to a boil. Then, remove from the heat.
3. In a shallow roasting pan, put the turkey and drizzle with the mixture of margarine.
4. Bake for 1 ½-2 hours, uncovered, at 325 °F, basting every 30 minutes.
5. Until carving, let it stand for 10 minutes.
Nutrition: Calories: 291 - Fat: 11 g - Protein: 44 g - Carbs: 2 g - Sodium: 221 mg

Thai Chili Chicken Wings
Preparation Time: 5 minutes **Cooking Time:** 16 minutes **Servings:** 2
Ingredients:
- ½ lb. chicken wings
- 1 teaspoon paprika
- ⅓ cup sugar-free Thai chili sauce
- 2 teaspoons garlic powder
- 2 teaspoons ginger powder
- 1 teaspoon cumin powder
- 2 ½ tablespoons low-sodium soy sauce
- A pinch pepper
- Cooking spray

Directions:
1. Toss chicken wings with soy sauce, paprika, cumin, garlic powder, ginger powder and pepper.
2. Add chicken wings into the air fryer greased basket and cook at 365 °F for 16 minutes.
3. Serve with Thai chili sauce and enjoy.
Nutrition: Calories: 259 - Fat: 14 g - Protein: 17 g - Carbs: 2 g - Sodium: 379 mg

BBQ Chicken Wings
Preparation Time: 5 minutes **Cooking Time:** 15 minutes **Servings:** 4
Ingredients:
- 1 lb. chicken wings
- ½ cup sugar-free BBQ sauce
- ¼ teaspoon garlic powder
- ½ teaspoon smoked paprika
- Pepper, to taste
- Cooking spray

Directions:
1. Preheat the air fryer to 412 °F.
2. Season chicken wings with garlic powder, paprika and pepper, and place into the air fryer basket greased with cooking spray.
3. Cook chicken wings for 15 minutes. Shake basket 3-4 times while cooking.
4. Transfer cooked chicken wings in a large mixing bowl.
5. Pour BBQ sauce over chicken wings and stir to coat.
Nutrition: Calories: 283 - Fat: 13 g - Protein: 15 g - Carbs: 12 g - Sodium: 429 mg

Chicken Jalapeño Poppers
Preparation Time: 10 minutes **Cooking Time:** 20 minutes **Servings:** 3
Ingredients:
- ½ cup chicken, cooked, and shredded
- 6 jalapeños, halved, and seed removed
- ¼ cup green onion, sliced
- ¼ cup low-fat Monterey Jack cheese, shredded
- ¼ teaspoon garlic powder
- 4 oz. low-fat cream cheese
- ¼ teaspoon dried oregano
- ¼ teaspoon dried basil
- ¼ teaspoon white pepper
- Cooking spray

Directions:
1. Preheat the air fryer to 372 °F and spray air fryer basket with cooking spray.
2. Mix all ingredients in a bowl except jalapeños.
3. Spoon 1 tablespoon mixture into each jalapeño halved and place into the air fryer basket.
4. Cook jalapeño for 20 minutes. Serve and enjoy.

Nutrition: Calories: 255 - Fat: 15 g - Protein: 17 g - Carbs: 2 g - Sodium: 485 mg

Chicken Alfredo

Preparation Time: 15 minutes **Cooking Time:** 16 minutes **Servings:** 4-6
Ingredients:
* 1 lb. chicken breasts, skinless, and boneless
* ½ lb. button mushrooms, sliced
* 1 medium-sized onion, chopped
* 5 oz. light Alfredo sauce
* ½ teaspoon dried thyme
* Black pepper, to taste
* Cooking spray

Directions:
1. Cut the chicken breasts into 1 inch cubes.
2. Mix chicken, onion, and mushrooms in a large bowl. Season with pepper and dried thyme, and mix well.
3. Preheat your air fryer to 370 °F and grease basket with cooking spray.
4. Transfer chicken and vegetables to the air fryer and cook for 12 minutes, stirring occasionally.
5. Stir in the Alfredo sauce. Cook for another 4 minutes.
Nutrition: Calories: 289 - Fat: 12 g - Protein: 13 g - Carbs: 19 g - Sodium: 493 mg

Cauliflower Chicken Burgers

Preparation Time: 10 minutes **Cooking Time:** 30 minutes **Servings:** 2
Ingredients:
* 1 ground chicken breast
* ½ jalapeño pepper
* ½ teaspoon cayenne pepper
* ½ tablespoon mustard powder
* ½ tablespoon oregano
* ½ tablespoon thyme
* ½ tablespoon smoked paprika
* 1 egg, beaten
* 1 small head cauliflower
* Black pepper, to taste

Directions:
1. Preheat the air fryer to 348 °F.
2. Add seasonings to a blender. Slice cauliflower into florets and add to blender.
3. Pulse until mixture resembles that of breadcrumbs.
4. Take out ¾ of cauliflower mixture, add into a bowl and set aside.
5. In another bowl, beat the egg and pepper, and set aside.
6. In a bowl, add ground chicken breast to remaining cauliflower mixture and mix well to combine.
7. Take the mixture and form burger shapes.
8. Roll each patty in cauliflower crumbs, then the egg, and back into crumbs again.
9. Place coated patties into the air fryer oven. Set temperature to 350 °F, and set time to 15 minutes.
10. Then, flip patties over and cook for additional 10-15 minutes. They are done when crispy!

Nutrition: Calories: 191 - Fat: 7 g - Protein: 12 g - Carbs: 9 g - Sodium: 351 mg

Crispy Honey Garlic Chicken Wings

Preparation Time: 10 minutes **Cooking Time:** 45 minutes **Servings:** 1
Ingredients:
* 2 chicken wings
* ⅛ cup water
* 1 tablespoon garlic, minced
* ¼ cup vegan butter
* ¼ cup raw honey, or honey substitute
* ¾ cup almond flour
* A pinch black pepper
* Cooking spray

Directions:
1. Rinse off and dry chicken wings well. Spray air fryer basket with olive oil.
2. Coat chicken wings with almond flour and add coated wings to the air fryer oven.
3. Set temperature to 380 °F, and set time to 25 minutes. Cook shaking every 5 minutes.
4. When the timer goes off, cook 5-10 minutes at 400 °F until skin becomes crispy and dry.
5. Meanwhile, melt butter in a saucepan and add garlic. Sauté garlic for about 5 minutes.
6. Add pepper and honey, simmering 20 minutes. Make sure to stir every so often, so the sauce does not burn. Add a bit of water after 15 minutes to ensure sauce does not harden.
7. Take out chicken wings from air fryer and coat in sauce. Enjoy!
Nutrition: Calories: 235 - Fat: 15 g - Protein: 17 g - Carbs: 15 - Sodium: 408 mg

Garlic Honey Chicken

Preparation Time: 10 minutes **Cooking Time:** 13 minutes **Servings:** 4
Ingredients:
* 1 pound chicken breast, boneless, skinless, and sliced
* ⅓ cup water
* ¼ cup low-sodium soy sauce
* ¼ cup raw honey, or honey substitute
* 2 garlic cloves, minced
* ¼ teaspoon black pepper
* 2 teaspoons cornstarch

Directions:
1. Combine chicken, water (saving 1 tablespoon for later), soy sauce, honey, garlic, and pepper in air fryer and cook at 350 °F for 10 minutes. Then, remove from air fryer and keep warm.
2. In a bowl, mix 2 teaspoons cornstarch and 1 tablespoon water and cook cornstarch mixture on SAUTÉ mode for 2-3 minutes.
3. Dip sliced chicken in sauce. Serve with rice and vegetable.
Nutrition: Calories: 267 - Fat: 10 g - Protein: 20 g - Carbs: 21 g - Sodium: 382 mg

Roasted Duck Breasts with Endives

Preparation Time: 10 minutes **Cooking Time:** 20 minutes **Servings:** 6

Ingredients:

- 6 (3-4 oz. each) duck breasts fillets
- 1 tablespoon raw sugar, or sugar substitute
- 1 tablespoon olive oil
- 3 endives, julienned
- 2 tablespoons cranberries
- 1 tablespoon garlic, minced
- 1 teaspoon juniper powder
- 1 cup light cream
- A pinch sea salt
- 1 teaspoon black pepper, divided

Directions:

1. Score duck bosoms and season them with salt, juniper and half of the pepper, place in preheated air fryer, and cook at 350 °F for 20 minutes flipping them midway cooking.
2. On the other hand, heat a skillet with the oil over medium heat.
3. Add in sugar and endives, blend, and cook for 2 minutes, or until endives are tender.
4. Stir in the remaining pepper, garlic, cream, and cranberries, blend, and cook for 3 minutes.
5. Slice and divide duck bosoms on plates, spread the endives sauce, and serve.

Nutrition: Calories: 314 - Fat: 17 g - Protein: 29 g - Carbs: 26 g - Sodium: 347 mg

Chicken Sausage with Nestled Eggs

Preparation Time: 10 minutes **Cooking Time:** 17 minutes **Servings:** 6

Ingredients:

- 4 low-sodium chicken sausages, chopped
- 6 eggs
- 2 bell peppers, seeded, and sliced
- 1 teaspoon dried oregano
- 1 teaspoon hot paprika
- 1 teaspoon freshly ground black pepper
- 1 teaspoon sea salt
- 1 ½ shallots, cut into wedges
- 1 teaspoon dried basil

Directions:

1. Take six ramekins and divide chicken sausages, shallot, and bell pepper among those ramekins.
2. Place in the air fryer and cook at 315 °F for about 12 minutes.
3. Now, crack an egg into each ramekin. Sprinkle the eggs with hot paprika, basil, oregano, salt, and black pepper.
4. Cook for 5 minutes more at 405 °F, and serve.

Nutrition: Calories: 285 - Fat: 14 g - Protein: 20 g - Carbs: 12 g - Sodium: 506 mg

Cornmeal Mush with Mushrooms and Chicken Sausage

Preparation Time: 10 minutes **Cooking Time:** 30-35 minutes **Servings:** 2

Ingredients:

- 4 oz. refrigerated corn meal mush
- 2 cooked all-natural chicken sausages, chunked
- 2 oz. mushrooms, sliced
- ½ garlic clove, minced
- 2 tablespoons extra-virgin olive oil
- ½ tablespoon light unsalted butter
- 1 sprig fresh sage
- Sea salt and pepper

Directions:

1. Put oil over medium heat. Add the garlic and sauté until golden.
2. Stir in mushrooms, sage, salt and pepper; cook for 3-5 minutes, or until mushrooms are golden brown. Then, remove from heat, cover to keep warm, and set aside.
3. In another skillet, melt butter over medium heat. Meanwhile, cut mush into two 1 inch slices and set aside.
4. Place mush, laying slices side by side, and cook for about 10 minutes, or until lightly browned on the side. Then, flip to brown other side.
5. At this point, add sausages into the skillet to warm throughout.
6. In the meantime, reheat the skillet with mushrooms, if needed.
7. Divide mush between plates, place sausage chunks on top and garnish with mushrooms.

Nutrition: Calories: 223 - Fat: 8 g - Protein: 14 g - Carbs: 24 g

Mozzarella Turkey Rolls

Preparation Time: 10 minutes **Cooking Time:** 10 minutes **Servings:** 4

Ingredients:

- 4 slices turkey breast
- 4 chive shoots (for tying rolls)
- 1 tomato, sliced
- ½ cup fresh basil, chopped
- 1 cup low-fat mozzarella, sliced

Directions:

1. Preheat your air fryer to 388 °F.
2. Place the slices of mozzarella cheese, tomato, and basil onto each slice of turkey. Roll up and tie with chive shoot.
3. Place into air fryer and cook for 10 minutes. Serve warm.

Nutrition: Calories: 215 - Fat: 12 g - Protein: 13 g - Carbs: 4 g - Fiber: 9 g

Spinach, Zucchini, and Sausage Pasta

Preparation time: 15 minutes **Cooking time:** 20 minutes **Servings:** 2

Ingredients:

- 4 oz. chicken sausage
- 1 cup baby spinach
- 1 small zucchini, sliced
- 1 garlic clove, grated
- ¼ cup parsley, minced
- 4 oz. whole-wheat pasta
- ⅛ cup Parmesan cheese, grated
- 2 tablespoons olive oil, divided
- A pinch sea salt

- A pinch pepper

Directions:

1. To prepare the pasta, fill a pot with water, placing it over medium-high heat.
2. While water comes to a boil, in a deep pan over medium-high heat, heat 1 tablespoon of olive oil.
3. Add garlic and cook for 1-2 minutes.
4. Add the sausage to pan, breaking apart the meat. Cook until meat begins browning.
5. Prepare pasta according to package directions.
6. When sausage is halfway cooked, add the zucchini and continue cooking until thoroughly cooked, about 6-7 minutes.
7. Stir in spinach, salt and pepper into sausage pan. Wait 2-3 minutes, until spinach is wilted.
8. Toss in cooked pasta, parsley and Parmesan. Serve and enjoy.

Nutrition: Calories: 360 - Fat: 19 g - Protein: 21 g - Carbs: 39 g - Cholesterol: 54 mg - Sodium: 780 mg - Fiber: 8 g

Thai Chicken Satay

Preparation Time: 20 minutes **Cooking Time:** 10 minutes **Servings:** 4

Ingredients:

- 1 pound chicken tenders
- ½ cup natural style crunchy peanut butter
- ⅓ cup low-sodium chicken broth
- 3 tablespoons low-sodium soy sauce
- 2 tablespoons lemon juice
- 2 garlic cloves, minced
- 2 tablespoons olive oil
- 1 teaspoon curry powder
- Cooking spray

Directions:

1. Set the grill to 390 °F.
2. combine the peanut butter, chicken broth, soy sauce, lemon juice, garlic, olive oil and curry powder, and mix well with a wire whisk until smooth.
3. Put 2 tablespoons of this mixture into a small bowl. Put remaining sauce into a serving bowl and set aside.
4. Add the chicken tenders to the bowl with the 2 tablespoons sauce and stir to coat. Let stand for a few minutes to marinate; then run a skewer through each chicken tender lengthwise.
5. Place the chicken in the lightly greased air fryer basket and cook for 8-10 minutes or until the chicken reaches 165 °F on a meat thermometer.
6. Serve the chicken with the reserved sauce.

Nutrition: Calories: 269 - Fat: 10 g - Protein: 12 g - Carbs: 15 g - Sodium: 413 mg

Butter and Orange Fried Chicken

Preparation Time: 10 minutes **Cooking Time:** 13 minutes **Servings:** 2

Ingredients:

- 4 chicken drumsticks, rinsed, and halved
- ½ tablespoon low-sodium Worcestershire sauce
- 1 teaspoon orange zest, finely grated
- 2 tablespoons light unsalted butter, melted

- ½ teaspoon smoked paprika
- ¼ teaspoon sea salt flakes
- 1 tablespoon cider vinegar
- ½ teaspoon mixed peppercorns, freshly cracked

Directions:

1. Firstly, pat the chicken drumsticks dry. Coat them with the melted butter on all sides.
2. In a bowl, mix all the other ingredients and stir well to combine.
3. Toss the chicken drumsticks with the mixture.
4. Transfer them to the air fryer cooking basket and roast for about 13 minutes at 345 °F.

Nutrition: Calories: 314 - Fat: 19 g - Protein: 24 g - Carbs: 24 g - Fiber: 2 g - Sodium: 421 mg

Lemon-Pepper Chicken Wings

Preparation Time: 10 minutes **Cooking Time:** 20 minutes **Servings:** 1

Ingredients:

- 2 whole chicken wings
- ½ lemon, juiced
- ½ teaspoon garlic powder
- 1 teaspoon onion powder
- A small pinch sea salt
- A pinch pepper
- ¼ cup low-fat buttermilk
- ½ cup all-purpose flour
- Cooking spray

Directions:

1. Place the wings in a sealed plastic bag. Drizzle with the lemon juice and season with the garlic powder, onion powder, salt and pepper.
2. Seal the bag. Shake thoroughly to combine the seasonings and coat the wings.
3. Pour the buttermilk and the flour into separate bowls, large enough to dip the wings.
4. One at a time, dip the wings in the buttermilk and then the flour.
5. Place the wings in the air fryer basket. Spray the wings with cooking oil, being sure to spray the bottom layer.
6. Set temperature to 360 °F and cook for 5 minutes.
7. Remove the basket and shake it to ensure all of the pieces will cook fully.
8. Return the basket to the air fryer and continue to cook the chicken.
9. Repeat shaking every 5 minutes until a total of 20 minutes has passed. Cool before serving.

Nutrition: Calories: 320 - Fat: 18 g - Protein: 20 g - Carbs: 12 g - Sodium: 649 mg

Honey and Wine Chicken Breast

Preparation Time: 5 minutes **Cooking Time:** 15 minutes **Servings:** 2

Ingredients:

- 2 chicken breasts, rinsed
- ½ tablespoon margarine, melted
- ½ teaspoon freshly ground pepper
- ¼ teaspoon sea salt
- 1 teaspoon paprika

- 1 teaspoon dried rosemary
- 1 tablespoon dry white wine
- ½ tablespoon raw honey, or honey substitute

Directions:
1. Pat the chicken breast dry.
2. Lightly coat them with the melted margarine.
3. Season with the remaining ingredients.
4. Transfer them to the air fryer basket and bake for about 15 minutes at 330 °F.
5. Serve warm and enjoy.

Nutrition: Calories: 247 - Fat: 14 g - Protein: 21 g - Carbs: 17 g - Sodium: 324 mg - Fiber: 1 g

Chicken Paté

Preparation Time: 5 minutes **Cooking Time:** 0 minutes
Servings: 4
Ingredients:
- 1 chicken breast or 1 package chicken slices, cooked, and diced
- 4 tablespoons low-fat plain Greek yogurt
- A pinch garlic powder
- ¼ teaspoon fresh sage, finely chopped
- A pinch black pepper

Directions:
1. Place the chicken breast in a mixer and pulse until soft.
2. Add all the other ingredients and continue mixing until a puréed consistency is reached.

Nutrition: Calories: 79 - Fat: 4 g - Protein: 12 g - Carbs: 1 g - Fiber: 0 g - Sodium: 136 mg

Turkey Breasts with Mustard Gravy

Preparation Time: 10 minutes **Cooking Time:** 20 minutes **Servings:** 4
Ingredients:
- 1 lb. turkey breast fillets
- 1 teaspoon dried sage
- 2 sprigs rosemary, chopped
- ½ onion, sliced
- 1 teaspoon garlic, minced
- A pinch sea salt
- ¼ teaspoon freshly ground black pepper
- 1 cup low-sodium turkey broth
- 4 tablespoons Dijon mustard
- 2 teaspoons lemon juice
- 1 tablespoon fresh parsley, chopped
- Cooking spray

Directions:
1. In a large saucepan greased with cooking spray, heat the oil over medium heat.
2. Season turkey with sage, rosemary, black pepper and salt, and place in the saucepan.
3. Cook the turkey about 2 minutes per side, or until lightly browned and cooked through.
4. Spray another pan with cooking oil and place over medium heat.
5. Stir in onion and garlic and sauté for about 3-4 minutes.

6. Increase the heat, pour in the broth and let it reduces by half.
7. Whisk in the mustard and lemon juice, and stir until thickened.
8. Place sauce on the turkey fillets, sprinkle with parsley, and serve.

Nutrition: Calories: 297 - Fat: 17 g - Protein: 35 g - Carbs: 13 g - Sodium: 483 mg

Dry-Rubbed Chicken Wings

Preparation Time: 5 minutes **Cooking Time:** 15 minutes
Servings: 6
Ingredients:
- 12 chicken wings
- 1 teaspoon garlic powder
- 1 teaspoon chili powder
- ½ teaspoon kosher salt
- ½ teaspoon black pepper
- A dash of paprika
- Cooking spray

Directions:
1. Preheat air fryer to 350 °F.
2. mix garlic powder, chili powder, paprika, salt and pepper.
3. Rinse and pat dry the chicken wings, and toss into the seasonings bowl to cover uniformly.
4. Place wings in a greased air fryer basket and cook for 15 minutes, or until golden brown, turning occasionally.

Nutrition: Calories: 215 - Fat: 10 g - Protein: 12 g - Carbs: 10 g - Sodium: 490 mg

Herbed Roast Chicken

Preparation Time: 15 minutes **Cooking Time:** 1 hour
Servings: 10-12
Ingredients:
- 1 (3.5 lbs.) whole chicken
- 2 tablespoons olive oil
- 1 teaspoon garlic powder
- 1 teaspoon paprika
- ½ teaspoon oregano
- Sea salt and black pepper, to taste
- 1 lemon, cut into quarters
- 5 garlic cloves

Directions:
1. Mix olive oil, garlic powder, paprika, oregano, salt, and pepper, and mix well to make a paste.
2. Rub the chicken with the paste and stuff lemon and garlic cloves into the cavity.
3. Place the chicken in the air fryer, breast side down, and tuck the legs and wings tips under.
4. Bake for 45 minutes at 360 °F.
5. Flip the chicken to breast side up and cook for another 15-20 minutes. Let rest for 5-6 minutes, then carve, and serve.

Nutrition: Calories: 280 - Fat: 5.7 g - Protein: 12.9 g - Carbs: 40.7 g - Fiber: 12.1 g

Za'atar Chicken

Preparation Time: 8 hours to marinate **Cooking Time:** 35 minutes **Servings:** 4

Ingredients:

- 4 chicken thighs
- 2 sprigs thyme
- 1 onion, cut into chunks
- 2 ½ tablespoon za'atar
- ½ teaspoon cinnamon
- 2 garlic cloves, smashed
- 1 lemon juice
- 1 lemon zest
- ¼ cup olive oil
- ¼ teaspoon pepper
- ½ teaspoon sea salt

Directions:

1. Add oil, lemon juice, lemon zest, cinnamon, garlic, pepper, 2 tablespoons za'atar, and salt in a large zip-lock bag and shake well.
2. Add chicken, thyme, and onion to the bag and shake well to coat. Place in refrigerator for overnight.
3. Preheat the air fryer to 378 °F.
4. Add marinated chicken in air fryer basket and cook at 380 °F for 15 minutes.
5. Turn chicken to other side, sprinkle with remaining za'atar spice and cook at 380 °F for 15-18 minutes more. Serve and enjoy.

Nutrition: Calories: 329 - Fat: 14 g - Protein: 20 g - Carbs: 16 g - Sodium: 368 mg

Spicy Asian Chicken

Preparation Time: 30 minutes to marinate **Cooking Time:** 20 minutes **Servings:** 4

Ingredients:

- 4 chicken thighs, skin-on, and bone-in
- 2 teaspoons ginger, grated
- 1 lime, juiced
- 2 tablespoons chili garlic sauce
- 2 tablespoons olive oil
- ⅓ cup low-sodium soy sauce

Directions:

1. Mix together ginger, lime juice, chili garlic sauce, oil, and soy sauce.
2. Add chicken in bowl and coat well with marinade and place in the refrigerator for 30 minutes.
3. Place marinated chicken in air fryer basket and cook at 400 °F for 15-20 minutes or until the internal temperature of chicken reaches at 165 °F. Turn chicken halfway through. Serve and enjoy.

Nutrition: Calories: 238 - Fat: 10 g - Protein: 22 g - Carbs: 21 g - Sodium: 437 mg

Air Fryer Turkey Bites

Preparation Time: 20 minutes **Cooking Time:** 40 minutes **Servings:** 4

Ingredients:

- 1 lb. turkey breast, diced
- 1 egg
- ½ teaspoon dried savory dill
- ⅔ cup walnuts, finely chopped
- ½ teaspoon ground allspice
- ¼ teaspoon black pepper

- 1 garlic clove, minced
- 1 tablespoon Dijon mustard
- 1 tablespoon liquid aminos
- 1 tablespoon tomato paste
- 2 tablespoons Parmesan cheese, grated
- 1 tablespoon onion flakes
- Cooking spray

Directions:

1. Preheat your air fryer to 363 °F. Grease a baking dish using cooking spray.
2. Whisk dill, egg, tomato paste, liquid aminos, mustard, garlic, allspice, and pepper.
3. Mix well and add diced turkey.
4. Mix again and add cheese, walnuts and onion flakes.
5. Put mixture into baking dish and bake for 40 minutes in air fryer. Serve hot.

Nutrition: Calories: 277 - Fat: 5 g - Protein: 22 g - Carbs: 15 g - Sodium: 411 mg

Cheesy Turkey Calzone

Preparation Time: 20 minutes **Cooking Time:** 10 minutes **Servings:** 6-8

Ingredients:

- 1 package frozen whole-wheat pizza dough
- 1 free-range egg, beaten
- ¼ cup low-fat mozzarella cheese, grated
- 1 cup low-fat cheddar cheese, grated
- 1 cooked turkey breast tenderloin, shredded
- 4 tablespoons tomato sauce
- Sea salt and pepper, to taste
- 1 teaspoon thyme
- 1 teaspoon basil
- 1 teaspoon oregano

Directions:

1. Roll the pizza dough out into 6-8 small circles, the same size as a small pizza.
2. Add thyme, oregano, basil into a bowl with tomato sauce and mix well.
3. Pour a small amount of sauce onto your pizza bases and spread across the surface.
4. Add the turkey and cheese. Brush the edge of dough with beaten egg, then fold over and pinch to seal. Brush the outside with more egg.
5. Place into air fryer and cook at 350 °F for 10 minutes. Serve warm.

Nutrition: Calories: 265 - Fat: 8 g - Protein: 16 g - Carbs: 27 g - Sodium: 372 mg

Turkey Juniper Paté

Preparation Time: 5 minutes **Cooking Time:** 0 minutes **Servings:** 2

Ingredients:

- 4 oz. cooked turkey breast slices
- 2 tablespoons low-fat mayonnaise
- ½ teaspoon fresh rosemary, finely chopped
- ¼ teaspoon juniper berries powder

Directions:

1. Place the turkey slices in a food processor and pulse until soft.

2.   Add all the other ingredients and continue mixing until a puréed consistency is reached.
Nutrition: Calories: 87 - Fat: 5 g - Protein: 13 g - Carbs: 2 g - Fiber: 1 g - Sodium: 148 mg

Korean Chicken Wings
Preparation Time: 10 minutes **Cooking Time:** 15 minutes
Servings: 4
Ingredients:
•   8 chicken wings
•   A pinch sea salt, to taste
•   1 teaspoon. sesame oil
•   ½ lemon, juiced
•   ¼ cup sriracha chili sauce
•   1 inch piece ginger, grated
•   1 teaspoon garlic powder
•   1 teaspoon sesame seeds
•   Cooking spray
Directions:
1.   Preheat air fryer to 370 °F.
2.   In a bowl, mix salt, ginger, garlic, lemon juice, sesame oil, and chili sauce.
3.   Add in the wings and coat them well.
4.   Cook in the air fryer for 15 minutes, flipping halfway through.
5.   Sprinkle with sesame seeds and serve.
Nutrition: Calories: 384 - Fat: 22 g - Protein: 17 g - Carbs: 15 g - Fiber: 10 g

Curry Chicken Wings
Preparation Time: 20 minutes to marinate **Cooking Time:** 20 minutes **Servings:** 4
Ingredients:
•   8 chicken wings
•   1 cup rice milk
•   1 tablespoon low-sodium soy sauce
•   1 tablespoon red curry paste
•   ½ tablespoon stevia
•   2 tablespoons fresh parsley, chopped
•   Cooking spray
Directions:
1.   Preheat air fryer to 380 °F.
2.   mix the ingredients, except for the parsley. Let marinate for 20 minutes.
3.   Meanwhile, grease the air fryer basket with cooking spray.
4.   After 20 minutes, drain the wings and reserve the marinade.
5.   Place wings in the air fryer basket and air fry for 18-20 minutes, flipping halfway through.
6.   Add the marinade to a saucepan over medium heat, and cook until thickened, about 8 minutes.
7.   Pour this sauce over the chicken, top with parsley, and serve.
Nutrition: Calories: 312 - Fat: 21 g - Protein: 23 g - Carbs: 15 g - Sodium: 546 mg

Chapter 10: Vegetarian Recipes

Chickpeas Salad

Preparation time: 15 minutes **Cooking time:** 15 minutes
Servings: 4
Ingredients:
Salad
- 1 can chickpeas, drained and rinsed
- 1 head butter lettuce, shredded
- 1 large cucumber, chopped
- 1 red bell pepper, seeded and chopped
- 1 cups tomatoes, chopped
- 1 red onion, chopped
- 2 tablespoons fresh cilantro leaves, chopped
- 2 tablespoons fresh mint leaves, chopped

Dressing
- 1 Serrano pepper, seeded and minced
- 1 garlic clove, minced
- 1/4 cup extra-virgin olive oil
- 3 tablespoons red wine vinegar
- 1 tablespoon fresh lemon juice
- 1/4 teaspoon red pepper flakes, crushed
- Salt and ground black pepper, as needed

Directions
1. Salad: In a salad bowl, add all ingredients and mix.
2. Dressing: In another bowl, add all ingredients and beat until well combined.
3. Pour dressing over salad and gently toss to coat well.
4. Serve immediately.

Nutrition
Calories 296
Total Fat 14.4 g
Saturated Fat 2 g
Cholesterol 0 mg
Sodium 380 mg
Total Carbs 37.4 g
Fiber 7.6 g
Sugar 6.1 g
Protein 7.5 g

Quinoa, Avocado and Mango Salad

Preparation time: 15 minutes **Cooking time:** 15 minutes
Servings: 4
Ingredients:
- 2 cups cooked quinoa
- 11/2 cups fresh mango; peeled, pitted, and chopped
- 1 avocado; peeled, pitted, and chopped
- 1 cup radishes, sliced
- 2 cups fresh baby arugula
- 1/4 cup fresh mint leaves, chopped
- 2 garlic cloves, minced
- 2 tablespoons fresh lemon juice
- 11/2 tablespoons olive oil
- Sea salt, as needed

Directions
1. In a glass salad bowl, put all the ingredients and gently stir to combine.
2. Refrigerate for about 1–2 hours before serving.

Nutrition
Calories 449 Total Fat 19.2 g
Saturated Fat 3 g
Cholesterol 0 mg
Sodium 78 mg Total Carbs 60.5 g
Fiber 11 g Sugar 11.4 g
Protein 11.5 g

Sweet Potato and Bell Pepper Soup

Preparation time: 15 minutes **Cooking time:** 35 minutes
Servings: 4
Ingredients:
- 2 tablespoons olive oil
- 1 medium white onion, chopped
- 1 red bell pepper, seeded and chopped
- 2 garlic cloves, minced
- 1 (1-inch) piece fresh ginger, grated
- 1 teaspoon dried rosemary, crushed
- 1 teaspoon dried thyme, crushed
- 1 teaspoon ground cinnamon
- 1/2 teaspoon cayenne pepper
- 1/2 cup tomato puree
- 1 tablespoon maple syrup
- 3 cups low-fat vegetable broth
- 2 large sweet potatoes, peeled and chopped
- 2 tablespoons fresh lemon juice
- Ground black pepper, as needed
- 1/4 cup fresh cilantro, chopped

Directions
1. In a soup pan, heat the oil over medium heat and sauté the onion for about 5 minutes.
2. Add the bell pepper, garlic, ginger, dried herbs, cinnamon, and cayenne pepper, and sauté for about 1 minute.
3. Stir in the tomato puree and maple syrup and cook for about 1 minute.
4. Stir in the sweet potatoes and broth and bring to a boil.
5. Simmer for about 10–15 minutes, stirring occasionally.
6. Remove from the heat and set aside to cool slightly.
7. In a blender, add the soup in 2 batches and pulse until smooth.
8. Return the soup in the same pan over medium-low heat and simmer for about 4–5 minutes or until heated completely.
9. Set in the lemon juice and black pepper and remove from the heat.
10. Serve hot with the garnishing of cilantro.

Nutrition
Calories 219
Total Fat 7.6 g
Saturated Fat 1.2 g
Cholesterol 0 mg
Sodium 268 mg
Total Carbs 37.7 g
Fiber 5.4 g
Sugar 8.5 g
Protein 2.6 g

Pumpkin and Black Beans Soup
Preparation time: 15 minutes **Cooking time:** 15 minutes
Servings: 6
Ingredients:
- 2 tablespoons olive oil
- 1 medium white onion, chopped
- 4 garlic cloves, minced
- 1 tablespoon ground cumin
- 1 teaspoon red chili powder
- Ground black pepper, as needed
- 2 cans black beans, rinsed and drained thoroughly
- 16 ounces canned sugar-free pumpkin puree
- 1 cup fresh tomatoes, chopped finely
- 2 cups low-fat chicken broth
- 1/4 cup fat-free plain Greek yogurt
- 1/4 cup fresh cilantro, chopped

Directions
1. In a soup pan, heat the oil over medium heat and sauté the onion for about 4–5 minutes.
2. Add the garlic, cumin, chili powder, and black pepper, and sauté for about 1 minute.
3. Add the black beans, pumpkin, tomatoes, and broth, and stir to combine.
4. Now adjust the heat to medium-high and bring to a boil.
5. Now adjust the heat to low and simmer, uncovered for about 25 minutes, stirring occasionally.
6. Remove from the heat and stir in yogurt.
7. With an immersion blender, blend the soup until smooth.
8. Serve hot with the garnishing of cilantro.

Nutrition
Calories 290 Total Fat 6.5 g
Saturated Fat 1.2 g
Cholesterol 0 mg
Sodium 65 mg
Total Carbs 44.7 g
Fiber 15.6 g
Sugar 4.1 g
Protein 16.3 g

Lentils and Quinoa Stew
Preparation time: 15 minutes **Cooking time:** 33 minutes
Servings: 6
Ingredients:
- 1 tablespoon extra-virgin olive oil
- 3 carrots, peeled and chopped
- 3 celery stalks, chopped
- 1 yellow onion, chopped
- 4 garlic cloves, minced
- 4 cups fresh tomatoes, chopped
- 1 cup red lentils, rinsed and drained
- 1/2 cup dried quinoa, rinsed and drained
- 11/2 teaspoons ground cumin
- 1 teaspoon red chili powder
- 5 cups low-fat vegetable broth
- 2 cups fresh spinach, chopped

Directions

1. In a heavy-bottomed saucepan, add olive oil and heat over medium heat.
2. Add the celery, onion, and carrot, and cook for about 8 minutes, stirring frequently.
3. Attach the garlic and sauté for about 1 minute.
4. Add the remaining ingredients (except spinach) and bring to a boil.
5. Now adjust the heat to low and simmer, covered for about 20 minutes.
6. Stir in spinach and simmer for about 3-4 minutes. Serve hot.

Nutrition
Calories 253
Total Fat 4 g
Saturated Fat 0.5 g
Cholesterol 0 mg Sodium 326 mg
Total Carbs 43.6 g
Fiber 13.9 g Sugar 7.1 g
Protein 12.4 g

Sweet Potato and Kale Stew
Preparation time: 15 minutes **Cooking time:** 45 minutes
Servings: 6
Ingredients:
- 2 tablespoons olive oil
- 1 medium onion, chopped
- 1 medium sweet potato, peeled and divide into 1/2-inch-sized cubes
- 1 teaspoon fresh ginger, minced
- 4 garlic cloves, minced
- 1 Serrano pepper, seeded and chopped
- 1/4 teaspoon red pepper flakes, crushed
- 1 teaspoon ground cumin
- 1/2 cup natural peanut butter
- 1 (6-ounce) can tomato paste
- 6 cups low-fat vegetable broth
- 3 cups fresh kale, tough ribs removed and chopped
- Salt and ground black pepper, as needed

Directions:
1. In a heavy-bottomed saucepan, add olive oil and heat over medium heat.
2. Add onion and sauté for about 4-6 minutes.
3. Add sweet potato and cook for about 5–8 minutes.
4. Add ginger, garlic, serrano pepper, and spices, and sauté for about 1 minute.
5. Add peanut butter and tomato paste and cook for about 2 minutes.
6. Add broth and bring to a boil.
7. Cover and cook for about 5 minutes.
8. Stir in kale, then adjust the heat to low.
9. Simmer for about 15 minutes.
10. Remove the pan of stew from heat and set aside to cool slightly.
11. With a potato masher, blend half of sweet potatoes.
12. Return the pan over medium heat and simmer for about 2–3 minutes.
13. Season with salt and black pepper and serve hot.

Nutrition
Calories 280

Total Fat 17.2 g
Saturated Fat 3.4 g
Cholesterol 0 mg
Sodium 924 mg
Total Carbs 22 g
Fiber 4.3 g
Sugar 8.7 g
Protein 13.4 g

Barley and Lentil Stew

Preparation time: 15 minutes **Cooking time:** 50 minutes
Servings: 8
Ingredients:
- 2 tablespoons olive oil
- 2 carrots, peeled and chopped
- 1 large onion, chopped
- 2 celery stalks, chopped
- 2 garlic cloves, minced
- 1 teaspoon ground coriander
- 2 teaspoons ground cumin
- 1 teaspoon cayenne pepper
- 1 cup barley
- 1 cup red lentils
- 1 (14-ounce) can diced tomatoes with liquid
- 8 cups low-fat vegetable broth
- 4 cups fresh spinach, torn
- Salt and ground black pepper, as needed

Directions
1. In a heavy-bottomed saucepan, warmth oil over medium heat and sauté carrots, onion, and celery for about 5 minutes.
2. Add garlic and spices and sauté for about 1 minute.
3. Add barley, lentils, tomatoes, and broth, and bring to a boil.
4. Now adjust the heat to low and simmer, covered for about 40 minutes.
5. Stir in spinach, salt, and black pepper, and simmer for about 3–4 minutes.
6. Serve hot.

Nutrition
Calories 265
Total Fat 6 g
Saturated Fat 1.1 g
Cholesterol 0 mg
Sodium 817 mg
Total Carbs 38.7 g
Fiber 13.2 g
Sugar 4.4 g
Protein 15.3 g

Mushroom and Corn Curry

Preparation time: 15 minutes **Cooking time:** 20 minutes
Servings: 4
Ingredients:
- 2 cups tomatoes, chopped
- 1 green chili, chopped
- 1 teaspoon fresh ginger, chopped
- 1/4 cup cashews

- 2 tablespoons olive oil
- 1/2 teaspoon cumin seeds
- 1/4 teaspoon ground coriander
- 1/4 teaspoon ground turmeric
- 1/4 teaspoon red chili powder
- 11/2 cups fresh shiitake mushrooms, sliced
- 11/2 cups fresh button mushrooms, sliced
- 1 cup frozen corn kernels
- 11/4 cups water
- 1/4 cup unsweetened coconut milk

Directions
1. In a food processor, add tomatoes, green chili, ginger, and cashews, and pulse until a smooth paste forms.
2. In a pan, heat oil over medium heat and sauté cumin seeds for about 1 minute.
3. Add spices and sauté for about 1 minute.
4. Add tomato paste and cook for about 5 minutes.
5. Stir in mushrooms, corn, water, and coconut milk, and cook for about 10–12 minutes, stirring occasionally.
6. Serve hot.

Nutrition
Calories 232
Total Fat 15.3 g
Saturated Fat 5.1 g
Cholesterol 0 mg
Sodium 145 mg
Total Carbs 24 g
Fiber 4.2 g
Sugar 7 g
Protein 5.3 g

Chickpeas and Pumpkin Curry

Preparation time: 15 minutes **Cooking time:** 35 minutes
Servings: 4
Ingredients:
- 1 tablespoon olive oil
- 1 onion, chopped
- 2 garlic cloves, minced
- 1 green chili, seeded and chopped finely
- 1 teaspoon ground cumin
- 1/2 teaspoon ground coriander
- 1 teaspoon red chili powder
- 2 cups fresh tomatoes, chopped finely
- 2 pounds pumpkin, peeled and cubed
- 2 cups vegetable broth
- 2 cups canned chickpeas, rinsed and drained
- Salt and ground black pepper, as needed
- 2 tablespoons fresh lemon juice
- 2 tablespoons fresh cilantro leaves, chopped

Directions
1. In a heavy-bottomed saucepan, warmth oil over medium-high heat and sauté onion for about 5–7 minutes. Add garlic, green chili, and spices, and sauté for about 1 minute.
2. Add tomatoes and cook for 2–3 minutes, crushing with the back of spoon.
3. Add pumpkin and cook for about 3–4 minutes, stirring occasionally.
4. Add broth and bring to a boil.

5.   Now adjust the heat to low and simmer for about 10 minutes.

6.   Stir in chickpeas and simmer for about 10 minutes. Stir in salt, black pepper, and lemon juice, and serve hot with the garnishing of cilantro.

Nutrition

Calories 304 Total Fat 6.7 g

Saturated Fat 1.3 g

Cholesterol 0 mg Sodium 805 mg

Total Carbs 53.3 g

Fiber 13.9 g Sugar 11.6 g

Protein 12.3 g

Beans and Sweet Potato Chili

Preparation time: 15 minutes **Cooking time:** 4 hours

Servings: 4

Ingredients:

- 2 tablespoons olive oil
- 1 onion, chopped
- 2 small bell peppers, seeds removed and chopped
- 4 garlic cloves, minced
- 1 teaspoon ground cumin
- 1 teaspoon cayenne pepper
- 1 tablespoon red chili powder
- 1 medium sweet potato, peeled and chopped
- 3 cups tomatoes, chopped finely
- 3 cups canned red kidney beans
- 1 cup canned corn kernels
- 2 cups vegetable broth
- Salt and ground black pepper, as needed

Directions

1.   In a Dutch oven, place olive oil and heat over medium-high heat.

2.   Put onion and peppers and sauté for about 3–4 minutes. Add garlic and spices and sauté for 1 minute. Add sweet potato and cook for about 4–5 minutes. Add remaining all ingredients and bring to a boil.

3.   Now adjust the heat to medium-low and simmer, covered for about 1–2 hours. Season with salt and black pepper and serve hot.

Nutrition

Calories 373 Total Fat 9.9 g

Saturated Fat 1.6 g

Cholesterol 0 mg Sodium 964 mg

Total Carbs 59.6 g Fiber 16.5 g

Sugar 15.4 g Protein 17.1 g

Arugula Lentil Salad

Preparation time: 5 minutes   **Cooking time:** 7 minutes

Servings: 2

Ingredients:

- 1-2 tbsp. balsamic vinegar
- 3/4 cups cashews
- 1 handful arugula/rocket
- 1 cup brown lentils, cooked.
- slices bread, whole wheat
- 5-6 sun-dried tomatoes in oil
- 1 chili / jalapeño
- 1 tbsp. olive oil
- 1 onion
- salt and pepper to taste

Optional:

- 1 tbsp. honey
- 1 small handful of raisins

Directions:

1.   Toast the cashews in a pan over low heat for about 3 to 4 minutes. Then dump them into a pot of salad. Dice and fry the onion in one-third of the olive oil over low heat for around 3 minutes.

2.   In the meantime, cut your chili / jalapeño and dried tomatoes. In the grill, add them and fry for the next 1-2 minutes.

3.   Slice the bread into large croutons. Shift the mixture of onions into a large container. Put the rest of the oil in your pan and cook the sliced bread until it's crispy with salt and pepper seasoning.

4.   Now clean the arugula and put it in the bowl.

5.   Bring in the lentils, too, and blend everything over. Use salt, pepper, and balsamic vinegar to season. With the croutons, eat. Super delicious!

Nutrition:

Calories: 270

Carbs: 27g

Fat: 15g

Protein: 12g

Tomato Avocado Toast

Preparation time: 5 minutes **Cooking time:** 5 minutes

Servings: 1 toast

Ingredients:

- 1 slice bread (ideally whole grain)
- 1/2 medium avocado
- 1 tbsp. lemon juice
- 1 tbsp. olive oil
- salt and pepper to taste
- cherry tomatoes

Directions:

1.   Split in half your cherry tomatoes. Dump them in a pan and let them cook until tender (about 5 minutes) with olive oil.

2.   In the meantime, mash and add some lemon with your avocado. Put it all together now, and season with salt and pepper. Perfect.

Nutrition:

Calories: 285

Carbs: 25g

Fat: 16g

Protein: 11g

Classic Tofu Salad

Preparation time: 5 minutes **Cooking time:** 15 minutes

Servings: 2

Ingredients:

- 8 oz. pineapple
- 1 handful spinach
- 1/2 bunch radishes
- 1/2 medium cucumber
- 1 cup bean sprouts

- 14 oz. firm tofu (ideally get fresh tofu from the supermarket)
- For the dressing:
- 1 tbsp. olive oil
- salt and pepper to taste
- 1 small handful of peanuts
- 1/2 chili pepper (e.g., jalapeño)
- 1/2 lime (juiced; lemon also works)
- 1 tbsp. sriracha (or equivalent)
- 1 tbsp. maple syrup

Directions:

1. Squeeze out some of the tofu block's excess moisture and split it (about one square centimeter) into tiny cubes. Heat some oil in a pan over low to medium heat and add it to your tofu.

2. Fry until golden brown for approximately 15 minutes. Rinse the vegetables!

3. Chop the radishes. Lengthwise, slice the cucumber in half, scrape the seeds with a big spoon, and cut what's left.

4. Also, cut the pineapple into smaller pieces. Put all together with the bean sprouts and spinach into a dish.

5. For the dressing, put the sugar, olive oil, sriracha, lime juice, salt, and pepper together and toss in the salad.

6. Get the pieces of tofu and put them in a separate bowl. Mix them to every serving of salad. Cut the chili and slightly crush or chop the peanuts for garnish as well. When served, dust them over the salad. Enjoy!

Nutrition:
Calories: 84
Carbs: 3g
Fat: 4g
Protein: 9g

Moroccan Couscous Salad

Preparation time: 15 minutes **Cooking time:** 0 minutes
Servings: 6
Ingredients:
- 2 tbsp. olive oil
- fig, fresh
- 1/2 orange's zest
- orange
- 1 medium zucchini
- 1 pomegranate
- 1 tbsp. ginger powder, chopped.
- 1 tbsp. cumin
- 1 tbsp. paprika powder
- 1 bell pepper, red
- 1/2 cup parsley, fresh
- 1 tbsp. salt
- salt and pepper to taste
- 1 cup of water
- 1/4 cup raisins
- 1 cup instant couscous

Optional:
- bunch radish (thinly sliced)

Directions:

1. Put water in a wide serving bowl and apply it to the couscous. Cover a tea towel or lid with the couscous and leave for 5 minutes.

2. Gently loosen the couscous with a fork and add the cumin, ginger, olive oil, and paprika powder. You want it dry and cool, no big clumps.

3. Wash the cherry, rub the zest. Peel and chop the orange and, along with the zest, add it to the salad.

4. Deseed and apply the seeds to the pomegranate. Finely cut the zucchini and thinly slice the red pepper, then put it in the salad.

5. Cut it up and add it to the salad if you've managed to find a fig. Clean the parsley and any other optional herbs, chop them, and then return them to the salad again. Give a decent toss to it. Serve.

Nutrition:
Calories: 206
Carbs: 34g
Fat: 5g
Protein: 7g

Eggplant Curry

Preparation time: 15 minutes **Cooking time:** 30 minutes
Servings: 2
Ingredients:
- 1/2 tbsp. pepper
- 1/2 cups of coconut milk
- 1 tin tomato chopped roughly.
- 1 tbsp. ground coriander
- 1 tbsp. turmeric
- 1 tbsp. gram masala powder or curry powder
- 1clove garlic
- 1 red onion
- 1 tbsp. olive oil
- 1/2 tbsp. salt
- 1 aborigine (medium)

Optional:
- 1-2 tbsp. sugar or mango chutney

Directions:

1. Cook as per packet directions when using rice. Break your aubergine into tiny cubes. Fry with olive oil in a wide pan over high heat for 3-4 minutes. Mix well enough that it won't smoke.

2. Meanwhile, chop the onion, and put it in as well. Put it back to medium heat and cook for 5-6 minutes. Crush the garlic or dice it.

3. Garlic, curry powder, turmeric, and ground cilantro should be mixed in. Cook, stirring well, for the next 3-4 minutes. Add in the sliced tomatoes and coconut milk. Add salt.

4. Boil for 15 minutes, roughly. The coconut milk gets thicker, so when it is at the right consistency for you, stop cooking.

5. If you like it a little sweeter, stir in the honey or mango chutney. Serve with salt plus pepper according to taste.

Nutrition:
Calories: 200
Carbs: 18g
Fat: 0g
Protein: 0g

Baked Zucchini Fries

Preparation Time: 15 Minutes **Cooking Time:** 20 Minutes **Servings:** 4

Ingredients:
- 1 Cup of Panko
- 1/2 Cup Parmesan Cheese
- 1 Tsp. Italian Seasoning
- Salt And Freshly Ground Black Pepper
- 4 Zucchini, Quartered Lengthwise
- 1/2 Cup of All-Purpose Flour
- 2 Large Eggs, Beaten
- 2 Tbsp. Chopped Fresh Parsley Leaves

Directions:
1. Preheat the oven to 425 degrees. Place a cooling rack on a baker, which has been coated with non-stick mist.
2. In a big mixing bowl, combine panko, parmesan and Italian with salt and pepper. Excluding the equation from it.
3. Dredge zucchini in flour, then plunge into eggs, cover with panko mixture and squeeze to stick.
4. Place the courgette on the prepared baking sheet. Bake in the oven, golden brown and dry, for 20-22 minutes.
5. Add parsley before serving, if necessary.

Nutrition:
Calories: 272
Total fat: 8g
Protein: 35g
Carbs: 15g
Fiber: 3g
Sugar: 3g
Sodium: 279mg

Best Eggplant Parmesan Pizza

Preparation Time: 15 Minutes **Cooking Time:** 20 Minutes **Servings:** 4

Ingredients:
- 1/2 A Medium Eggplant
- 1/2 Cup of Grated Parmesan
- 2 Tbsp. Unsalted Butter
- 1/3 Cup of Italian Panko Breadcrumbs
- 1 Pkg. Store-Bought
- 1/2 Cup of Pizza Sauce
- 2 Cups of Shredded Whole Milk Mozzarella
- 1 Roma Thinly Sliced Tomato
- Fresh Basil Leaves, Torn

Directions:
1. Warmth the oven to 400 degrees Fahrenheit before cutting it into 1/8-inch trimmings and removing the ends of the eggplant. Around 8-10 slices are required. Put the eggplant in a single layer on a parchment-lined pan. Drizzle with olive oil and mix with Parmigiano-Reggiano rubber and salt and pepper seasoning. Bake for 10-15 minutes or until mildly wilted eggplant and browned.
2. As the aubergine roasts, prepare the bread crumbs. Melt the butter over medium heat in a shallow saucepan. Toast the breadcrumbs in Italian Panko to golden and scented. Keep an eye on it and always stir it to avoid it burning. Excluding the equation from it.
3. Place the pizza along with the ingredients. Place the pizza dough to the instructions of the box. You'll need a circle with a diameter of about 10-12 inches and I want a grated pizza pan.
4. Turn the sauce into the center of the middle pizza dough. Disseminate the sauce to the edges of the dough and leave for a crust a narrow border. Sprinkle the tomatoes, eggplant, and breadcrumbs on top approximately 2/3 of the mozzarella and spread thinly. Terminate with the leftover mozzarella and parmesan sprinkling.
5. Bake on top for 15-18 minutes, or until brown golden. Serve on top of new ripped basil.

Nutrition
Calories 449 Total Fat 19.2 g
Saturated Fat 3 g Cholesterol 0 mg
Sodium 78 mg Total Carbs 60.5 g

Tomato, Basil, and Feta Salad

Preparation Time: 15 Minutes **Cooking Time:** 15 Minutes **Servings:** 2

Ingredients:
- 6 Roma Diced Tomatoes
- 1 Small Cucumber
- 3 Green Onions
- 1/4 Cup of Fresh Basil Leaves
- 3 Tbsp. Olive Oil
- 2 Tbsp. Balsamic Vinegar
- 3 Tbsp. Crumbled Feta Cheese
- Salt And Freshly Ground Black Pepper As need

Directions
1. Toss the tomatoes, cucumber, green onions, basil, olive oil, balsamic vinegar, and feta cheese in a large mixing bowl. Salt and pepper to taste.

Nutrition:
Calories: 315 Fat: 4.3 g
Protein: 30.5 g
Carb: 36.1 g

Easy Black Bean Chipotle Dip

Preparation Time: 15 Minutes **Cooking Time:** 15 Minutes **Servings:** 4

Ingredients:
- 30 Ounce Can Black Beans
- 1/2 Cup of Cilantro Leaves
- 2 Tsp. Minced Garlic
- 2 Tbsp. Olive Oil
- 3 Tbsp. Lime Juice
- 1/2 Tsp. Salt
- 2–4 Tsp. Canned Chipotle Peppers + 2–4 Adobo Sauce
- Additional Cilantro For Garnish And Olive Oil For Drizzling On Top

Directions
1. In a food processor or blender, merge all ingredients until smooth, excluding the chipotle peppers.
2. Blend in 1-2 Chipotle Peppers and 1-2 Tbsp Adobo Sauce from the can. Taste the dip and, if necessary, add another 1-2 peppers and 1-2 tablespoons adobo sauce to make it more spicy.
3. Set a little olive oil over the top of the dip before serving if desired. Serve with fresh vegetables like bell peppers

and cucumbers, as well as tortilla chips, crackers, and pita bread.

Nutrition:
Calories: 206
Carbs: 34g
Fat: 5g
Protein: 7g

Easy, Classic Roasted Root Vegetables

Preparation Time: 15 Minutes **Cooking Time:** 45 Minutes **Servings:** 4
Ingredients
• 3 Pounds Root Vegetables
• 1 Red Onion
• 1/4 Cup Olive Oil
• 1 1/2 Tsp. Kosher Salt
• 1/4 Tsp. Freshly Ground Black Pepper
• 2 Tbsp. Coarsely Chopped Fresh Rosemary Leaves

Directions:
1. Preheat the oven to 423 Fahrenheit and place a rack in the middle.
2. If desired, peel 3 pounds of root vegetables and cut them into rough 1-inch chunks. 1 small red onion, chopped into 1-inch chunks On a rimmed baking sheet, arrange the root vegetables and red onion. Toss with 1/5 cup olive oil, 1 1/2 teaspoon Kosher salt, and 1/4 teaspoon ground black pepper to evenly coat. In an even layer, spread out the ingredients.
3. 30 minutes of roasting Meanwhile, chop the rosemary leaves coarsely until you have 2 tablespoons.
4. Detach the baking sheet from the oven, toss the vegetables with the rosemary, and return to the oven to finish cooking. Re-spread the mixture in an even layer.
5. Continue to roast for another 10 to 15 minutes, or until the vegetables are tender and caramelized.

Nutrition:
Calories: 162
Total fat: 7g
Protein: 18g
Carbs: 8g
Fiber: 2g
Sugar: 5g
Sodium: 261mg

Healthy Cauliflower Rice

Preparation Time: 15 Minutes **Cooking Time:** 10 Minutes **Servings:** 4
Ingredients:
• 24 Ounces Cauliflower Florets
• 2 Tbsp. Reduced Sodium Soy Sauce
• 1 Tbsp. Sesame Oil
• 1 Tbsp. Freshly Grated Ginger
• 1/4 Tsp. White Pepper
• 2 Tbsp. Divided Vegetable Oil
• 2 Large Eggs, Beaten
• 2 Minced Cloves Garlic
• 1 Diced Onion
• 6 Ounces Broccoli Florets, Chopped
• 2 Carrots, Peeled And Grated
• 1/2 Cup of Frozen Corn
• 1/2 Cup of Frozen Peas
• 2 Green Thinly Sliced Onions
• 1/2 Tsp. Sesame Seeds

Directions:
1. To make the cauliflower rice, push the cauliflower in a food processor bowl until it looks like rice, about 2-3 minutes; set aside.
2. Whisk together the soy sauce, sesame oil, ginger, and white pepper in a small bowl; set aside.
3. In a medium skillet, heat 1 tablespoon vegetable oil over low heat. Cook, flipping just once, until eggs are cooked through, around 2-3 minutes per hand. Set to cool completely before dicing into small pieces and setting aside.
4. Heat is still there. Heat 1 tablespoon vegetable oil in a big saucepan or wok over medium heat. Add the garlic and onion to the skillet and cook, stirring often, for 3-4 minutes, or until the onions are translucent. Stir in the broccoli, carrots, corn, peas, and cook, stirring constantly, for 3-4 minutes, or until the vegetables are tender.
5. In a large mixing bowl, merge the cauliflower, eggs, green onions, and soy sauce mixture. Cook, stirring constantly, for 3-4 minutes, or until heated through and the cauliflower is tender.
6. If desired, garnish with sesame seeds and serve right away.

Nutrition:
Calories: 206
Total fat: 9g;
Protein: 25g
Carbs: 11g;
Fiber: 1g
Sugar: 9g
Sodium: 111mg

Roasted Vegetable Quinoa Salad

Preparation Time: 15 Minutes **Cooking Time:** 20 Minutes **Servings:** 4
Ingredients:
• 1 1/2 Cups of Cooked Quinoa
• 1 14 Oz. Can Chickpeas, Cooked And Drained
• 1 Zucchini, Diced Small
• 1 Red Bell Pepper, Diced Small
• 1/2 A Red Onion, Diced Small
• 1 Tbsp. Olive Oil
• 1/2 Tsp. Salt
• 1 Tsp. Dried Basil
• 1/2 Tsp. Oregano
• 1/2 Tsp. Onion Powder
• 1/2 Tsp. Garlic Powder
• Generous Pinch Of Black Pepper
• 2 Tbsp. Chopped Fresh Parsley
• Additional Tbsp. Of Olive Oil
• 2 Tsp. Of Fresh Lemon Juice, About 1/4 Of A Lemon

Directions
1. As guided to the box, Cook Quinoa. I salt the waters for a more flavorful result.
2. Preheat the oven to Fahrenheit 400 and put in a big baker with parchment paper while the quinoa cooks.

3. Before adding to a big mixing bowl, chickpeas should be drained and rinsed. Chop all vegetables and add to the bowl.

4. Put the Veggies in a mixer until they have been uniformly coated and add 1 tablespoon of olive oil and seasoning (salt, basil, oregano, onion powder, garlic powder and a pinch of pepper). On a parchment-lined baker's pan, bake for 20 minutes.

5. When ready, combine the vegetables and quinoa with fresh pepper, lemon juice, and more olive oil

6. . Season to taste and eat warm with salt and pepper.

Nutrition:
Calories: 32
Fat: 0 g
Protein: 0 g
Carb: 3 g

Taco Stuffed Summer Squash Boats

Preparation Time: 15 Minutes **Cooking Time:** 20 Minutes **Servings:** 4

Ingredients
- 4 Medium Squash, Cut In Half
- 1/2 Cup of Salsa
- 1 Pound Lean Ground Turkey
- 1 Tbsp. Taco Seasoning
- 1/2 Small Onion, Chopped Fine
- 1/4 Cup of Bell Pepper, Chopped Fine
- 4 Oz Can Tomato Sauce
- 1/4 Cup of Water
- 1/2 Cup of Reduced Fat Mexican Blend Shredded Cheese
- 1/4 Cup of Chopped Scallions

Directions
1. 400 degrees Celsius to Preheat the oven.. Save 3/4 of a cup.

2. Place the squash on a paper towel for 1 minute in boiling water before draining.

3. Place 1/4 of a cup of salsa on the bottom of a big baking platter and place the squash face up. Excluding the equation from it.

4. Brown the turkey in a big skillet until it's not pink anymore. Add the onion, pepper, sliced squash, tomato and bath, reserved for 3 / 4 cup.

5. Stir in seasoning. Cook on the cover for twenty minutes.

6. Complete the turkey mixture in each squash boat and complete the cheese half way. Cook until squash is tender and the cheese melts for 35 minutes. As a garnish, serve with salsa.

Nutrition:
Calories 261
Fat 19 g
Carbohydrates 2 g
Sugar 0 g
Protein 18 g

The Best Broccoli Cheese Soup

Preparation Time: 60 Minutes **Cooking Time:** 15 Minutes **Servings:** 4

Ingredients:
- 1 Tbsp. + 4 Tbsp. Divided Unsalted Butter
- 1 Sweet Yellow Onion, Diced Small
- 1 Clove Garlic
- 1/4 Cup of All-Purpose Flour
- 2 Cups of Low-Sodium Vegetable Stock
- 2 Cups of Half-And-Half
- 2 To 3 Cups of Broccoli Florets, Diced Into Bite-Size Pieces + 1 Cups of Stems
- 2 Large Carrots
- 3/4 Tsp. Salt
- 3/4 Tsp. Freshly Ground Black Pepper
- 1/2 Tsp. Smoked Paprika
- 1/2 Tsp. Dry Mustard Powder
- Pinch Cayenne Pepper
- A Small Amount Reserved For Garnishing With 8 Ounces Grated High Quality Extra-Sharp Cheddar Cheese

Directions:
1. Merge 1 Tbsp. Butter, 1 Diced Onion, 1 Tbsp. Butter, 1 Tbsp. Butter, 1 Tbsp. Butter, 1 Tbsp. Butter, 1 Tbsp. Butter, 1 Tbsp. Butter, 1 Tbsp. Butter, 1 Tbsp. Butter, 1 Tbsp Butter In between stirrings, add a pinch of salt and a pinch of black pepper.

2. Cook. Take the pan off the heat and place it on the left.

3. 4 Tbsp Butter, Flour, And Cook Over Medium Heat For Around 3 To 5 Minutes, Whisking Constantly, Until Flour Is Thickened (I Use This Le Creuset Signature Enameled Cast-Iron 6-3/4-Quart Oval French (Dutch) Oven) you're making a roux, and the mixture must be thick, or else the soup won't thicken properly later.

4. Slowly whisk in the vegetable stock.

5. Slowly whisk in the half-and-half.

6. Allow the mixture to simmer for 15 to 20 minutes over low heat, or until it has reduced and thickened slightly. This Is Natural. Whisk Every Now and Then To Re-Incorporate The 'Skin' That Inevitably Forms.

7. Chop the broccoli and carrots while the mix is simmering. Mix broccoli, carrots, onion and garlic that you set aside after 15 to 20 minutes of simmering.

8. Season with salt, pepper, paprika, dry mustard powder, and cayenne pepper, if desired. It's fine if you don't have these seasonings on hand; however, they do add subtle flavor depth. whisk them together To combine ingredients,.

9. Set the soup to simmer for 20 to 25 minutes over low heat, or until it has reduced and thickened slightly. This Is Natural. Whisk Now and Then To Re-Incorporate The 'Skin' That Inevitably Forms.

10. Grate The Cheese As Soup Simmers Since the soup's flavor is dependent on it, it is critical to use a high-quality cheese (not the cheapest one available). Pre-grated cheese won't melt and won't mix well in ziptop bags. Add the most of the cheese after 20 to 25 minutes of simmering, reserving a small amount for garnishing the bowls. In less than one minute, stir in the cheese until fully melted and incorporated.

11. Serve right.

Nutrition
Calories 275
Fat 7 g
Carbohydrates 14 g
Sugar 13 g
Protein 36 g
Cholesterol 95 mg

Turmeric Red Lentil Soup with Kale

Preparation Time: 60 Minutes **Cooking Time:** 30 Minutes **Servings:** 4

Ingredients:
- 1 1/2 Tbsp. Vegetable Oil
- 1 Large Yellow Onion
- 2 Cloves Large Garlic
- 3 Tsp. Ground Turmeric
- 1 Tsp. Ground Cumin
- 1 15-Ounce Can Peeled Roma Tomatoes
- 3 1/2 Cups of Vegetable Stock
- 3/4 Cup of Red Lentils
- 3 Cups of Chopped Kale Leaves
- 1 Tbsp. Fresh Lemon Juice
- Salt And Pepper As need

Directions
1. Heat the oil medium heat in a big kettle. Sprinkle onions and hairy garlic until transparent and scented.
2. Apply the turmeric and cumin for about 1 minute or before it is scented. With a wooden spoon.
3. In a big mixing bowl, combine diced tomatoes, vegetables and red lens. Mix thoroughly to combine. Boil the ingredients by heating up to a high level.
4. Reduce to low heat and simmer until legumes tender, uncovered, about 20 minutes.
5. Take the sweet pot out of the fire and whisk into the bowl until wilted. Combine thoroughly with the lemon juice. Season the soup with salt and pepper, if required.
6. In the pots, pour the broth and eat immediately.

Nutrition:
Calories 215
Fat 10 g
Carbohydrates 1 g
Sugar 1 g
Protein 31 g
Cholesterol 90 mg

Mushroom Barley Risotto

Preparation Time: 15 Minutes **Cooking Time:** 1 hour 5 Minutes **Servings:** 4

Ingredients:
- 1 Tbsp. Olive Oil
- 1 Small Onion Chopped
- 2 Cloves Garlic Minced
- 1/2 Cup of Dry White Wine
- 8 Ounces Mixed Mushrooms Cleaned And Sliced
- 3-4 Cups of Chicken Broth
- 1 Cup of Pearl Barley
- 1 Tbsp. Fresh Parsley Chopped
- 1/4 Cup of Parmesan Cheese
- 1/2 Tbsp. Truffle Oil
- Salt and Pepper As need

Directions
1. Put the olive oil. Cook for 4 minutes,
2. Cook for 5 minutes, stirring sometimes, after adding the mushrooms and garlic. Cook for 2 minutes after adding the barley.

3. Set in the white wine and cook until it has all evaporated.
4. Get 3 cups of chicken broths to a boil. Cook for 55 minutes, or until liquid has evaporated. Add the remaining broth if the liquid evaporates before the barley is cooked.
5. Stir in 12 oz. cheese, salt, and parsley once the barley is soft.
6. Finish with the remaining cheese and truffle oil, if desired.

Nutrition:
Calories: 188
Total fat: 3g
Protein: 22g
Carbs: 16g

Coconut Curry Tofu Bowl

Preparation Time: 10 Minutes **Cooking Time:** 30 Minutes **Servings:** 2

Ingredients:
- 1-15 Ounce Can Chickpeas Rinsed, Drained, And Patted Dry
- 1 Cup of Frozen Green Peas
- 1/2 Tbsp. Olive Oil
- 1-16 Ounce Package Extra Firm Tofu Pressed And Cubed
- 1 Tsp. Ground Cumin
- 1 Tsp. Paprika
- 1 Tsp. Ground Coriander
- 1 Tbsp. Maple Syrup
- 1/2 Tsp. Salt
- 3 Cups of Vegetable Broth
- 2 Cups of Butternut Squash Cubed
- 2 Cups of Fresh Cauliflower Florets
- 1/2 Cup of Onion Diced
- 2 Large Garlic Cloves Minced
- 1 Tbsp. Olive Oil
- 1-1.2 Tbsp. Curry Powder
- 3 Tbsp. Flour
- 1/2 Tsp. Salt
- Pepper As need
- 1 Cup of Light Coconut Milk
- 1/2 Cup of Chopped Cilantro
- 1/2 Cup of Chopped Peanuts
- Lime Wedges
- Jalapeño Slices

Directions
1. heat the oven to 450 degrees.
2. In a medium mixing bowl, combine tofu cubes, 1 tablespoon oil, cumin, paprika, ground coriander, salt and maple syrup.
3. Spread chickpeas on one side of a big bakery plate. Rinse over the top 1/2 tbsp of olive oil and mix. Spread the tofu mixture on the other side of the big baking sheet. Stirring regularly in a hot oven for 15 minutes. Drop the chick peas into the frozen green peas. Return to the oven 15 minutes, or toasted chickpeas and peas.
4. Prepare the stew as the peas and tofu roast. Preheat the big oven at 350°F in the Netherlands. In a mixing bowl, merge olive oil, onion dike and hair-thin garlic. Warmth up to medium heat and cook until ovation is soft for 1 to 2 minutes.

In a mixing bowl, combine curry powder, meal, salt and pepper. Mix and simmer for a minute in the onion mix. Gradually whisk in the broth of vegetables. Cauliflower and squash can be included. Simmer for twenty minutes, or tenderly to the squash. Add the milk and blend properly. Mix well. Delete from heat, reserve for 10 minutes.

5.   Pour the serving into a serving bowl, add 1-1/2 cups of stew. Tofu, chickpeas, cilantro, lime, jalapeo, and cilantro are all top-quality (If Desired).

Nutrition:
Calories: 660kcal
Carbohydrates: 50g
Protein: 80g
Fat: 15g
Saturated Fat: 7g
Cholesterol: 191mg

Eggplant Rollatini

Preparation Time: 60 Minutes **Cooking Time:** 30 Minutes **Servings:** 4
Ingredients:
- 1 Large Eggplant
- 1 Tbsp. Salt
- 1 Small Onion, Chopped
- 1/4 Cup of Olive Oil
- 2 Minced Garlic Cloves
- 1 Can Tomato Sauce
- 1 Can Diced Tomatoes
- 1/2 Cup of Chicken Broth
- 1/4 Cup of Tomato Paste
- 2 Tbsp. Minced Fresh Parsley
- 2 Tsp. Sugar
- 1/2 Tsp. Salt
- 1/2 Tsp. Dried Basil
- 1/4 Tsp. Pepper
- 1/8 Tsp. Crushed Red Pepper Flakes
- 1 Carton Ricotta Cheese
- 1 Cup of Shredded Part-Skim Mozzarella Cheese
- 1/2 Cup of Grated Parmesan Cheese
- 1/4 Cup of Minced Fresh Parsley
- 1 Large Egg, Lightly Beaten
- 1/8 Tsp. Pepper
- 3 Large Eggs, Lightly Beaten
- 1 Cup of Seasoned Bread Crumbs
- 1 Cup of Divided Grated Parmesan Cheese
- 2 Minced Garlic Cloves
- 2 Tbsp. Minced Fresh Parsley
- Dash Every Salt And Pepper
- Oil For Frying

Directions

1.   Peel and cut the eggplant into fifteen 1/8-inch thick slices lengthwise. Sprinkle with salt and toss in a colander over a plate. Allow 30 minutes for cooling.

2.   Meanwhile, sauté the onion in oil in a large saucepan for the sauce. Cook for an additional minute after adding the garlic. Combine the rest of the sauce with a bowl. Get the water to a boil. Reduce heat to low and cook, stirring occasionally, for 20-25 minutes, until the flavors have blended. Drain and rinse the eggplant.

3.   Mix the filling ingredients in a large mixing bowl and set aside.

4.   In a shallow bowl, crack the eggs. Mix bread crumbs, 1/2 cup Parmesan cheese, garlic, parsley, salt, and pepper in a shallow bowl. Eggplant is dipped in eggs, then in a bread crumb mixture.

5.   An Electric Skillet is a kind of electric skillet that is used to cook food. Preheat the oil to 375°F. Eggplant should be fried in batches until golden brown, around 2-3 minutes per hand. Using paper towels, soak up the excess liquid.

6.   375 degrees Fahrenheit Heat the oven to. 1 cup sauce in a 13x9-inch baking dish that hasn't been greased Fill each eggplant slice with 2 rounded tbsp filling. Roll up the dough carefully and place seam side down in the baking dish. Pour the remaining sauce over the rolls. The remaining Parmesan cheese should be sprinkled on top. Bake for 33 minutes, or until bubbly.

Nutrition:
Calories: 133
Total fat: 3g
Protein: 19g
Carbs: 7g
Fiber 2g
Sugars: 4g
Sodium: 356mg

Onion Soup

Preparation Time: 10 minutes Cooking Time: 35 minutes Servings: 2
Ingredients:
- 2 large white onions, peeled, and sliced
- ½ cup squash, cubed
- 1 sprig thyme
- 1 tablespoon grapeseed oil
- 2 cups spring water
- ½ teaspoon sea salt
- ¼ teaspoon cayenne pepper

Directions:

1.   Take a medium pot and add oil, place over medium heat.

2.   Add onion and cook for 10 minutes.

3.   Add thyme sprig, switch heat to the low level and then cook onions for 15 to 20 minutes until soft, covering the pan with its lid.

4.   Add remaining ingredients, stir until mixed and simmer for 5 minutes.

5.   Ladle soup into bowls and serve.

Nutrition: Calories: 226 - Fat: 10 g - Protein: 9 g - Carbs: 11 g - Fiber: 2.5 g

Baked Parmesan Herbs Tomatoes

Preparation Time: 5 minutes Cooking Time: 20 minutes Servings: 4
Ingredients:
- 4 medium Roma tomatoes, sliced
- ½ teaspoon dried oregano
- ½ teaspoon dried rosemary
- 1 teaspoon onion powder
- 1 teaspoon garlic powder
- 1 teaspoon sea salt

- 1 teaspoon black pepper
- ½ cup Parmesan cheese, shredded
- 2 tablespoon fresh parsley, chopped
- Cooking spray

Directions:

1. Preheat the oven to 423 °F and lightly grease a baking dish with cooking spray.
2. In a small bowl, stir together dried oregano, rosemary, onion powder, garlic powder, sea salt and black pepper.
3. Place the tomato slices on the baking dish and season with the herbs blend.
4. Top with parmesan and transfer to the oven.
5. Bake in the oven for about 20 minutes and serve.

Nutrition: Calories: 63 - Fat: 4 g - Protein 4 g - Carbs: 5 g - Cholesterol: 6 mg - Fiber: 1 g - Sodium: 98 mg

Greek Chickpeas Cucumber Salad

Preparation Time: 15 minutes **Cooking Time:** 0 minutes
Servings: 4
Ingredients:

- 1 medium English cucumber, chopped
- 1 cup cherry tomatoes, halved
- ½ onion, diced
- ½ cup canned no-salt added chickpeas, drained, and rinsed
- ½ red bell pepper, seeded, and diced
- ½ cup low-salt feta cheese, crumbled
- ½ cup pitted Kalamata olives, roughly chopped
- 1 ½ tablespoon fresh lemon juice

Directions:

1. In a large bowl, combine the cucumber, tomatoes, onion, chickpeas, bell pepper, olives, and feta cheese with the lemon juice, and serve.

Nutrition: Calories: 203 - Fat: 13 g - Protein: 8 g - Carbs: 14 g - Fiber: 4 g - Sugar: 6 g - Sodium: 861 mg

Roasted Veggies

Preparation Time: 15 minutes **Cooking Time:** 30 minutes **Servings:** 2
Ingredients:

- 1 small carrot, peeled, and sliced
- 1 small bell pepper, cut into strips
- 1 small onion, halved, and sliced
- 1 tomato, sliced
- 1 small zucchini, sliced into rounds
- 2 tablespoons extra-virgin olive oil
- 1 teaspoon dried rosemary
- A pinch sea salt
- A pinch ground black pepper

Directions:

1. Preheat the oven to 400 °F.
2. In a large baking sheet, place the vegetables without overlapping.
3. In a small bowl, mix together oil, salt, pepper and rosemary.
4. Drizzle the olive oil mixture over the veggies, and stir to season.

5. Bake in the oven, stirring halfway through, for 20-30 minutes, or until all the vegetables are soft.

Nutrition: Calories: 91 - Fat: 5 g - Protein: 2 g - Carbs: 15 g - Fiber: 6 g - Sugar: 6 g - Sodium: 52 mg

Cabbage Salad

Preparation Time: 10 minutes **Cooking Time:** 0 minutes
Servings: 2
Ingredients:

- 2 ½ cups cabbage, shredded
- 1 carrot, shredded
- 1 teaspoon sea salt
- 2 tablespoons low-fat mayonnaise
- 2 teaspoons Dijon mustard
- 1 tablespoon fresh lemon juice

Directions:

1. In a bowl, add the cabbage, carrot, salt, lemon juice, mustard and mayonnaise, and stir all ingredients together until well coated.

Nutrition: Calories: 113 - Fat: 5.8 g - Protein: 3 g - Carbs: 8 g - Fiber: 1.9 g

Potato Salad

Preparation Time: 2 hours to chill **Cooking Time:** 0 minutes **Servings:** 4
Ingredients:

- 3 cup potatoes, cubed, boiled, and cold
- 2 hard-boiled eggs, sliced
- 1 tablespoon red onion, finely chopped
- ¾ cup low-fat mayonnaise
- 1 tablespoon Dijon mustard
- ¼ cup light French dressing
- 2 tablespoons parsley, finely chopped
- 1 tablespoon lemon juice
- A dash sea salt
- A dash black pepper

Directions:

1. Put potatoes and onion in a bowl, season with salt, pepper and French dressing, and stir to coat.
2. Place the bowl in the fridge and let chill for 2 hours.
3. Add the sliced eggs, mayonnaise, mustard, parsley and lemon juice.
4. Mix gently until well combined and serve.

Nutrition: Calories: 165 - Fat: 4 g - Protein: 5 g - Carbs: 23 g - Fiber: 4 g

Spaghetti Squash Chow Mein

Preparation Time: 10 minutes **Cooking Time:** 55 minutes **Servings:** 4
Ingredients:

- 1 small spaghetti squash
- 2 cups cabbage, shredded (or coleslaw mix)
- ¼ cup low-sodium soy sauce
- 1 teaspoon vinegar
- 2 garlic cloves, minced
- 1 inch ginger root, peeled, and minced
- 1 small white onion, diced
- 1 green bell pepper, thinly sliced
- 2 celery stalks, thinly sliced

- Cooking spray

Directions:

1. Preheat the oven to 350 °F. Coat a baking sheet with cooking spray.
2. Halve the spaghetti squash, remove and discard the seeds, and place the halves cut-side down on the prepared baking sheet.
3. Bake for 43 minutes, or until the flesh is tender.
4. Remove from the oven, and let cool. Scrape out the flesh with a fork, creating small noodles. Set aside.
5. In a small bowl, whisk together the soy sauce, garlic, vinegar and ginger.
6. Coat a large skillet with cooking spray and place over medium heat. Put onion and celery, and cook, stirring, until soft, for 3-4 minutes.
7. Add bell pepper and cook for about 2 minutes.
8. Stir in the cabbage, and cook, stirring, for 1-2 minutes more.
9. Add in the spaghetti squash and sauce mixture. Stir to coat and continue cooking for another 2 minutes. Serve immediately.

Nutrition: Calories: 226 - Fat: 9 g - Protein: 6 g - Carbs: 29 g - Fiber: 7 g - Sugar: 13 g - Sodium: 650 mg

Italian Zucchini Roll-Ups

Preparation Time: 10 minutes **Cooking Time:** 35 minutes **Servings:** 2

Ingredients:

- 1 zucchini, trimmed and sliced lengthwise into thick strips
- 4 oz. fresh spinach
- 2 teaspoons onion, diced
- ¾ cup low-fat ricotta
- ⅓ cup Parmesan cheese, grated
- 1 large egg white
- 1 garlic clove, minced
- 1 cup no-sugar added marinara sauce, divided
- ½ cup low-fat mozzarella, shredded
- A pinch sea salt
- A pinch black pepper
- Cooking spray

Directions:

1. Preheat the oven to 400 °F.
2. Lay the zucchini slices flat on a paper towel-lined baking sheet and sprinkle with salt. Let sit for 15 minutes.
3. Meanwhile, spray a small skillet with non-stick cooking spray, and set over medium heat.
4. Add the onion and sauté for 2 minutes. Then, stir in the spinach, and cook for 2 minutes more, or until wilted. Remove from the heat and let cool.
5. mix the spinach, ricotta, Parmesan, egg white, garlic, and pepper, until well combined.
6. Pat the zucchini dry, removing excess salt.
7. Spread half of marinara in the bottom of a baking dish.
8. Spread each zucchini slice with a spoonful of ricotta mixture, then gently roll up and place in the prepared baking dish, seam-side down. Repeat with the remaining zucchini and filling.

9. Top with the remaining marinara, and sprinkle with the mozzarella cheese.
10. Bake for 25-30 minutes, or until the rolls are heated through and the cheese begins to brown. Serve immediately.

Nutrition: Calories: 190 - Fat: 9 g - Protein: 20 g - Carbs: 18 g - Fiber: 5 g - Sugar: 8 g - Sodium: 839 mg

Roasted Vegetable Quinoa Salad with Chickpeas

Preparation Time: 15 minutes **Cooking Time:** 30 minutes **Servings:** 4

Ingredients:

- ⅓ cup packaged quinoa
- 1 small eggplant, diced
- 1 small zucchini, diced
- 1 small yellow summer squash, diced
- ½ cup grape tomatoes, halved
- 1 can chickpeas, drained, and rinsed
- 3 tablespoons extra-virgin olive oil, divided
- 1 cup low-sodium vegetable broth
- 2 tablespoons freshly squeezed lemon juice
- 1 teaspoon fresh garlic, minced
- 1 tablespoon dried basil
- 1 teaspoon dried oregano

Directions:

1. Preheat the oven to 425 °F. Line a baking sheet with parchment paper.
2. Place the eggplant, zucchini, yellow squash, tomatoes, and chickpeas on the baking sheet and toss them with 1 tablespoon of olive oil.
3. Bake for 30 minutes, stirring once halfway through. The finished vegetables should be tender and the tomatoes should be juicy. The chickpeas will be firm and crispy.
4. While the vegetables and chickpeas are roasting, place the quinoa and broth in a small saucepan over medium-high heat. Cover and bring to a boil. cook for about 15 minutes, or until all liquid has absorbed.
5. Remove the pan from the heat and fluff the quinoa with a fork.
6. In a small dish, whisk together the lemon juice, garlic, and remaining 2 tablespoons of olive oil. Mix in the basil and oregano.
7. In a large serving bowl, combine the quinoa, roasted vegetables with chickpeas, and dressing. Gently stir to combine. Serve and enjoy.

Nutrition: Calories: 250 - Fat: 13 g - Protein: 8 g - Carbs: 21 g - Fiber: 8 g - Sugar: 5 g - Sodium: 160 mg

Mexican Stuffed Summer Squash

Preparation Time: 5 minutes **Cooking Time**: 35 minutes **Servings:** 2

Ingredients:

- 1 yellow summer squash
- ½ cup canned fat-free refried pinto beans, seasoned with 1 teaspoon taco seasoning
- ½ cup quinoa, cooked
- ¼ cup low-fat Colby Jack cheese, shredded
- 1 small tomato, diced
- 1 tablespoon black olives, sliced
- 1 scallion, chopped, for garnish

- Cooking spray

Directions:

1. Preheat the oven to 400 °F. Coat an 8-by-8-inch baking dish with the cooking spray.

2. Cut the ends off of the summer squash and discard. Cut lengthwise; then use a spoon to remove and discard the seeds. Place the squash halves cut-side down in the baking dish. Gently poke a couple of holes in the squash to vent. Add 1 tablespoon of water to the dish. Microwave for about 3 minutes or until slightly tender. Discard any leftover water.

3. When cool enough to handle, turn the squash so they are skin-side down and spaced evenly apart in the dish.

4. Layer ¼ cup of the beans in each squash, then ¼ cup of the quinoa.

5. Top the whole thing with the Colby Jack cheese.

6. Cover with aluminum foil and bake for 25 minutes. Remove the foil and bake for 5 minutes more, or until the cheese is bubbly and the squash is tender.

7. Garnish each squash with the tomatoes, olives, and scallions just before serving.

Nutrition: Calories: 213 - Fat: 8 g - Protein: 9 g - Carbs: 17 g - Fiber: 4 g - Sugar: 3 g - Sodium: 140 mg

Tomato Bruschetta

Preparation Time: 1 hour to marinate **Cooking Time:** 5 minutes **Servings:** 2

Ingredients:

- 6 thick baguette slices
- 3 medium tomatoes, coarsely chopped, and drained
- ½ small red onion, finely chopped
- 2 garlic cloves, crushed
- 6 leaves fresh basil, finely chopped
- ⅛ cup balsamic vinegar
- ¼ cup extra-virgin olive oil
- Sea salt and pepper, to taste

Directions:

1. Mix the onions, tomatoes, garlic, and basil in a big bowl, taking care not to crush or break the tomatoes up too much.

2. Season with balsamic vinegar, salt, pepper and extra-virgin olive oil, and stir to combine. Cover and let sit for 1 hour, so that the flavors can mix.

3. Lightly toast the bread slices until both sides are light brown.

4. Spoon the mixture on the warm bread slices and enjoy.

Nutrition: Calories: 180 - Fat: 10 g - Protein 5 g - Carbs 20 g - Sugar: 4 g - Fiber: 3 g

Roasted Garlic Zucchini and Tomatoes

Preparation Time: 15 minutes **Cooking Time:** 20 minutes **Servings:** 4

Ingredients:

- 2 zucchinis cut into half-moons
- 1 carrot cut in half lengthwise, then cut into half-moons
- 2 cups ripe tomatoes, quartered
- ½ onion, minced
- 2 garlic cloves, minced
- ½ teaspoon red pepper flakes, crushed

- ¼ cup olive oil
- ½ cup Parmesan cheese, grated
- 1 tablespoon fresh basil, chopped
- Sea salt and pepper, as needed
- Cooking spray

Directions:

1. Heat the oven to 450 °F. Lightly grease a baking dish measuring 9x13 inches with cooking spray.

2. In the prepared baking dish, combine the zucchini, carrot, tomatoes, onion, garlic, and red pepper flakes. Add the olive oil, season with salt and pepper, and blend well.

3. Set in a preheated oven. Roast for about 20 minutes, until the vegetables are tender and slightly golden. sprinkle with basil and Parmesan cheese.

Nutrition: Calories: 190 - Fat: 14 g - Protein: 7 g - Carbs: 9 g - Cholesterol: 10 mg - Sodium: 270 mg

Stuffed Acorn Squash with Cheese

Preparation Time: 5 minutes **Cooking Time:** 40 minutes
Servings: 2

Ingredients:

- 1 acorn squash
- ½ cup reduced-fat Cheddar cheese, shredded
- 1 (8 oz.) can no-salt added tomato sauce
- ⅛ cup olive oil
- 1 cup fresh mushrooms, sliced
- 1 cup onion, chopped
- 1 cup celery, diced
- 1 teaspoon garlic powder
- 1 teaspoon basil
- 1 teaspoon oregano
- A pinch black pepper
- ⅛ teaspoon sea salt

Directions:

1. Program the oven temperature to 350 °F.

2. Slice the squash in half and remove the seeds. Arrange the squash, cut side down, in a dish and microwave on high for 20 minutes.

3. While the squash is baking, sauté onion and celery in olive oil for 2-3 minutes, or until clear.

4. Blend in the mushrooms and sauté for about 4 minutes. Then add the sauce and seasonings, and cook until the sauce begins to thicken.

5. Divide and spoon into the squash. Cover and bake for 15 minutes.

6. Garnish with the cheese and bake until the cheese has melted.

Nutrition: Calories: 332 - Fat: 13 g - Protein: 14 g - Carbs: 33 g

Carrot, Zucchini and Leeks Purée

Preparation Time: 10 minute **Cooking Time:** 25 minutes
Servings: 4-6

Ingredients:

- 1 leek, stems removed, and roughly chopped
- 3. carrots, chopped
- 1 zucchini, chopped
- 1 cup low-sodium vegetable broth, warmed
- 1 tablespoon Parmesan cheese, grated

- 1 tablespoon extra-virgin olive oil
- A pinch black pepper
- A pinch sea salt
- Water

Directions:

1. Over medium heat, bring a pot of salted water to a boil.
2. Add the leeks and the carrots and cook for about 10 minutes. Then, add the zucchini and cook for 5 minutes more. Drain and set aside.
3. In a saucepan over medium heat, add the oil and stir in the vegetables, cooking for 1-2 minutes.
4. Pour in the broth and cook for 4-5 minutes, or until most of the broth has been absorbed.
5. Transfer to a mixer and pulse until smooth.
6. Return the mixture in the saucepan over low heat, add Parmesan and black pepper, stir well, and serve hot.

Nutrition: Calories: 162 - Fat: 4 g - Protein: 4 g - Carbs: 20 g - Sodium: 376 mg

Chickpea and Feta Salad

Preparation Time: 5 minutes **Cooking Time:** 0 minutes
Servings: 4
Ingredients:

- ½ cucumber, sliced
- 6 oz. no-salt added chickpeas, drained, and rinsed
- ¾ cup low-sodium feta cheese, crumbled
- ½ cup cherry tomatoes, halved
- ½ red onion, diced
- 1 avocado, peeled, pitted, and diced
- 2 teaspoons low-salt capers
- 2 tablespoons lemon juice
- 2 tablespoons olive oil
- 1 teaspoon dried basil
- A dash pepper
- A dash sea salt

Directions:

1. combine all the ingredients and stir until well mixed.

Nutrition: Calories: 185 - Fat: 10 g - Protein: 12 g - Carbs: 20 g - Sodium: 406 mg

Eggplant Pesto Mini Pizza

Preparation Time: 15 minutes **Cooking Time:** 25 minutes
Servings: 4
Ingredients:

- 1 eggplant, cut into ⅓-½ inch thick round slices
- 1 tablespoon coarse sea salt
- 2 garlic cloves, minced
- 1 tablespoon extra-virgin olive oil
- 1 cup low-fat vegan pesto sauce
- ¼ cup hummus
- 1 cup low-fat mozzarella cheese
- Ground black pepper

Directions:

1. Place the eggplant on paper towels and sprinkle with salt. Let sit for 15 minutes to lose excess water. Then, pat them dry and remove the salt.
2. Set the oven to 400 °F.

3. In a bowl, mix olive oil, garlic and black pepper, and mix well.
4. With the mixture, season both sides of the eggplant slices and place in the oven for 15 minutes.
5. Take the eggplants out of the oven, turn them over, spread with a tablespoon pesto sauce and top with mozzarella.
6. Put back in the oven and bake for 10 minutes more.

Nutrition: Calories: 295 - Fat: 18 g - Protein: 15 g - Carbs: 21 g

Lentil Vegetarian Loaf

Preparation Time: 10 minutes **Cooking Time:** 1 ½ hour
Servings: 8
Ingredients:

- ½ cup canned no-salt added lentils, drained, and rinsed
- 2 yellow onions, diced
- 2 cups brown rice, cooked
- 2 tablespoons canola/olive oil
- ½ cup no-added sugar ketchup
- 1 (6 oz.) can tomato sauce
- 1 teaspoon marjoram
- 1 teaspoon garlic powder
- 1 teaspoon sage
- ½ cup cherry tomatoes, quartered
- A pinch sea salt
- A pinch black pepper
- 3-4 cups water
- Cooking spray

Directions:

1. Preheat the oven to 350 °F.
2. heat oil over medium heat. Add the onions and sauté until golden.
3. In a large pot, combine the sautéed onions, lentils, tomato sauce, rice, cherry tomatoes, salt, pepper and spices. Mix well.
4. Press the mixture into a cooking spray greased baking dish with ½ cup of ketchup over the top.
5. Bake for 1 hour.

Nutrition: Calories: 226 - Fat: 4.4 g - Protein: 11 g - Carbs: 36 g

Spinach Lasagna

Preparation Time: 10 minutes **Cooking Time:** 1 ½ hour
Servings: 12
Ingredients:

- 10 oz. frozen baby spinach
- 9 lasagna noodles oven ready
- 1 large egg
- 2 cups low-fat cottage cheese
- 2 cups low-fat mozzarella cheese
- ½ cup Parmesan cheese, grated
- 1 jar marinara tomato sauce
- 1 cup water
- ⅛ teaspoon black pepper
- Cooking spray

Directions:

1. Program the oven temperature to 350 °F.

2.   Combine the thawed and drained spinach, one cup of mozzarella, cottage cheese, egg, and pepper in a large mixing bowl.

3.   Spray a 9x13x2 inch casserole dish with some cooking spray.

4.   Layer ½ cup of the sauce, 3 noodles, and ½ of the cheese mixture. Repeat, and top with the noodles, one cup of mozzarella and grated Parmesan.

5.   Pour water around the edges and toothpicks on top to place a piece of aluminum foil over the noodles.

6.   Bake covered 1 hour-1 ½ hour. Let it rest 15 minutes.

Nutrition: Calories: 317 - Fat: 12.6 g - Protein: 26.4 g - Carbs: 24 g

Vegetarian Frittata

Preparation Time: 15 minutes **Cooking Time:** 30-35 minutes **Servings:** 2

Ingredients:

- 2 oz. button mushrooms
- 4 oz. asparagus
- ⅓ shallot, minced
- ½ garlic clove, minced
- 1 tablespoon olive oil
- ½ small zucchini
- 2 large eggs
- 2 tablespoons low-fat milk
- ½ tablespoon chives, chopped
- ½ small tomato, thinly sliced
- ¼ cup freshly Parmesan cheese, grated
- A dash nutmeg
- A pinch freshly ground black pepper
- A pinch sea salt

Directions:

1.   Set the oven to 348 °F.

2.   Wash and trim the asparagus, and cut it into 1 inch pieces.

3.   Blanche cut asparagus for 1-2 minutes. Shock it by adding it to ice water. Drain and set to the side.

4.   Clean and slice the mushrooms. Sauté them in the oil for 5 minutes using medium heat.

5.   Add in the shallot and garlic and cook 2 minutes more. Transfer the mushrooms to a plate and set aside.

6.   Slice the zucchini lengthwise and into half-moon shapes.

7.   Whisk the eggs, milk, chives, pepper, salt, and nutmeg in a large bowl. Add the mushroom mixture, asparagus, and zucchini.

8.   add the egg-veggie mixture.

9.   Arrange the thinly sliced tomatoes on top and sprinkle with the Parmesan cheese.

10.   Bake 30-35 minutes. You can place the frittata under the broiler for 2-3 minutes to brown the top.

Nutrition: Calories: 148 - Fat: 9 g - Protein: 10.6 g - Carbs: 8 g - Sodium: 135 mg

Seitan Buffalo Bites

Preparation Time: 15 minutes **Cooking Time:** 15 minutes **Servings:** 2

Ingredients:

- 1 (8 oz.) package seitan, cut into strips or small, 2 inch pieces
- 1 large egg
- ½ cup flaxseed meal
- 1 ½ tablespoons garlic powder
- 1 ½ tablespoons onion powder
- ½ cup sugar-free buffalo wing sauce
- ¾ tablespoon parsley, chopped
- A pinch sea salt
- A pinch black pepper
- Cooking spray

Directions:

1.   Preheat the oven to 350 °F. Coat a baking sheet with cooking spray.

2.   In a medium bowl, whisk the egg, salt and pepper.

3.   In another medium bowl, mix together the flaxseed meal, garlic powder, and onion powder.

4.   One by one, coat each seitan piece in egg, allowing the excess egg to drip off, then lightly coat with the dry mixture.

5.   Gently transfer coated pieces to the prepared baking sheet. Bake for 12-15 minutes, or until crispy, flipping halfway through.

6.   Transfer to a large bowl, coat with the buffalo wing sauce, and sprinkle with parsley. Serve immediately.

Nutrition: Calories: 87 - Fat: 4 g - Protein: 8 g - Carbs: 5 g - Fiber: 2 g - Sodium: 517 mg

Veggie Sloppy Joes in Lettuce

Preparation Time: 10 minutes **Cooking Time:** 35 minutes **Servings:** 2

Ingredients:

- 1 cup dry green lentils, well rinsed
- 2 cups low-sodium vegetable broth
- 1 tablespoon extra-virgin olive oil
- ½ small yellow onion, minced
- ½ small green bell pepper, minced
- 1 garlic cloves, minced
- 1 (8 oz.) can no-salt added tomato sauce
- 1 teaspoon sugar substitute
- 1 tablespoon low-sodium Worcestershire sauce
- 2 teaspoons chili powder
- 1 teaspoon ground cumin
- 1 teaspoon paprika
- Lettuce leaves, sliced jalapeños and red onion, for serving (enough for 2)

Directions:

1.   In a small saucepan over medium-high heat, combine the broth and lentils. cook uncovered for about 18 minutes, or until tender. Drain any excess liquid.

2.   In a large skillet over medium heat, heat the oil. Add the onion, bell pepper, and garlic, and cook for 4-5 minutes, until tender.

3.   Add the tomato sauce, sugar substitute, Worcestershire, chili powder, cumin, paprika, and lentils. Stir to combine.

4.   Continue cooking for 5-10 minutes over medium heat until warmed through and thickened.

5.   Serve in lettuce leaves with sliced jalapeños and red onion.

Nutrition: Calories: 263 - Fat: 9 g - Protein: 10 g - Carbs: 20 g - Sugar: 6 g - Fiber: 8 g - Sodium: 525 mg

Backed Brussels Sprouts with Parmesan

Preparation Time: 10 minutes **Cooking Time:** 30 minutes **Servings:** 4

Ingredients:

- 1 lb. fresh Brussels sprouts, stems removed
- 1 garlic clove, minced
- 3 tablespoons Parmesan cheese, grated
- 1 tablespoon margarine
- A pinch sea salt
- A pinch black pepper
- Cooking spray

Directions:

1. Preheat the oven to 390 °F.
2. bring salted water to a boil.
3. Add Brussels sprouts and blanch for 3 minutes. Drain and set aside.
4. Ina saucepan over medium heat, add the garlic and margarine, and sauté for 2 minutes.
5. Stir in the blanched Brussels sprouts and cook for 2-3 minutes.
6. Grease a baking dish with cooking spray and add in the garlic and Brussels sprouts mixture.
7. Top with Parmesan and black pepper and bake in the oven for 15-20 minutes.

Nutrition: Calories: 127 - Fat: 6 g - Protein: 8 g - Carbs: 12 g - Sugar: 3 g - Fiber: 7 g - Sodium: 346 mg

Chapter 11: Seafood Recipes

Shrimp, Zucchini and Cherry Tomato Sauce

Preparation Time: 5 minutes **Cooking Time:** 25 minutes
Servings: 2
Ingredients:
- 1 medium zucchini, diced
- 3 oz. shrimp, cleaned
- 5 cherry tomatoes, chopped
- 1 garlic clove
- ½ teaspoon curry powder
- Sea salt and pepper, to taste
- Cooking spray

Directions:
1. Grease the air fryer with cooking.
2. Add the garlic clove and diced zucchini.
3. Cook for 15 minutes at 300 °F.
4. Add the shrimps, tomato, salt, pepper and curry. Stir well.
5. Cook for 5-10 minutes, or until the shrimp water evaporates, and serve.

Nutrition: Calories: 214 - Fat: 8 g - Protein: 27 g - Carbs: 8 g - Cholesterol: 232 mg - Sugar: 5 g

Monkfish with Olives and Capers

Preparation Time: 15 minutes **Cooking Time:** 40 minutes **Servings:** 1
Ingredients:
- 1 monkfish fillet, cleaned
- 6 cherry tomatoes, chopped
- 2 oz. cailletier olives
- 1 tablespoon capers
- ½ teaspoon oregano
- 1 teaspoon olive oil
- A pinch black pepper

Directions:
1. Spread aluminum foil inside the air fryer basket and place the monkfish clean and skinless.
2. Add chopped tomatoes, olives, capers, oil, oregano and pepper.
3. Set the temperature to 350 °F. Cook the monkfish for about 40 minutes. Serve and enjoy.

Nutrition: Calories: 246 - Fat: 14 g - Protein: 14 g - Carbs: 12 g - Cholesterol: 36 mg - Sugar: 7 g

Baked Garlic Scallops

Preparation Time: 15 minutes **Cooking Time:** 10 minutes
Servings: 4
Ingredients:
- 16 sea scallops, rinsed, and drained
- 3 garlic cloves, minced
- 2 small shallots, chopped
- 1 cup breadcrumbs
- 2 tablespoons olive oil
- ¼ cup parsley, chopped
- 1 tablespoon dried oregano
- ½ teaspoon chili powder
- A pinch ground black pepper
- Cooking spray

Directions:
1. In a mixing bowl, add shallots, garlic, scallops, oil, and pepper. Combine to mix well with each other.
2. In another bowl, add oregano, parsley, chili powder and breadcrumbs. Combine to mix well with each other.
3. Place air fryer lid on top. Press AIR FRY, set the temperature to 375 °F, and set the timer to 5 minutes to preheat. Press START and allow it to preheat for 5 minutes.
4. Take air fryer basket; grease it with some cooking spray. In the basket, add a scallop mixture and top with the crumb mixture. Place the basket in the inner pot, close air fryer lid on top.
5. Press the BAKE setting. Set temperature to 390 °F and set the timer to 10 minutes. Press START. Cook until the top is light brown.
6. Open air fryer lid after cooking time is over. Serve warm with the parsley on top.

Nutrition: Calories: 251 - Fat: 16 g - Protein: 17 g - Carbs: 10 g - Fiber: 1 g - Sodium: 458 mg

Ranch Tilapia

Preparation Time: 15 minutes **Cooking Time:** 13 minutes
Servings: 4
Ingredients:
- 4 tilapia fillets
- ¾ cup cornflakes, crushed
- 1 (1 oz.) packet dry ranch-style dressing mix
- 2 tablespoons vegetable oil
- ½ lemon, zested, and juiced
- 2 eggs
- Cooking spray

Directions:
1. beat the eggs.
2. In another bowl, add the cornflakes, ranch dressing, lemon zest, and oil and mix until a crumbly mixture form.
3. Dip the fish fillets into eggs and then coat with the breadcrumbs mixture.
4. Press POWER button of air fryer oven and turn the dial to select the AIR FRY mode. Press TIME button and again turn the dial to set the cooking time to 13 minutes. Now, push TEMPERATURE button and rotate the dial to set the temperature at 356 °F. Press START/PAUSE button to start.
5. When the unit beeps to show that it is preheated, open the lid.
6. Arrange the tilapia fillets in oil sprayed air fryer basket, and insert in the oven.
7. Remove from the air fryer, drizzle with lemon juice and serve.

Nutrition: Calories: 267 - Fat: 12 g - Protein: 22 g - Carbs: 18 g - Sodium: 768 mg

Easy Crab Sticks

Preparation Time: 5 minutes **Cooking Time:** 10 minutes
Servings: 2
Ingredients:
- 1 package crab sticks
- Cooking spray

Directions:

1. Take each of the sticks out of the package and unroll it until the stick is flat. Tear the sheets into thirds.
2. Arrange them on the air fryer basket and lightly coat using cooking spray.
3. Set the timer for 10 minutes, and serve.

Nutrition: Calories: 169 - Fat: 5 g - Protein: 11 g - Carbs: 15 g - Sodium: 184 mg

Vinegar Spice Prawns

Preparation Time: 10 minutes **Cooking Time:** 8 minutes
Servings: 1-2
Ingredients:
- 12 prawns, shelled, and deveined
- 1 tablespoon white wine vinegar
- 1 tablespoon no-added sugar ketchup
- ½ teaspoon black pepper
- 1 teaspoon chili flakes
- 1 teaspoon chili powder
- 1 teaspoon fresh parsley, chopped
- Cooking spray

Directions:
1. Place air fryer lid on top. Press AIR FRY, set the temperature to 375 °F and set the timer to 5 minutes to preheat. Press START and allow it to preheat for 5 minutes.
2. Take air fryer basket; grease it with some cooking spray. In the basket, add all ingredients and combine well.
3. Place the basket in the inner pot, close air fryer lid on top. Press the AIR FRY setting. Set temperature to 390 °F and set the timer to 8 minutes. Press START.
4. Stir mixture halfway through.
5. Open air fryer lid after cooking time is over. Serve warm.

Nutrition: Calories: 178 - Fat: 4 g - Protein: 21 g - Carbs: 9 g - Fiber: 1 g - Sodium: 581 mg

Herbed Baked Shrimp

Preparation Time: 10 minutes **Cooking Time:** 10 minutes
Servings: 4
Ingredients:
- 1 lb. shrimp, defrosted
- 1 tablespoon garlic, minced
- 2 teaspoons red pepper flakes
- 3 tablespoons margarine
- 1 tablespoon lemon juice
- 1 tablespoon chives, chopped
- 1 tablespoon basil leaves, minced
- 2 tablespoons low-sodium chicken stock
- Cooking spray

Directions:
1. Place air fryer lid on top. Press AIR FRY, set the temperature to 375 °F and set the timer to 5 minutes to preheat. Press START and allow it to preheat for 5 minutes.
2. Take air fryer basket; grease with cooking spray.
3. In the basket, add shrimp and margarine.
4. Place the basket in the inner pot, close air fryer lid on top. Press the BAKE setting. Set temperature to 330 °F and set the timer to 2 minutes. Press START.
5. Open air fryer lid after cooking time is over. Mix in red pepper flakes and garlic. Press the BAKE setting. Set

temperature to 330 °F and set the timer to 3 minutes. Press START.
6. After 3 minutes, add other ingredients and combine them. Press the BAKE setting. Set temperature to 330 °F and set the timer to 5 minutes. Press START. Serve warm.

Nutrition: Calories: 253 - Fat: 10 g - Protein: 23 g - Carbs: 3 g - Fiber: 0.5 g - Sodium: 594 mg

Breaded Coconut Shrimp

Preparation Time: 10 minutes **Cooking Time:** 15 minutes
Servings: 4
Ingredients:
- 1 lb. shrimp, peeled, and deveined
- 1 cup low-carb breadcrumbs
- 1 cup coconut, shredded
- 2 eggs
- ⅓ cup all-purpose flour
- 1 teaspoon white pepper
- 1 teaspoon dried coriander
- Cooking spray

Directions:
1. Fix the temperature of the air fryer at 360 °F.
2. In a dish, whisk the coriander and white pepper with the flour. In another dish, whisk the eggs. In a third container, combine the breadcrumbs and coconut.
3. Dip the cleaned shrimp into the flour, eggs, and finish with the coconut mixture.
4. Lightly spray the basket of the fryer and set the timer for 10-15 minutes.
5. Cook until golden brown before serve.

Nutrition: Calories: 235 - Fat: 5 g - Protein: 10 g - Carbs: 20 g - Sodium: 378 mg

Lemon Cod Meal

Preparation Time: 10 minutes **Cooking Time:** 15 minutes
Servings: 4
Ingredients:
- 4 cod fillets
- A bunch basil, chopped
- 1 lemon, juiced
- ¼ cup olive oil
- 1 teaspoon marjoram
- ½ tablespoon fresh parsley, finely chopped
- Ground black pepper, to taste
- Cooking spray

Directions:
1. Season cod fillets with black pepper.
2. In a mixing bowl, add other ingredients. Combine to mix well with each other. Add fish and coat well.
3. Place air fryer lid on top. Press AIR FRY, set the temperature to 375 °F and set the timer to 5 minutes to preheat. Press START and allow it to preheat for 5 minutes.
4. Take air fryer basket; grease with cooking spray. In the basket, add fish.
5. Place the basket in the inner pot, close air fryer lid on top. Press the AIR FRY setting. Set temperature to 350 °F and set the timer to 15 minutes. Press START.
6. Flip cod halfway through.

7. Open air fryer lid after cooking time is over. Serve warm with some vinaigrette on top.

Nutrition: Calories: 326 - Fat: 15 g - Protein: 16 g - Carbs: 2 g - Fiber: 1 g - Sodium: 387 mg

Oregano and Thyme Scallops

Preparation Time: 10 minutes **Cooking Time:** 10 minutes **Servings:** 4

Ingredients:
- 1 lb. sea scallops, cleaned, and patted dry
- 2 tablespoons dried thyme
- 1 tablespoon dried oregano
- 2 teaspoons chipotle pepper
- 1 tablespoon ground coriander
- 1 tablespoon ground fennel
- 1 dried chilies
- A pinch ground black pepper
- Cooking spray

Directions:
1. In a mixing bowl, add scallops and other ingredients. Combine to mix well.
2. Place air fryer lid on top. Press AIR FRY, set the temperature to 375 °F and set the timer to 5 minutes to preheat. Press START and allow it to preheat for 5 minutes.
3. Take air fryer basket; grease with cooking spray. In the basket, add scallops.
4. Place the basket in the inner pot, close air fryer lid on top. Press the AIR FRY setting. Set temperature to 390 °F and set the timer to 10 minutes. Press START.
5. Open air fryer lid after cooking time is over. Serve warm.

Nutrition: Calories: 257 - Fat: 14 g - Protein: 18 g - Carbs: 12 g - Fiber: 1 g - Sodium: 588 mg

Crispy Breaded Tilapia

Preparation Time: 10 minutes **Cooking Time:** 15 minutes **Servings:** 2

Ingredients:
- 2 tilapia fillets
- 1 egg
- 1 cup low-carb breadcrumbs
- A pinch black pepper
- A dash sweet paprika
- ¼ lemon, juiced
- 2 teaspoons parsley, chopped
- Cooking spray

Directions:
1. beat the egg and season to taste with pepper and sweet paprika. Mix well and set aside.
2. In another bowl, place breadcrumbs.
3. Dip each tilapia fillet in the egg mixture, and then in the breadcrumbs. Coat entire fillet well, removing any excess of egg or breadcrumbs.
4. Spray your air fryer with cooking oil, place tilapia fillets in, and cook for 10 minutes at 350 °F.
5. After 10 minutes, flip fillets and cook for 5 minutes more.
6. Remove tilapia from air fryer and garnish with lemon juice and parsley.

Nutrition: Calories: 249 - Fat 12 g - Protein: 24 g - Carbs: 15 g - Sodium: 462 mg

Sweet and Sour Glazed Salmon

Preparation Time: 2 hours to marinate **Cooking Time:** 12 minutes **Servings:** 4

Ingredients:
- 4 (3 ½ oz.) salmon fillets
- ⅓ cup low-sodium soy sauce
- ⅓ cup raw honey, or honey substitute
- 3 teaspoons rice wine vinegar
- 1 teaspoon dried dill
- 1 teaspoon water
- Cooking spray

Directions:
1. Mix the soy sauce, honey, vinegar, dill and water together in a bowl.
2. In another small bowl, reserve about half of the mixture.
3. Add salmon fillets in the remaining mixture and coat well. refrigerate to marinate for about 2 hours.
4. Press POWER button of air fryer oven and turn the dial to select the AIR FRY mode. Press the TIME button and again turn the dial to set the cooking time to 12 minutes. Now, push the TEMPERATURE button and rotate the dial to set the temperature at 355 °F. Press START/PAUSE button to start.
5. When the unit beeps to show that it is preheated, open the lid.
6. Arrange the salmon fillets in greased air fryer basket and put them in the oven.
7. Flip the salmon fillets once halfway through and coat with the reserved marinade after 3 minutes. Serve hot.

Nutrition: Calories: 271 - Fat: 12 g - Protein: 32 g - Carbs: 10 g - Sodium: 416 mg

Fried Catfish

Preparation Time: 5 minutes **Cooking Time:** 25 minutes **Servings:** 4

Ingredients:
- 4 catfish fillets
- 1 tablespoon olive oil
- ¼ cup seasoned fish fry
- A pinch ground black pepper
- ½ lemon, juiced
- 1 tablespoon chives, chopped

Directions:
1. Heat the air fryer to reach 400 °F before fry time.
2. Rinse the catfish and pat dry using a paper towel.
3. Dump the seasoned fish fry, oil and black pepper into a sizeable zipper-type bag. Add the fish and shake to cover each fillet.
4. Remove fish from the bag and add to the basket. Set the timer for 10 minutes.
5. After 10 minutes, flip the fillets and reset the timer for 10 additional minutes.
6. Then, turn the fish once more and cook for 2-3 minutes.
7. Once it reaches the desired crispiness, transfer into plates, drizzle with lemon juice, sprinkle with chives, and serve.

Nutrition: Calories: 356 - Fat: 11 g - Protein: 35 g - Carbs: 25 g - Sodium: 678 mg

Baked Tilapia Cheese
Preparation Time: 10 minutes **Cooking Time:** 15 minutes
Servings: 2
Ingredients:
- 2 tilapia fillets
- 2 teaspoons Dijon mustard
- 1 teaspoon horseradish
- 3 tablespoons fat-free mayonnaise
- 1 tablespoon lemon juice
- ¼ cup low-carb breadcrumbs
- 2 teaspoons light unsalted butter, melted
- 2 tablespoons Parmesan cheese, grated
- Cooking spray

Directions:
1. In a mixing bowl, add mayo, lemon juice, mustard, 1 tablespoon cheese, and horseradish. Combine to mix well.
2. In another bowl, combine remaining cheese, melted butter, and breadcrumbs.
3. Place air fryer lid on top. Press AIR FRY, set the temperature to 375° F and set the timer to 5 minutes to preheat. Press START and allow it to preheat for 5 minutes.
4. Take air fryer basket; grease with cooking spray. In the basket, add fish and top with the mayo mixture and then with the crumb mixture.
5. Place the basket in the inner pot, close air fryer lid on top. Press the BAKE setting. Set temperature to 390° F and set the timer to 15 minutes. Press START.
6. Open air fryer lid after cooking time is over. Serve warm.
Nutrition: Calories: 238 - Fat: 13 g - Protein: 26 g - Carbs: 6 g - Fiber: 0.5 g - Sodium: 324 mg

Breaded Cod Sticks
Preparation Time: 10 minutes **Cooking Time:** 12 minutes
Servings: 4
Ingredients:
- 1 lb. cod fillets
- 2 large eggs
- 3 tablespoons low-fat milk
- 2 cups breadcrumbs
- 1 cup almond flour
- 1 teaspoon paprika
- Black pepper, to taste

Directions:
1. Heat the air fryer at 350 °F.
2. Cut the cod into strips about 1 inch wide.
3. Prepare three bowls: one with almond flour, one with the milk, black pepper and eggs, and another with the breadcrumbs and paprika.
4. Dip the sticks in the flour, egg mixture, and breadcrumbs.
5. Place in the basket and set the timer for 12 minutes. Toss the basket halfway through the cooking process. Serve with your favorite sauce.
Nutrition: Calories: 286 - Fat: 8 g - Protein: 26 g - Carbs: 25 g - Sodium: 512 mg

Honey Glazed Salmon
Preparation Time: 5 minutes **Cooking Time:** 8 minutes
Servings: 2
Ingredients:
- 2 (4 oz.) salmon fillets
- 1 tablespoon raw honey, or honey substitute
- 2 teaspoons sesame seeds
- A pinch black pepper
- 2 teaspoons chives, finely chopped
- Cooking spray

Directions:
1. Brush the honey to coat the salmon, and sprinkle with sesame seeds and pepper.
2. Press POWER button of air fryer oven and turn the dial to select the AIR FRY mode. Press the TIME button and again turn the dial to set the cooking time to 8 minutes. Now, push TEMPERATURE button and rotate the dial to set the temperature at 355 °F. Press START/PAUSE button to start.
3. When the unit beeps to show that it is preheated, open the lid.
4. Arrange the salmon fillets in greased air fryer basket and insert them in the oven.
5. Remove from the air fryer, sprinkle with chives and serve.
Nutrition: Calories: 258 - Fat: 11 g - Protein: 33 g - Carbs: 7 g - Sodium: 225 mg

Crumbled Chives Sole
Preparation Time: 10 minutes **Cooking Time:** 12 minutes
Servings: 4
Ingredients:
- 4 sole fillets
- 1 cup breadcrumbs
- 2 tablespoons chives, finely chopped
- 1 egg, beaten
- 1 lemon, juiced
- A pinch pepper
- Cooking spray

Directions:
1. Heat the air fryer to reach 356 °F.
2. In a bowl, place the breadcrumbs.
3. beat the egg with pepper and chives.
4. Dip the fish into the egg, then into the breadcrumbs.
5. Arrange the sole fillets in the spray greased air fryer and cook for 12 minutes.
6. Remove from the air fryer and season with lemon juice.
Nutrition: Calories: 320 - Fat: 15 g - Protein: 27 g - Carbs: 20 g - Sodium: 341 mg

Lime Marinated Salmon
Preparation Time: 30 minutes to chill **Cooking Time:** 12 minutes **Servings:** 2
Ingredients:
- 2 (4 oz.) salmon fillets
- 3 tablespoons lime juice
- 3 tablespoons low-sodium soy sauce
- 1 teaspoon garlic powder

- 2 tablespoons Dijon mustard
- 1 tablespoon chives, finely chopped
- 2 teaspoons olive oil
- Cooking spray

Directions:

1. mix together lime juice, soy sauce, garlic powder, mustard and olive oil.
2. Place salmon fillets in the bowl, cover them with the mixture, seal the bowl with plastic wrap, and let marinate for 30 minutes in the fridge.
3. Coat the air fryer basket with cooking spray and add the salmon.
4. Set the air fryer to 380 °F. Cook everything for 10-12 minutes.
5. Remove the fish from air fryer and serve with chives on top.

Nutrition: Calories: 278 - Fat: 12 g - Protein: 34 g - Carbs: 8 g - Sodium: 455 g

Cod Fish Nuggets

Preparation Time: 10 minutes **Cooking Time:** 20 minutes **Servings:** 4

Ingredients:

- 1 lb. cod fillet
- 2 eggs
- 1 cup almond flour
- 1 cup low-carb breadcrumbs
- 1 tablespoon dried thyme
- A pinch black pepper

Directions:

1. Warm the air fryer at 390 °F.
2. Slice the cod into nuggets.
3. Prepare three bowls. Whisk the eggs and black pepper in one. Stir in the breadcrumbs and thyme in another. Sift the almond flour into the third one.
4. Cover each of the nuggets with the flour, dip in the eggs and the breadcrumbs.
5. Arrange the nuggets in the basket and set the timer for 20 minutes.
6. Serve the fish with your favorite dips or sides.

Nutrition: Calories: 272 - Fat: 8 g - Protein: 23 g - Carbs: 7 g - Sodium: 458 mg

Creamy Yogurt Salmon

Preparation Time: 5 minutes **Cooking Time:** 10 minutes **Servings:** 2

Ingredients:

- 2 salmon fillets
- ½ tablespoon dill, chopped
- 1 tablespoon olive oil
- 3 tablespoons low-fat plain Greek yogurt
- 1 teaspoon coriander
- A pinch black pepper

Directions:

1. Heat the air fryer and wait for it to reach 285 °F.
2. Add salmon to the fryer basket with the olive oil, and cook for 10 minutes.
3. In a bowl, whisk the yogurt, coriander, black pepper, and dill.

4. Garnish salmon with sauce and serve with your favorite sides.

Nutrition: Calories: 325 - Fat: 21 g - Protein: 32 g - Carbs: 5 g Sodium: 265 mg

Baked Onion Cod

Preparation Time: 15 minutes **Cooking Time:** 10 minutes **Servings:** 4

Ingredients:

- ½ lb. thick-cut cod loin
- ¼ lemon, juiced
- 2 tablespoons margarine, melted
- ¼ sleeve round crackers, crushed
- 2 garlic cloves, minced
- 1 ½ teaspoon parsley, chopped
- 1 ½ teaspoon green onion, chopped
- 2 tablespoons dry white wine
- ¼ teaspoon black pepper
- Cooking spray

Directions:

1. In a mixing bowl, add half margarine and crackers. Combine to mix well.
2. In another bowl, add lemon juice, white wine, parsley, garlic, black pepper, and green onion. Combine to mix well with each other.
3. Coat cod with remaining margarine.
4. Place air fryer lid on top. Press AIR FRY, set the temperature to 375 °F and set the timer to 5 minutes to preheat. Press START and allow it to preheat for 5 minutes.
5. Take air fryer basket and grease with cooking spray.
6. In the basket, add cod. Top with the dressing and then add the cracker mixture.
7. Place the basket in the inner pot, close air fryer lid on top. Press the BAKE setting. Set temperature to 390 °F and set the timer to 10 minutes. Press START.
8. Open air fryer lid after cooking time is over. Serve warm.

Nutrition: Calories: 219 - Fat: 13 g - Protein: 16 g - Carbs: 4 g - Fiber: 2 g - Sodium: 324 mg

Mussels with Pepper

Preparation Time: 15 minutes **Cooking Time:** 12 minutes **Servings:** 4

Ingredients:

- 1 ½ lb. fresh mussels
- 2 garlic cloves, crushed
- 1 teaspoon oil
- 2 tablespoons parsley, chopped
- 1 dried chili
- Pepper, to taste

Directions:

1. Clean and scrape the mold cover and remove the byssus (the "beard" that comes out of the mold).
2. Pour the oil, clean mussels, dried chili and crushed garlic in the air fryer basket. Set the temperature to 390 °F and simmer for 12 minutes.
3. Towards the end of cooking, add black pepper and chopped parsley.

4.   Finally, distribute the mussels' juice well at the bottom of the basket, stirring the basket.

Nutrition: Calories: 194 - Fat: 8 g - Protein: 25 g - Carbs: 9 g - Sodium: 235 mg

Cajun Salmon

Preparation Time: 5 minutes **Cooking Time:** 7 minutes
Servings: 1
Ingredients:
• 1 salmon fillet, 0.75-inches thick
• Cajun seasoning, to taste
• ¼ lemon, juiced
• Cooking spray

Directions:
1.   Set the air fryer at 356 °F to preheat for 5 minutes.
2.   Rinse and dry the salmon with a paper towel. Cover the fish with the Cajun coating mix.
3.   Coat the air fryer basket with cooking spray.
4.   Place the fillet in the air fryer for 7 minutes with the skin side up.
5.   Serve with a sprinkle of lemon.

Nutrition: Calories: 315 - Fat: 18 g - Protein: 34 g - Carbs: 4 g - Sodium: 673 mg

Lemon Juice Salmon with Quinoa

Preparation time: 15 minutes **Cooking time:** 25 minutes
Servings: 2
Ingredients:
• 2 (4 oz. each) salmon fillets, boneless
• ½ cup quinoa
• 1 lemon, juiced
• 6 cherry tomatoes, halved
• 3 white button mushrooms, thinly sliced
• 8-10 asparagus spears
• 2 tablespoon dill, roughly chopped
• 1 teaspoon dried oregano
• 2 garlic cloves, minced
• 2 teaspoons olive oil
• A pinch sea salt
• A pinch pepper
• 2 teaspoons low-salt capers

Directions:
1.   Preheat oven to 350 °F.
2.   On a baking dish lined with parchment paper, place minced garlic. Top garlic with the asparagus and arrange salmon fillets on the asparagus.
3.   Place the mushrooms and cherry tomatoes on the salmon and season with half lemon juice and half olive oil. Sprinkle with salt, pepper, dill, oregano and capers.
4.   Bake for 20-25 minutes, or until salmon is flaky.
5.   Meanwhile, in a saucepan, bring 1 cup water to a boil.
6.   Add quinoa and cook for 12-15 minutes, until the water is absorbed.
7.   Place quinoa into a bowl and season with remaining lemon juice and oil.
8.   Serve salmon with veggies over the quinoa.

Nutrition: Calories: 388 - Fat: 20 g - Protein: 30 g - Carbs: 16 g - Cholesterol: 88 mg - Sodium: 634 mg

Breaded Flounder

Preparation Time: 15 minutes **Cooking Time:** 12 minutes
Servings: 1
Ingredients:
• 1 (3-4 oz.) flounder fillet
• 1 egg
• 1 cup low-carb breadcrumbs
• ⅛ teaspoon red pepper
• ⅛ teaspoon black pepper
• ½ teaspoon garlic powder
• ¼ lemon, sliced
• Cooking spray

Directions:
1.   beat the egg.
2.   In another bowl, add the breadcrumbs, black pepper, red pepper, garlic powder and mix until well combined.
3.   Dip flounder fillets into the beaten egg and then, coat with the breadcrumb mixture.
4.   Press POWER button of air fry oven and turn the dial to select the AIR FRY mode. Press the TIME button and again turn the dial to set the cooking time to 12 minutes. Then, push the TEMPERATURE button and rotate the dial to set the temperature at 356 °F. Press START/PAUSE button to start.
5.   When the unit beeps to show that it is preheated, open the lid.
6.   Arrange the flounder fillets in greased air fry basket and insert them in the oven.
7.   Plate with lemon slices and serve hot.

Nutrition: Calories: 365 - Fat: 17 g - Protein: 27 g - Carbs: 23 g - Fiber: 1.5 g - Sodium: 363 mg

Puréed Tuna with Chives

Preparation Time: 5 minutes **Cooking Time:** 0 minutes
Servings: 2
Ingredients:
• 4 oz. canned tuna in water, drained
• 2 tablespoons low-fat cream cheese
• 1 teaspoon lemon juice
• 2 teaspoons chives, chopped
• A pinch white pepper

Directions:
1.   Put all in a mixer and process until smooth and creamy.

Nutrition: Calories: 80 - Fat: 3.5 g - Protein: 12 g - Carbs: 2 g - Cholesterol: 18 mg - Sugar: 1.5 g - Sodium: 100 mg

Salmon Butter Crumbed

Preparation Time: 10 minutes **Cooking Time:** 10 minutes
Servings: 2
Ingredients:
• 2 (3-4 oz. each) salmon fillets
• 1 tablespoon thyme, chopped
• 1 tablespoon onion powder
• 1 ½ cups soft low-carb breadcrumbs
• 2 tablespoons parsley, minced
• 1 teaspoon lemon zest, grated
• 1 teaspoon lemon juice
• ¼ teaspoon paprika
• 2 teaspoons coriander

- 1 tablespoon light unsalted butter, melted
- ¼ teaspoon black pepper
- Cooking spray

Directions:

1. In a mixing bowl, add breadcrumbs, fresh parsley, thyme, onion powder, lemon zest, lemon juice, coriander, black pepper, and paprika.

2. Place air fryer lid on top. Press AIR FRY, set the temperature to 375 °F and set the timer to 5 minutes to preheat. Press START and allow it to preheat for 5 minutes.

3. Take air fryer basket; grease with cooking spray. In the basket, add salmon fillets skin side down, and top with the crumb mixture.

4. Place the basket in the inner pot, close air fryer lid on top. Press the BAKE setting. Set temperature to 390 °F and set the timer to 10 minutes. Press START.

5. Open air fryer lid after cooking time is over. Serve warm.

Nutrition: Calories: 312 - Fat: 17 g - Protein: 27 g - Carbs: 10 g - Fiber: 1 g - Sodium: 340 mg

Seasoned Fish Fry Shrimp

Preparation Time: 5 minutes **Cooking Time:** 5 minutes
Servings: 2

Ingredients:

- 6-8 oz. Tiger shrimp
- ¼ teaspoon seasoned fish fry
- ¼ teaspoon smoked paprika
- ¼ teaspoon cayenne pepper
- Cooking spray

Directions:

1. Set the air fryer at 387 °F.

2. Season shrimp with cooking oil and spices. Toss them into the air fryer basket and set the timer for 5 minutes.

3. Serve with your favorite side dish.

Nutrition: Calories: 169 - Fat: 5 g - Protein: 24 g - Carbs: 3 g - Sodium: 343 mg

Halibut with Vegetables and Egg

Preparation Time: 10 minutes **Cooking Time:** 15 minutes
Servings: 2

Ingredients:

- 2 (3 oz. each) halibut fillets
- 4 oz. mixed vegetables
- 2 hard-boiled eggs, sliced
- Ground black pepper, to taste
- 1 teaspoon fresh parsley, chopped
- 1 lime, juiced
- Cooking spray

Directions:

1. Season the halibut with black pepper.

2. Place air fryer lid on top. Press AIR FRY, set the temperature to 375 °F and set the timer to 5 minutes to preheat. Press START and allow it to preheat for 5 minutes.

3. Take air fryer basket; grease with cooking spray. In the basket, add fish and arrange the mixed vegetables around.

4. Place the basket in the inner pot, close air fryer lid on top. Press the AIR FRY setting. Set temperature to 375 °F and set the timer to 15 minutes. Press START.

5. Stir the mixture halfway through.

6. Open air fryer lid after cooking time is over and remove.

7. Serve warm in a bowl mixed with eggs, and season with lime juice and parsley.

Nutrition: Calories: 316 - Fat: 11 g - Protein: 35 g - Carbs: 13 g - Fiber: 2 g - Sodium: 328 mg

Air Fried Prawns

Preparation Time: 15 minutes **Cooking Time:** 8 minutes
Servings: 1-2

Ingredients:

- 12 small prawns
- 1 egg
- Whole-wheat flour, for coating
- Low-carb breadcrumbs, for coating
- ½ teaspoon turmeric
- A pinch white pepper
- Low-fat plain Greek yogurt or low-fat mayonnaise, for serving
- Cooking spray

Directions:

1. Preheat the air fryer to 312 °F. Lightly spray the basket with cooking oil.

2. Remove the head of the prawns and shell carefully.

3. In a small bowl, whisk the egg and pepper. In another bowl, mix breadcrumbs and turmeric.

4. Pass the prawns first in the flour, then in the beaten egg and finally in the breadcrumbs.

5. cook for 4.5 minutes.

6. Turn the prawns and cook for another 4 minutes.

7. Serve with a yogurt or mayonnaise sauce.

Nutrition: Calories: 245 - Fat: 8 g - Protein: 27 g - Carbs: 17 g - Sodium: 512 mg

Salmon with Pistachio Bark

Preparation Time: 10 minutes **Cooking Time:** 25 minutes **Servings:** 2

Ingredients:

- 2 (3-4 oz. each) salmon fillets
- 1 oz. low-salt pistachios
- 2 tablespoons Dijon mustard
- 1 teaspoon dried dill
- Cooking spray

Directions:

1. Preheat the air fryer to 348 °F.

2. Put the parchment paper on the bottom of the air fryer basket.

3. Cut the pistachios to your preferred thickness.

4. Lightly grease the fish with cooking spray.

5. Spread the mustard on each fillet, sprinkle with pistachios and top with dill.

6. Place the salmon fillets in the air fryer and cook for 25 minutes.

Nutrition: Calories: 303- Fat: 18 g - Protein: 26 g - Carbs: 6 g - Sodium: 372 mg

Grilled Herbed Sardines

Preparation Time: 5 minutes **Cooking Time:** 14 minutes
Servings: 2
Ingredients:
- 6 small sardines
- 1 tablespoon herbs of Provence seasoning
- 1 tablespoon fresh parsley, chopped
- Cooking spray

Directions:
1. Preheat the air fryer to 317 °F.
2. Lightly grease the sardines with cooking spray, sprinkle with the herbs seasoning and place in the air fryer.
3. Set the timer for 14 minutes. After 7 minutes, turn the sardines and continue cooking.
4. Sprinkle with parsley and serve.

Nutrition: Calories: 189 - Fat: 8 g - Protein: 13 g - Carbs: 3 g - Sodium: 309 mg

Rangoon Crab Dip

Preparation Time: 10 minutes **Cooking Time:** 16 minutes
Servings: 6-8
Ingredients:
- 1 ½ cup crab meat
- ½ cup low-fat mozzarella cheese, shredded
- ½ teaspoon garlic powder
- ¼ cup pimentos, drained, and diced
- ¼ teaspoon stevia
- ½ lemon, juiced
- 2 teaspoons coconut amino
- 2 teaspoons low-fat mayonnaise
- 2 oz. fat-free cream cheese, softened
- 1 tablespoon green onion
- ¼ teaspoon pepper
- A pinch sea salt

Directions:
1. Preheat the air fryer to 321 °F.
2. Add all ingredients except half mozzarella cheese into a large bowl and mix until well combined.
3. Transfer bowl mixture into the air fryer baking dish and sprinkle with remaining mozzarella cheese.
4. Place into the air fryer and cook for 16 minutes. Serve and enjoy.

Nutrition: Calories: 147 - Fat: 15 g - Protein: 5 g - Carbs: 4 g - Sodium: 322 mg

Perfect Crab Dip

Preparation Time: 5 minutes **Cooking Time:** 7 minutes
Servings: 6
Ingredients:
- 1 ½ cup crab meat
- 2 tablespoons parsley, chopped
- 2 tablespoons fresh lemon juice
- 2 tablespoons low-carb hot sauce
- ½ cup green onion, sliced
- 1 cup low-fat cheese, grated
- ¼ cup low-fat mayonnaise
- ¼ teaspoon pepper
- A pinch sea salt

Directions:
1. In a 6 inch dish, mix together crab meat, hot sauce, onion, cheese, mayo, pepper, and salt.
2. Place dish in air fryer basket and cook dip at 400 °F for 7 minutes.
3. Remove dish from air fryer.
4. Drizzle dip with lemon juice and garnish with parsley. Serve and enjoy.

Nutrition: Calories: 288 - Fat: 23 g - Protein: 13 g - Carbs: 6 g - Sodium: 431 mg

Herb-Crusted Salmon

Preparation Time: 10 minutes **Cooking Time:** 15 minutes
Servings: 2
Ingredients:
- 2 (3-4 oz. each) salmon fillets
- 2 teaspoons garlic, minced
- 1 tablespoon dried parsley
- ½ teaspoon dried thyme
- ½ teaspoon dried dill
- ½ teaspoon marjoram
- 2 teaspoons freshly squeezed lemon juice
- 2 tablespoons Parmesan cheese, grated
- A pinch black pepper
- Cooking spray

Directions:
1. Set the oven to 425 °F.
2. Place the salmon skin-side down on the baking dish, transfer to the preheated oven and bake for 10 minutes.
3. Meanwhile, in a small bowl, stir in garlic, parsley, thyme, dill, marjoram, black pepper, lemon juice, and Parmesan cheese.
4. Remove salmon from the oven, spread the mixture on the fillets, and return into the oven.
5. Cook for another 5 minutes and serve.

Nutrition: Calories: 217 - Fat: 9 g - Protein: 26 g - Carbs: 7 g - Sodium: 209 mg

Shrimp Kabobs

Preparation Time: 10 minutes **Cooking Time:** 8 minutes
Servings: 1
Ingredients:
- ½ cup shrimp
- ½ lime, juiced
- ½ garlic clove, minced
- ¼ teaspoon paprika
- ¼ teaspoon ground cumin
- ¼ teaspoon pepper

Directions:
1. Preheat the air fryer to 348 °F.
2. Add shrimp, lime juice, garlic, pepper, paprika, and cumin into a bowl and mix well until coated.
3. Thread shrimp onto wooden skewers and place into the air fryer basket.
4. Cook for 8 minutes and turn halfway through. Serve and enjoy.

Nutrition: Calories: 75 - Fat: 3 g - Protein: 13 g - Carbs: 4 g - Sodium: 467 mg

Crab-Stuffed Mushrooms

Preparation Time: 10 minutes **Cooking Time:** 8 minutes
Servings: 2
Ingredients:
- 4 oz. mushrooms, cleaned, and stems chopped
- ¼ teaspoon chili powder
- ¼ teaspoon onion powder
- ¼ cup low-fat mozzarella cheese, shredded
- 2 oz. crab meat, chopped
- 2 oz. fat-free cream cheese, softened
- 1 teaspoon garlic, minced
- 1 tablespoon green onion, finely chopped
- ¼ teaspoon pepper

Directions:
1. Preheat the air fryer to 368 °F. Line the air fryer basket with baking paper.
2. In a mixing bowl, stir stems, chili powder, onion powder, pepper, mozzarella, crab meat, cream cheese, and garlic until well combined.
3. Stuff mushroom caps with bowl mixture and place into the air fryer basket.
4. Cook for 8 minutes.
5. top with green onion. Serve and enjoy.

Nutrition: Calories: 139 - Fat: 8 g - Protein: 5 g - Carbs: 4 g - Sodium: 228 mg

Yogurt Salmon Paté

Preparation Time: 5 minutes **Cooking Time:** 0 minutes
Servings: 1
Ingredients:
- 2 oz. canned salmon in water, drained
- 1 tablespoon low-fat plain Greek yogurt
- 1 teaspoon fresh parsley, chopped
- ½ teaspoon balsamic vinegar
- A pinch red pepper

Directions:
1. blend until smooth and well combined.

Nutrition: Calories: 82 - Fat: 6 g - Protein: 11 g - Carbs: 1 g - Sugar: 2 g - Sodium: 118 mg

Pesto-Topped Swordfish

Preparation Time: 5 minutes **Cooking Time:** 10 minutes
Servings: 2
Ingredients:
- 2 (3-4 oz. each) swordfish steaks
- 2 tablespoons low-fat basil pesto
- 6 cherry tomatoes, halved
- ½ garlic clove, minced
- A pinch white pepper
- Cooking spray

Directions:
1. Grease a skillet with cooking spray over medium heat.
2. Add in swordfish, garlic and tomatoes and cook for about 4-5 minutes.
3. Reduce the heat to low, turn the swordfish steaks, spread with pesto, and season with white pepper.
4. Cook the other side for about 4-5 minutes. Serve and enjoy.

Nutrition: Calories: 215 - Fat: 11 g - Protein: 23 g - Carbs: 4 g - Sodium: 140 mg

Baked Halibut Mediterranean Style

Preparation Time: 5 minutes **Cooking Time:** 30 minutes
Servings: 2
Ingredients:
- 2 (3-4 oz. each) halibut fillets, deboned
- 1 tablespoon extra-virgin olive oil
- ⅓ onion, chopped
- 1 teaspoon garlic, minced
- 6 oz. grape tomatoes, halved
- 4 black olives, pitted, and sliced
- 1 tablespoons capers
- ¼ teaspoon dried thyme
- Freshly ground black pepper

Directions:
1. Put the olive oil over medium heat. Add the onion and sauté until golden and softened, 3-5 minutes.
2. Add the garlic and cook until fragrant, 1-2 minutes.
3. Stir in the tomatoes and cook for 5 minutes, or until they start to soften.
4. Stir in the capers and olives.
5. add the fish and sprinkle with thyme and pepper. Cover the fillets with the tomato, capers and olives mixture.
6. Cook for about 15 minutes, or until the fish flakes easily with a fork.

Nutrition: Calories: 246 - Fat: 9 g - Protein: 26 g - Carbs: 6 g - Sodium: 196 mg

Cod with Leek, Bell Pepper and Kalamata Olives

Preparation Time: 10 minutes **Cooking Time:** 25 minutes **Servings:** 4
Ingredients:
- 4 (3-4 oz. each) cod fillets
- ½ leek, sliced
- 2 teaspoons extra-virgin olive oil
- 1 red bell pepper, sliced
- 1 teaspoon freshly ground black pepper
- ¼ cup Kalamata olives, pitted
- 1 tablespoon fresh basil, chopped

Directions:
1. heat oil over medium heat.
2. Stir in leek and sauté until golden.
3. Add bell pepper and cook for about 5 minutes. Stir in the olives and reduce the heat.
4. Place cod in the saucepan, season with black pepper, and cover the fish with bell pepper and olives mixture.
5. Cook for about 15 minutes, sprinkle with fresh basil, and serve.

Nutrition: Calories: 236 - Fat: 8 g - Protein: 23 g - Carbs: 11 g - Sodium: 241 mg

Cucumber Tuna Salad

Preparation Time: 5 minutes **Cooking Time:** 0 minutes
Servings: 2
Ingredients:
- 8 oz. light tuna, drained

- ¾ cup cucumber, diced
- 2 tablespoons light mayonnaise
- ½ teaspoon dried dill
- 1 teaspoon fresh lemon juice
- A pinch black pepper

Directions:

1. mix until well combined.

Nutrition: Calories: 193 - Fat: 11 g - Protein: 15 g - Carbs: 7 g - Sodium: 211 mg

Creamy Salmon Salad

Preparation Time: 10 minutes **Cooking Time:** 0 minutes
Servings: 4
Ingredients:

- 6 oz. canned no-salt added salmon, drained
- 1 celery stalk, sliced
- 1 avocado, chopped
- ½ bell pepper, chopped
- 2 tablespoons low-fat yogurt
- 2 tablespoons Dijon mustard
- ¼ cup onion, minced
- 1 tablespoon lime juice
- 1 teaspoon sesame seeds
- A pinch black pepper

Directions:

1. whisk together yogurt and mustard.
2. Add remaining ingredients and stir to combine.

Nutrition: Calories: 399 - Fat: 25 g - Protein: 28 g - Carbs: 15 g - Sodium: 392 mg

Baked Dijon Salmon

Preparation Time: 10 minutes **Cooking Time:** 10 minutes **Servings:** 4
Ingredients:

- 4 (3-4 oz. each) salmon fillets
- 2 tablespoons olive oil
- 2 tablespoons Dijon mustard
- 1 teaspoon juniper powder
- 1 teaspoon dried parsley
- ½ teaspoon pepper
- Cooking spray

Directions:

1. Preheat the oven to 400 °F.
2. mix together oil, mustard, juniper, parsley and pepper.
3. Spray a baking dish with cooking oil and set aside.
4. Place salmon on the baking dish and spread the mixture over salmon evenly.
5. Bake salmon for 10 minutes. Serve and enjoy.

Nutrition: Calories: 235 - Fat: 13 g - Protein: 29 g - Carbs: 2 g - Sodium: 345 mg

Broiled Fish Fillet

Preparation Time: 5 minutes **Cooking Time:** 12 minutes
Servings: 2
Ingredients:

- 2 (3-4 oz. each) cod fish fillets
- ⅛ teaspoon curry powder
- 2 teaspoons light unsalted butter
- ¼ teaspoon paprika
- ⅛ teaspoon pepper
- A small pinch cloves
- Cooking spray

Directions:

1. Preheat the broiler.
2. Spray broiler pan with cooking oil and set aside.
3. In a small bowl, mix together paprika, curry powder, pepper and cloves.
4. Coat fish fillet with paprika mixture and place on broiler pan.
5. Broil fish for 10-12 minutes. Top with butter and serve.

Nutrition: Calories: 204 - Fat: 5 g - Protein: 27 g - Carbs: 2 g - Sodium: 340 mg

Baked Lemon Tilapia

Preparation Time: 10 minutes **Cooking Time:** 12 minutes
Servings: 2
Ingredients:

- 2 (3-4 oz. each) tilapia fillets
- 1 tablespoon fresh lemon juice
- ½ teaspoon garlic, minced
- 1 tablespoon olive oil
- 1 tablespoon fresh parsley, chopped
- ½ lemon, zested
- A pinch black pepper
- Cooking spray

Directions:

1. Preheat the oven to 425 °F.
2. Spray a baking dish with cooking oil and set aside.
3. In a small bowl, whisk together olive oil, lemon zest, lemon juice, and garlic.
4. Season fish fillets with pepper and place in the baking dish. Pour olive oil mixture over fish fillets.
5. Bake fish fillets in the oven for 10-12 minutes. Garnish with parsley and serve.

Nutrition: Calories: 252 - Fat: 13 g - Protein: 32 g - Carbs: 2 g - Sodium: 145 mg

Garlic Shrimp

Preparation Time: 10 minutes **Cooking Time:** 50 minutes **Servings:** 2
Ingredients:

- ½ lb. large shrimp, peeled and deveined
- ¼ tablespoon parsley, minced
- ⅛ teaspoon chili flakes, crushed
- ¼ teaspoon paprika
- 2 garlic cloves, sliced
- 1 tablespoon olive oil
- 1 tablespoon lemon juice
- ¼ teaspoon pepper

Directions:

1. Add all ingredients except shrimp, lemon juice and parsley into the slow cooker and stir.
2. Cover and cook for 31 minutes.
3. Add shrimp and stir well. Cover and cook on HIGH for 20 minutes.

4. Garnish with parsley and lemon juice, and serve.
Nutrition: Calories: 208 - Fat: 14 g - Protein: 21 g - Carbs: 3 g - Sodium: 215 mg

Chili Garlic Salmon

Preparation Time: 5 minutes **Cooking Time:** 2 minutes **Servings:** 2
Ingredients:
- 2 (3-4 oz. each) salmon fillets
- ½ teaspoon red chili powder
- 1 garlic clove, minced
- ½ teaspoon ground cumin
- ¾ cup water
- A pinch black pepper

Directions:
1. Pour water into your multi-cooker and place trivet into the pot.
2. mix together chili powder, garlic, cumin, and pepper.
3. Rub salmon fillets with spice mixture and place on top of the trivet.
4. Seal the multi-cooker with a lid and cook on STEAM mode for 2 minutes.
5. Once done, release pressure using the quick-release method; then open the lid. Serve and enjoy.
Nutrition: Calories: 275 - Fat: 17 g - Protein: 30 g - Carbs: 4 g - Sodium: 442 mg

Salmon Salad with Marinade

Preparation Time: 15 minutes **Cooking Time:** 10 minutes **Servings:** 4
Ingredients:
- 1 lb. skinless salmon fillets
- Cooking spray

Marinade/Dressing:
- 2 tablespoons olive oil
- 2 tablespoons fresh orange juice
- 1 tablespoon fresh parsley, chopped
- 2 teaspoons garlic, minced
- 1 teaspoon dried oregano
- ¼ teaspoon sea salt
- Ground black pepper, as need

Salad:
- 4 cups Romaine (or Cos) lettuce leaves, washed, dried, and shredded
- 1 fennel, diced
- 2 Roma tomatoes, diced
- 1 red onion, sliced
- 1 avocado, sliced
- ½ cup Parmesan cheese, flaked

Directions:
1. In a big jug, whisk all the marinade/dressing ingredients.
2. Into a big, shallow dish, pour half of the marinade. Refrigerate the remaining marinade.
3. With the reserved half marinade, coat the salmon.
4. Grease a skillet with cooking spray and heat oil over medium-high heat. Cook both sides of salmon until crispy and cooked through.
5. While the salmon is cooking, prepare all the salad ingredients, and combine them in a large bowl.
6. Place the salad into plates and top with salmon.
7. Drizzle with the remaining refrigerated marinade.
Nutrition: Calories: 391 - Fat: 24 g - Protein: 26 g - Carbs: 14 g - Sodium: 139 mg

Salmon Mini Patties

Preparation Time: 20 minutes **Cooking Time:** 20 minutes **Servings:** 2
Ingredients:
- ½ lb. fresh salmon fillet
- ⅛ teaspoon black pepper
- 1 tablespoon extra-virgin olive oil
- ½ cup onion, finely diced
- ½ cup low-carb breadcrumbs
- 1 large egg, lightly beaten
- 1 ½ tablespoon low-fat mayonnaise
- ½ teaspoon low-sodium Worcestershire sauce
- 1 tablespoon fresh parsley, minced
- ½ tablespoon fresh dill, chopped
- Cooking spray

Directions:
1. Preheat the oven to 423 °F.
2. Place skin-side down salmon, brush with 1 tablespoon olive oil and season with black pepper.
3. Bake for 10-15 minutes.
4. Remove from the oven. Clean the salmon, discarding the skin and bones, and flake it with a fork. Let cool.
5. In a large bowl, combine flaked salmon, onion, breadcrumbs, Worcestershire sauce, egg, mayonnaise, black pepper, dill and parsley and stir until well combined.
6. From the mixture, shape 6-8 small patties.
7. In a saucepan greased with cooking spray, heat oil over medium heat.
8. Add in the salmon patties and cook until golden.
9. Remove from heat, pat them dry with a paper towel, and serve.
Nutrition: Calories: 250 - Fat: 11 g - Protein: 20 g - Carbs: 8 g - Sodium: 472 mg

Salmon Lime Cream

Preparation Time: 5 minutes **Cooking Time:** 0 minutes **Servings:** 2
Ingredients:
- 6 oz. fresh smoked salmon, roughly chopped
- ¼ cup fat-free plain Greek yogurt
- 2 teaspoons parsley, finely chopped
- 2 teaspoons chives, finely chopped
- 2 tablespoons fresh lime juice
- 2 teaspoons extra-virgin olive oil
- ¼ teaspoon ground black pepper

Directions:
1. Place the salmon, parsley, lime juice, olive oil, chives and pepper into a blender and pulse until all ingredients are well combined.
2. Remove the mixture from the blender and place it in a bowl.
3. Add the yogurt to the bowl and stir until creamy.

Nutrition: Calories: 94 - Fat: 5 g - Protein: 15 g - Carbs: 4 g - Sodium: 545 mg

Chapter 12: Dessert Recipes

Brown Sugar
PREP TIME: 15 min **COOK TIME:** none **YIELD:** 1 cup
INGREDIENTS:
- 1/4 cup sugar-free maple syrup
- 1 cup SPLENDA No Calorie Sweetener, granular
DIRECTIONS:
- In a small mixing dish, combine all of the ingredients and stir thoroughly..
NUTRITION:
130 Cal; 0g Protein; 0g Tot Fat; 36g Carb; 0g Fiber; 4g Sugar; 100mg Sodium

Powdered Sugar
PREP TIME: 5 min **COOK TIME:** none **YIELD:** 1/2 cup
INGREDIENTS:
- 2 Tbsp. cornstarch
- 3/4 cup SPLENDA granular
DIRECTIONS:
- In a blender jar, combine all of the ingredients. Cover and mix until the SPLENDA granular powder are extremely fine.
NUTRITION:
20 Cal; 0g Protein; 0g Tot Fat; 5g Carb; 0g Fiber; 4g Sugar; 0mg Sodium

Healthy Amazing Dessert
PREP TIME: 15 min **COOK TIME:** none **YIELD:** 4 Serve
INGREDIENTS:
Crust:
- 2 tablespoons Splenda
- 1 cup almonds, finely chopped, lightly toasted in a dry skillet
Filling:
- zest of 2 limes
- 3oz. ultra low fat cream cheese (softened, to blend better)
- 3 oz. firm silken tofu
- 1/2 cup Splenda
- 1/3 cup lime juice (lemon OR orange juice will work as well)
DIRECTIONS:
- Crust: Splenda and groundnuts are mixed and pressed onto the bottom of a pie dish. (the filler will keep them in place)
- Filling: In a blender, combine all ingredients and pour over ground nuts. Refrigerate for at least one night. You may use a mix of nuts for the crust or whatever you have on hand.
NUTRITION:
58 Cal; 4g Protein; 3g Tot Fat; 3g Carb; 0g Fiber; 3g Sugar; 12mg Sodium

Plain Peanut Butter Cookies
PREP TIME: 15 min **COOK TIME:** 12 min **YIELD:** 6 Serve
INGREDIENTS:
- 1 egg
- 1 cup Splenda
- 1 cup peanut butter
DIRECTIONS:
- Combine all of the ingredients and bake at 350 degrees for 10-12 minutes. They are easily broken, so be careful!
NUTRITION:
69 Cal; 4g Protein; 7g Tot Fat; 3g Carb; 0g Fiber; 4g Sugar; 44mg Sodium

Protein Rich Dessert
PREP TIME: 15 min **COOK TIME:** none **YIELD:** 4 Serve
INGREDIENTS:
- 1 small container of low-fat cool whip
- 1 pt. container of low-fat cottage cheese
- 4 tbsp. of skim milk
- 2 tbsp of vanilla or chocolate powder
- 1 pkg. of jell sugar-free, no fat pudding mix
DIRECTIONS:
- In a blender, combine the first four ingredients. Remove the cool whip and place it in a small bowl. Divide into four equal pieces and enjoy!
NUTRITION:
150 Cal; 5g Protein; 4g Tot Fat; 7g Carb; 0g Fiber; 2g Sugar; 89mg Sodium

Cream Cheese Nibblers
PREP TIME: 15 min **COOK TIME:** 15 min **YIELD:** 12-15 Serve
INGREDIENTS:
Crust:
- 1/4 cup Splenda
- 1 tablespoon butter
- 1 cup Pecans, finely chopped
Filling:
- skim milk
- 1 container low fat/fat-free cool whip
- 1/2 cup chopped Strawberries
- 1 small box Sugar-Free Jell-O gelatin (strawberry)
- 1 8-ounce package Cream Cheese (room temp)
DIRECTIONS:
- Crust: To make the crust, combine all ingredients and distribute them equally on the bottom of an 8-inch square pan.
- Filling: In a hand blender (or a mixer, although more effort), combine all ingredients. If the mixture is too thick, add a little quantity of milk until it is pourable. Pour evenly into the filling. Chill until the mixture is solid. 12-15 equal squares should be cut out.
NUTRITION:
98 Cal; 2g Protein; 9g Tot Fat; 4g Carb; 0g Fiber; 4g Sugar; 32mg Sodium

Tropical Dream
PREP TIME: 15 min **COOK TIME:** none **YIELD:** 20 Serve
INGREDIENTS:
- 1 medium banana, diced
- 1 small box lime-flavored Sugar-free Jell-O Gelatin
- 8 ounces ultra-low-fat cream cheese, divided

- 1 and 1/2 cups cold water
- 1 20-ounce can Dole Crushed Pineapple, no sugar added
- 2 cups boiling water
- 1 12-ounce container fat-free Cool Whip
- 1 large box Orange flavored Sugar-free Jell-O Gelatin

DIRECTIONS:
- One big box of orange-flavored gelatin and 1 tiny lime gelatin, plus 2 cups boiling water, in a mixing bowl Stir for 2 minutes, or until the entire gelatin has dissolved. Microwave 8 ounces of cubed cream cheese for 45 to 60 seconds, or until malleable but not runny.
- Blend into the heated gelatin mixture for approximately 2 minutes, or until completely dissolved. 1 and 1/2 cup ice-cold water Stir in the crushed pineapple, juice, and chopped banana until everything is thoroughly mixed. Refrigerate until softly set, then fold in the Cool Whip until creamy but not whipped (you don't want to deflate the cool whip). Chill for another 2 to 3 hours.

NUTRITION:
105 Cal; 3g Protein; 4g Tot Fat; 5g Carb; 0g Fiber; 5g Sugar; 76mg Sodium

Butterscotch and Pumpkin Pudding

PREP TIME: 15 min **COOK TIME:** none **YIELD:** 6 Serve
INGREDIENTS:
- 1 tsp. vanilla
- 1 package sugar-free butterscotch pudding mix
- 1/2 tsp. nutmeg
- 1 tsp. cinnamon
- 1 cup canned or fresh cooked pumpkin
- Cool Whip or Dream Whip
- 1 1/2 cup of low-fat milk

DIRECTIONS:
- Combine the pudding mix, cinnamon, pumpkin, milk, and nutmeg in a mixing bowl and whisk until smooth. Pour into individual pudding containers. Cool whip and vanilla ice cream on top.

NUTRITION:
76 Cal; 3g Protein; 3g Tot Fat; 3g Carb; 0g Fiber; 3g Sugar; 47mg Sodium

Fruit Smoothie Cheesecake

PREP TIME: 15 min **COOK TIME:** none **YIELD:** 3 Serve
INGREDIENTS:
- 2 cups of frozen non-sweetened fruit
- 1 pack graham crust
- 1 package of light cream cheese
- 1/2 cup Splenda

DIRECTIONS:
- Combine 1 package of light cream cheese and 1/2 cup Splenda in a mixing bowl. Blend in a food processor until completely smooth. Mix the drained fruit into the cheese and Splenda mixture well. Three cups light whipping cream, folded in. Fill the pie crust with the mixture. Enjoy!

NUTRITION:
52 Cal; 5g Protein; 2.5g Tot Fat; 4.5g Carb; 0g Fiber; 4g Sugar; 45mg Sodium

Yogurt Parfait

PREP TIME: 15 min **COOK TIME:** none **YIELD:** 1 Serve
INGREDIENTS:
- 1/3-cup granola or other breakfast cereal
- 3/4 cup plain or flavored yogurt,
- 1 peach or nectarine, chopped
- Artificially sweetened yogurt

DIRECTIONS:
- Put 4 tablespoons of yogurt in a large glass. 2 tbsp. granola, followed with 1/3 of the sliced peach. Make two more layers of each component for a total of three layers.

NUTRITION:
70 Cal; 6g Protein; 4g Tot Fat; 3g Carb; 0g Fiber; 3g Sugar; 32mg Sodium

Fudge Brownies

PREP TIME: 15 min **COOK TIME:** 15 min **YIELD:** 16 Serve
INGREDIENTS:
- 2 tbsp. unsweetened applesauce
- 2 tbsp. butter
- 1/2 tbsp. baking powder
- 1 cup sugar
- 1/2 cup plus 2 tbsp. all-purpose flour
- 1/4 cup unsweetened cocoa powder
- Pinch salt
- 1 1/2 tbsp. canola oil
- 2 large white eggs
- 2 oz. semi-sweet chocolate

DIRECTIONS:
- Preheat your stove to 325 degrees Fahrenheit. Set aside an 8x8 pan that has been sprayed with cooking spray. Combine butter, chocolate, and oil in a medium saucepan over low heat; simmer until the chocolate is melted, stirring constantly. Remove from the heat and let it cool slightly.
- Stir in the sugar and cocoa powder to the chocolate mixture. Stir in the flour and the other ingredients until smooth. Pour the butter into the pan. Bake for 30 minutes at 325°F, or until a knife inserted in the center of the brownies comes out clean. Remove the dish from the oven. Cool on a rack in the pan. Cut the squares into 2x2 squares.

NUTRITION:
89 Cal; 2.2g Protein; 3.9g Tot Fat; 6.4g Carb; 0g Fiber; 3.4g Sugar; 26mg Sodium

Strawberry Angel Pie

PREP TIME: 15 min **COOK TIME:** 15 min **YIELD:** 6 Serve
INGREDIENTS:
- 1/4 cup (50 ml) ice water
- 1 cup (250 ml) water
- 1/2 tsp. (2 ml) almond extract
- 1 tbsp. (15 ml) cornstarch
- 1 tsp. (5 ml) vanilla
- 1/3 cup Splenda
- 1 egg, separated
- 1/4 cup (50 ml) instant skim milk powder
- 1 packet unflavored gelatin
- 9 inch Graham Cracker Crust

- 3 cups (750 ml) frozen unsweetened or fresh strawberries

DIRECTIONS:
- Strawberries should be sliced. Allow strawberries to soak in water for 1 hour at room temperature. Strawberries should be drained into a saucepan and set aside. 2 tbsp. (25 ml) of the liquid drained from the strawberries is sprinkled with gelatin. In the remaining water, whisk together cornstarch and egg yolk. Over medium heat, cook and stir until the mixture boils and thickens slightly. Remove the pan from the heat.
- Stir in the softened gelatin, sweetener, vanilla, and almond extract until the gelatin and sweetener are completely dissolved. Strawberries should be added last. Refrigerate for 30 minutes or until the mixture has partly set. In a cold bowl, whisk together the egg white; skim milk powder, and ice water. Into the thickened strawberry mixture, fold in. Fill Graham Cracker Crust with filling. Refrigerate until fully set.

NUTRITION:
66 Cal; 4g Protein; 3g Tot Fat; 2g Carb; 0g Fiber; 2g Sugar; 36mg Sodium

Sugar-Free Graham Cracker Crust

PREP TIME: 15 min **COOK TIME:** none **YIELD:** 8 Serve
INGREDIENTS:
- 1/4 tsp. (1 ml) each of cinnamon and nutmeg
- 3 tbsp. (45 ml) melted butter or margarine
- 3/4 cup (200 ml) graham wafer crumbs

DIRECTIONS:
- Combine the graham cinnamon, butter, wafer crumbs, and nutmeg in a big mixing bowl. Fill a 9-inch (1 L) pie dish, an 8-inch square pan, or a 9-inch spring form pan with the mixture. Before filling, chill for 2 hours in the refrigerator. Reserve 2 tbsp. (25 ml) of the crumb mix to sprinkle over the filling if preferred.

NUTRITION:
50 Cal; 10g Protein; 6g Tot Fat; 7g Carb; 0g Fiber; 4g Sugar; 41mg Sodium

Strawberry Cheesecake

PREP TIME: 15 min **COOK TIME:** 15 min **YIELD:** 6 Serve
INGREDIENTS:
- Fresh Strawberries
- 2 cups sugar-free low-fat whipped topping
- 1 pkg. sugar-free Strawberry Banana Jell-O
- 1 graham cracker crust made with Splendaï
- 1 pkg low-fat cream cheese

DIRECTIONS:
- 1/2 cup boiling water to dissolve jelly. Make sure there are no lumps in the cream cheese. Incorporate the whipped topping into the mixture. Cut your strawberries (and bananas) lengthwise and flatten the slices.
- Fruit should be used to line the bottom of the crust. Cover with a layer of cheesecake batter. Let's say you want to put another fruit layer in the center. That's all right. Serve with quartered fresh strawberries on top. Refrigerate until ready to use.

NUTRITION:
98 Cal; 2g Protein; 9g Tot Fat; 4g Carb; 0g Fiber; 4g Sugar; 32mg Sodium

Blueberry-Peach Crisp

PREP TIME: 15 min **COOK TIME:** 45 min **YIELD:** 6 Serve
INGREDIENTS:
- 1/4 cup apple juice
- 1 lb. of peach slices
- 10 oz. fresh or frozen blueberries

Topping:
- 1/2 tsp. cinnamon
- 1/2 cup almonds
- 2 TBS apple juice
- 1 cup pitted dates
- 1/2 cup oats

DIRECTIONS:
Preheat your stove to 350 degrees Fahrenheit. Fill the bottom of an 8-inch square baking pan with blueberries. If you're using frozen vegetables, make sure they're fully thawed and drained. On top of the blueberries, arrange peach slices. If they've been frozen, make sure they've been thawed, and any extra water has been drained. Drizzle a quarter cup of apple juice over the fruit.
Remove the pits from the dates and combine them with the oats, almonds, and cinnamon in the bowl of a food processor. After a minute of running, the dates are combined with the oats and cinnamon, and then apple juice is added and well mixed. Bake uncovered for 45 minutes, spreading the mixture evenly over the peaches and blueberries. Serve hot or cold.

NUTRITION:
67 Cal; 1.6g Protein; 0.5g Tot Fat; 3g Carb; 0g Fiber; 2g Sugar; 18mg Sodium

Peanut Butter Oatmeal Protein Balls

PREP TIME: 15 min **COOK TIME:** none **YIELD:** 12 Serve
INGREDIENTS:
- 3 packets of Splenda
- 2 scoops of unbury chocolate
- 1/4 c chopped nuts pecans, walnuts, almonds
- oatmeal
- 3 tbsp. of sugar-free maple syrup
- 1/2 c low carb special K
- 1 1/2 c peanut butter

DIRECTIONS:
- In a bowl, combine all ingredients, shape them into walnut-sized balls, and then roll them in oats.

NUTRITION:
37 Cal; 2.3g Protein; 0.9g Tot Fat; 1.4g Carb; 1.2g Fiber; 0.34g Sugar; 13mg Sodium

Peanut Butter Protein Balls

PREP TIME: 15 min **COOK TIME:** none **YIELD:** 6 Serve
INGREDIENTS:
- 1 cup protein powder
- 1 cup quick rolled oats
- 1 cup natural smooth peanut butter

DIRECTIONS:
- Combine the ingredients and roll into walnut-sized balls. Roll them in crushed almonds or oats for added protein and to prevent them from sticking together. Keep the container sealed. Keep refrigerated until ready to use.

NUTRITION:
45 Cal; 2.9g Protein; 3.6g Tot Fat; 2.5g Carb; 0.2g Fiber; 0.4g Sugar; 33mg Sodium

Vanilla & Peanut Butter Cookies
PREP TIME: 15 min **COOK TIME:** 12 min **YIELD:** 12 Serve
INGREDIENTS:
- 1 tbsp. vanilla (Optional)
- 1 cup Peanut Butter
- 1 egg
- 1 cup SplendaÂ

DIRECTIONS:
- Mix and drop roll or press out the mixture. Preheat oven to 348°F and bake for 11 minutes.

NUTRITION:
43 Cal; 2g Protein; 2g Tot Fat; 0.3g Carb; 0.1g Fiber; 4g Sugar; 13mg Sodium

Flourless Chewy Oatmeal Cookies
PREP TIME: 15 min **COOK TIME:** 15 min **YIELD:** 12 Serve
INGREDIENTS:
- 1 Egg
- 1/3 cup unsalted butter
- 1/8 tsp. Salt
- 1/4 cup SplendaÂ Brown sugar - scant, firmly packed
- 1/2 cup SplendaÂ
- 1 tsp. Vanilla extract
- 1 1/2 cups Rolled oats

DIRECTIONS:
- put the butter aside to cool. In a medium-sized mixing dish, place the oats. Blend in both the sugars and the salt to break up any chunks. Whisk together all the softened butter, vanilla, and egg in a different dish.
- Stir this into the oat mixture, working in the ingredients with your hands or a big wooden spoon. Form into a big dough ball. Allow the dough to chill for 20 minutes. Preheat your stove to 350 degrees Fahrenheit.
- In the meanwhile, line a baking sheet with parchment paper. Form the cold dough into 1-inch balls and gently flatten it on a baking sheet. Bake for 13–17 minutes, or until the edges of the cookies are well browned, and the tops are a medium golden color.
- Allow cooling completely on the baking sheet (approximately 10 minutes) before removing with a metal spatula or icing knife. To create a big, crisp, lace-like cookie, bring the dough to room temperature and flatten it further before placing it on the baking pan. Keep the cookies in the fridge.

NUTRITION:
98 Cal; 2g Protein; 9g Tot Fat; 4g Carb; 0g Fiber; 4g Sugar; 45mg Sodium

Amazing Pecan Pie
PREP TIME: 15 min **COOK TIME:** 35 min **YIELD:** 10 Serve
INGREDIENTS:
- Whipped cream sweetened with Splenda
- 3 large eggs

- Â½ cup chopped pecans, plus 10 halves One 9-inch homemade unbaked pie shell
- Pinch of table salt
- Â¾ cup Sugar-Free Country Syrup
- 4 tablespoons salted butter, melted
- 1 tsp. vanilla extract
- Â¾ cup Splenda Granular

DIRECTIONS:
- Preheat oven to 350 degrees Fahrenheit. beat the eggs until well combined, then add the Splenda, salt, vanilla, butter, and syrup. Pour the filling into the pie crust after adding the chopped pecans.
- Arrange the pecan halves equally on top of the custard and bake for 30 to 35 minutes, or until the edges are set, but the center is still soft. Allow it cool to room temperature before serving with Splenda-sweetened whipped cream in tiny slices.

NUTRITION:
171 Cal; 3g Protein; 14.5g Tot Fat; 7.5g Carb; 0g Fiber; 4g Sugar; 21mg Sodium

Crestless Pumpkin Pie
PREP TIME: 15 min **COOK TIME:** 55 min **YIELD:** 6 Serve
INGREDIENTS:
- 1 tsp. vanilla
- 1 cup Egg Beaters
- 1 cup fat-free evaporated milk
- 1 (15 ounces) can Libby's pure pumpkin
- 3/4 cup Splenda
- 3 teaspoons pumpkin pie spice

DIRECTIONS:
- Preheat your stove to 425 degrees Fahrenheit. Combine the ingredients in a pie dish that has been coated with Pam. Bake for 15 minutes at 425 degrees, then lower to 350 degrees and bake for another 40 minutes, or until a knife inserted in the center comes out clean. Others swear by Libby's pumpkin can recipe on the back. Replace the sugar with Splenda and leave out the pie crust.

NUTRITION:
148 Cal; 3g Protein; 7g Tot Fat; 7g Carb; 0g Fiber; 5g Sugar; 32mg Sodium

Chocolate Peanut Brittle
PREP TIME: 15 min **COOK TIME**: none **YIELD:** 6 Serve
INGREDIENTS:
- 2 tablespoons creamy peanut butter
- 3 ounces (6 squares)Valor 70% Sugar-Free Imported Dark chocolate, chopped
- 1 recipe Susan Peanut Brittle

DIRECTIONS:
- Microwave your chocolate in 20-second intervals, stirring after each. Stir in the peanut butter. Allow to cool and set on parchment paper after dipping broken pieces of peanut brittle halfway into the chocolate. Keep the container sealed.

NUTRITION:
98 Cal; 2g Protein; 9g Tot Fat; 4g Carb; 0g Fiber; 45g Sugar; 45mg Sodium

Spritz Cookies

PREP TIME: 15 min **COOK TIME:** 15 min **YIELD:** 6 Serve
INGREDIENTS:
* Food coloring
* 1 cup butter softened
* 2 1/2 cups flour
* 1 tsp. vanilla
* 3 egg yolks
* Sanding sugar
* 2/3 cup Nature Sweet Crystals

DIRECTIONS:
* Preheat your stove to 400 degrees Fahrenheit. cream the butter, Nature Sweet, egg yolks, and vanilla until frothy. If you want the dough to be colored, add a single drop of food coloring. Pulse in the flour until it is well incorporated, then gather into a smooth ball.
* Fill the cookie press halfway with dough, insert the chosen die, and press the cookies onto an ungreased baking sheet. If you don't have a cookie press, shape the dough into 1 inch balls, place it on an oiled baking sheet, and then flatten it with a fork in a cris-cross pattern, similar to peanut butter cookies.
* Add a pinch of colored sugar to each cookie. Do not over bake; bake for 8 to 10 minutes, or until firm and light golden brown around the edges. Place on a wire rack to cool.

NUTRITION:
108 Cal; 4g Protein; 7g Tot Fat; 3g Carb; 0g Fiber; 5g Sugar; 25mg Sodium

Rum Balls

PREP TIME: 15 min **COOK TIME:** none **YIELD:** 12 Serve
INGREDIENTS:
* 1/4 cup dark rum
* 2 1/2 cups sugar-free cookies, Chocolate Walnut or Pecan Shortbread
* 2 tablespoons Dutch-processed cocoa powder
* 1 cup Splenda granular
* 2 tablespoons Honey Sweet Maple Syrup
* 1 1/2 cups chopped pecans

DIRECTIONS:
* In a food processor, coarsely grind the cookies (you should end up with 1/2 cup of fine crumbs). add 3/4 cup Splenda. Blend in the syrup and rum until thoroughly blended. Make 1-inch balls out of the dough. Roll the rum balls in the remaining 1/4 cups Splenda in a small dish until lightly coated. Refrigerate the mixture in an airtight jar. It's ideal if you make them a few days ahead of time so the flavors can mix. Allow cooling before serving.

NUTRITION:
63 Cal; 4g Protein; 2g Tot Fat; 1.7g Carb; 0g Fiber; 0.5g Sugar; 36mg Sodium

Almond Flour Cookies

PREP TIME: 15 min **COOK TIME:** 12 min **YIELD:** 32 Serve
INGREDIENTS:
* 1 cup California blanched almond flour
* 1 cup peanut butter
* 1/2 tsp. salt
* 1 cup Nature Sweet Crystals
* 1 large egg

DIRECTIONS:
* Preheat your stove to 350 degrees Fahrenheit. Combine peanut butter, egg, Nature Sweet Crystals, salt, and almond flour in a mixing bowl until thoroughly combined.
* Using a tablespoon, scoop the mixture and shape it into balls. Place the dough on two ungreased cookie sheets, leaving 1 inch to spread slightly during baking.
* To flatten, press down with a fork in one direction, then the other. Bake for 10-12 minutes, or until a fingertip inserted into the center comes out slightly stiff. Allow for cooling for 4-5 minutes before transferring to a wire rack to cool completely.

NUTRITION:
62 Cal; 3g Protein; 6g Tot Fat; 1.4g Carb; 0g Fiber; 0.5g Sugar; 57mg Sodium

Sugar-Free Peanut Brittle

PREP TIME: 15 min **COOK TIME:** 15-18 min **YIELD:** 6 Serve
INGREDIENTS:
* 1 1/2 cups roasted salted peanuts
* 1 cup butter
* 1/2 tsp. vanilla extract
* 1 cup Nature Sweet Crystals

DIRECTIONS:
* Set aside a cookie sheet. In a large nonstick skillet, melt the butter. Stir in the Nature Sweet Crystals and simmer, stirring continuously, over medium heat. The mixture will initially look gritty and separate before blending easily.
* Cook for 15-18 minutes, or until the syrup darkens to a golden caramel color similar to the peanuts (a hard crack stage in a cup of cold water), and then remove from heat. Stir in the vanilla extract first, and then mix in the nuts rapidly.
* Transfer to the prepared baking sheet and pat nuts and candy into a single layer with the cooking spoon. Allow the mixture to cool to room temperature before using. Break the brittle into bite-sized chunks and store it in a sealed jar after it has fully cooled.

NUTRITION:
60 Cal; 2g Protein; 6g Tot Fat; 2g Carb; 0g Fiber; 4g Sugar; 54mg Sodium

Gingerbread Cookies

PREP TIME: 15 min **COOK TIME:** 15 min **YIELD:** 6 Serve
INGREDIENTS:
* 1/4 tsp. ground nutmeg
* 1/4 cup butter
* 1 tsp. ground cinnamon
* 1/4 cup dark molasses
* 3/4 tsp. salt
* 1/2 tsp. baking soda
* 2 cups all-purpose flour
* 1 tsp. ground ginger
* 1/4 cup Steels Country Syrup or Honey Sweet
* 1/4 tsp. ground cloves
* 1/2 cup Nature Sweet, powder or crystals

DIRECTIONS:
* Combine the butter and Nature Sweet in a mixing bowl. Add the molasses, Country Syrup, and 1/4 cup water

and mix well. Salt, in a different bowl, combine the baking soda, flour, salt, ginger, cloves, cinnamon, and nutmeg; add to the wet ingredients. Blend until you get soft dough.

- Place tiny round pieces 1 inch apart on a lined or well-greased cookie sheet using a 1/2 tsp. metal ice cream type scoop or a teaspoon. Bake at 375 degrees until virtually no impression remains when gently touched with a finger. Remove to a cooling rack after 2-3 minutes on the baking sheet.
- To gently dust, toss in a dish with 1 cup Nature Sweet Powder and store in an airtight container. Alternatively, refrigerate the dough for a few hours or overnight. Roll out to a thickness of 14 inches. Cookie cutters may be used to make circles, trees, or gingerbread men. Place on a baking sheet that has been buttered. And then bake as directed above.

NUTRITION:
46 Cal; 1.5g Protein; 1.5g Tot Fat; 3g Carb; 0g Fiber; 2g Sugar; 33mg Sodium

Beatrice's Apricot Cream Cheese Cookies
PREP TIME: 15 min **COOK TIME:** 15 min **YIELD:** 30 Serve

INGREDIENTS:
- Natures Hollow sugar-free apricot preserves
- 4 ounces cream cheese
- 1/4 tsp. salt
- 1 cup flour, plus additional for rolling
- 1/2 cup butter

DIRECTIONS:
- Cream together the cream cheese and butter. Blend in flour and salt. Form the dough into a smooth ball, wrap it in plastic wrap, and place it in the refrigerator for 1-2 hours. Preheat your stove to 375 degrees Fahrenheit.
- Roll out 1/2 of the dough to 1/8 inch thickness on the counter and carefully cut into 2-inch squares, reserving scraps to re-roll. With a spoon, blend the preserves until they have a smooth consistency. dab a quarter tsp. of preserves.
- Fold two opposing corners of the square to the center, slightly overlapping and pushing so they stay together, and the jam squishes out a little. Transfer each cookie to an ungreased cookie sheet, approximately 1 inch apart, after folding. Bake until the bottoms are golden brown.
- Any overlapped edges that have opened during baking should be gently pressed down. Place on a wire rack to cool. Rep with the rest of the dough.

NUTRITION:
35 Cal; 2g Protein; 3g Tot Fat; 2g Carb; 0g Fiber; 6g Sugar; 47mg Sodium

Almond Cookies
PREP TIME: 15 min **COOK TIME:** 15 min **YIELD:** 36 Serve

INGREDIENTS:
- Parchment paper
- 1/2 tsp. vanilla extract
- 3/4 cup Nature Sweet Crystals
- 1 egg white, slightly beaten
- 1/2 stick butter, melted
- 1/4 cup all-purpose flour
- Sliced dried cranberries

- 2 1/4 cups sliced unblanched almonds, about 10 ounces

DIRECTIONS:
- Using nonstick veggie cooking spray, lightly coat each of the two baking sheets. Preheat your stove to 350 degrees Fahrenheit.
- In a big mixing bowl, combine almonds, Nature Sweet crystals, flour, butter, egg white, and vanilla, gently tossing to coat the mixture and wet the mixture equally.
- Place tablespoonfuls on a cookie sheet that has been prepped. Press a dried cranberry slice into each biscuit gently. Preheat oven to 348°F and bake for 10-12 minutes, or until golden brown. Allow cooling for 10 minutes before gently transferring to a wire rack. Keep the container sealed.

NUTRITION:
36 Cal; 1.5g Protein; 1.5g Tot Fat; 3g Carb; 0g Fiber; 2g Sugar; 33mg Sodium

Chocolate Truffles
PREP TIME: 15 min
COOK TIME: 11 min
YIELD: 8 Serve

INGREDIENTS:
- 1/4 cup almond flour blended with 1/2 tsp. cinnamon and Nature Sweet Powder to roll truffles in.
- 1 tablespoon butter
- 4 ounces (8 squares) Valor 70% Sugar-Free Imported Dark chocolate
- 2 tablespoons DaVinci Sugar-Free Raspberry Syrup
- Unsweetened cocoa powder, unsweetened coconut,
- 3 tablespoons heavy cream

DIRECTIONS:
- In a medium glass dish, combine the cream and DaVinci syrup. 30 to 40 seconds in the microwave, or until heated but not boiling. Allow 3 minutes for the chocolate and butter to melt in the heated mixture. Stir until everything is melted and smooth. Allow cooling to room temperature, stirring once in a while.
- It has to be strong but not too hard. Scoop out teaspoon-sized mounds with a spoon or melon ball maker and put them on a parchment paper-lined baking sheet. Allow 30 minutes for chilling. Roll or shape uneven balls with care, then roll in unsweetened cocoa powder and other coatings. For presentation, each truffle may be put in its candy cup.

NUTRITION:
148 Cal; 2g Protein; 6g Tot Fat; 4g Carb; 0g Fiber; 21g Sugar; 23mg Sodium

Cinnabliss Lace Cookies
PREP TIME: 15 min **COOK TIME:** 15 min **YIELD:** 6 Serve
INGREDIENTS:
- 1/3 cup finely chopped pecans
- 1/4 cup real butter
- 1/4 t. vanilla extract
- 1/2 tsp. instant coffee granules
- 1/4 cup Cinnamon Bliss SF Sauce
- 1/2 cup flour
- 1/4 cup Nature Sweet Crystals

DIRECTIONS:

• Preheat your stove to 350 degrees Fahrenheit. In a small saucepan, melt the butter. Combine Nature Sweet and caramel sauce in a mixing bowl. Over medium heat, bring to a boil. Whisk in the coffee, vanilla, flour, and pecans after removing the pan from the heat. Allow cooling slightly before serving. Spray a cookie sheet with Pam and place shiny foil side down.

• Drop the batter one tsp. at a time onto a baking sheet, 6 to a sheet. Bake for 6–7 minutes, or until the edges are golden brown. (Keep an eye on them since them burn fast.) Allow cooling on a baking sheet until hard enough to pull off, and then transfer to a wire rack to cool completely.

NUTRITION:
198 Cal; 12g Protein; 7g Tot Fat; 21g Carb; 0g Fiber; 9g Sugar; 37mg Sodium

Double Chocolate Protein Pudding

PREP TIME: 15 min **COOK TIME:** 15 min **YIELD:** 6 Serve
INGREDIENTS:
• One package 1 ounce Jell-O Sugar-Free Instant Pudding Mix, Chocolate
• 2 cups Chocolate ready to drink a protein shake

DIRECTIONS:
• Whisk the pudding mix for 2 minutes in a shallow bowl with a wire whisk into the lukewarm ready-to-drink proteins. Chill immediately after pouring into separate serving plates. Within 5 minutes, the pudding will be soft set and ready to consume.

NUTRITION:
98 Cal; 2g Protein; 9g Tot Fat; 4g Carb; 0g Fiber; 45g Sugar; 45mg Sodium

Cinnamon Bliss Pumpkin Mousse

PREP TIME: 15 min **COOK TIME:** none **YIELD:** 6 Serve
INGREDIENTS:
• 1/2 cup pecan pieces
• 1 cup cold Micellar Milk Vanilla
• 1 1/2 cups sugar-free Cool Whip, thawed
• One 15 ounces can of pure pumpkin
• Â½ tsp. ground nutmeg
• 1 tsp. ground cinnamon
• Â¼ cup Cinnamon Bliss sugar-free topping
• Two 4-serving size packages Jell-O Sugar-Free Vanilla Instant Pudding Mix

DIRECTIONS:
• Whisk together Micellar Milk, dry pudding mixes, pumpkin, cinnamon, and nutmeg until well combined. Lastly, fold in the whipped topping. If desired, serve with extra whipped topping in a deep serving bowl or individual serving plate. Let it sit for 1 hour in the refrigerator.

NUTRITION:
189 Cal; 8g Protein; 4g Tot Fat; 7g Carb; 2g Fiber; 9g Sugar; 56mg Sodium

Ricotta Apple Pancake

PREP TIME: 15 min **COOK TIME:** 12 min **YIELD:** 8 Serve
INGREDIENTS:
• 1 cup grated apple
• 3 eggs, separated
• 1 Tablespoon Splenda
• 1 cup Ricotta
• 1/4 tsp. salt
• 1/4 tsp. baking soda
• 1/4 tsp. Apple Pie Spice OR Cinnamon
• 1/2 tsp. Vanilla
• 1/4 cup flour
• 1 whole egg

DIRECTIONS:
• Set aside 3 egg whites that have been stiffened. Combine the remaining ingredients in a small mixing bowl and stir just until combined. In a different bowl, whisk together the egg whites. Heat a pan with nonstick spray over medium-low heat. In a heated skillet, drop batter by tablespoonful's and fry until golden brown, flipping once.

NUTRITION:
94 Cal; 7 g Protein; 5 g Tot Fat; 4 g Carb; 0 g Fiber; 2 g Sugar; 119 mg Sodium

Cappuccino Custard

PREP TIME: 15 min **COOK TIME:** 30 min **YIELD:** 6-8 Serve
INGREDIENTS:
• pinch of salt
• Â½ tsp. vanilla
• 2 1/3 cup milk
• 2 tablespoon instant coffee granules
• Â½ cup Splenda Granular
• 1/8 tsp. cinnamon
• 4 eggs, beaten

DIRECTIONS:
• Mix all ingredients and pour into 6-6 ounce custard cups OR 8-4 ounce cups. Fill a 9X13 baking pan halfway with boiling water. Preheat oven to 325°F and bake for 25-30 minutes. Don't overcook. In the center, it should still be jiggle. Serve chilled or heated.

NUTRITION:
189 Cal; 8g Protein; 4g Tot Fat; 7g Carb; 2g Fiber; 9g Sugar; 56mg Sodium

Black Forest Mocha Cake

PREP TIME: 15 min **COOK TIME:** 26 min **YIELD:** 8 Serve
INGREDIENTS:
• Whipped cream
• 3/4 cup butter, cut into pieces
• 1/4 tsp. cinnamon
• 2 teaspoons instant coffee granules
• 1 tsp. vanilla extract
• 2/3 cup Nature Sweet powdered or Splenda
• 1/3 cup flour
• 4 large eggs
• Splenda-sweetened cherry pie filling or sugar-free raspberry jam, warmed
• Six ounces sugar-free dark or 70% cocoa chocolate

DIRECTIONS:
• Preheat your stove to 400 degrees Fahrenheit. Grease eight 4-ounce custard cups generously. Microwave the butter, chocolate, and instant coffee together for one minute or until the butter has completely melted. Stir until the chocolate is fully melted. Allow cooling before serving. In a

medium mixing basin, beat eggs, sugar substitute, and vanilla with an electric mixer for 3-4 minutes or until light and fluffy.

• Incorporate the chocolate mixture. Mix together the flour and cinnamon, and stir into the batter until combined. Using a spatula, evenly distribute the batter among the prepared cups. Bake for 10 minutes or until hard around the edges and soft in the middle, on a cookie sheet. Allow 5 minutes for cooling before inverting onto a dessert dish. Top with Splenda sweetened whipped cream and a layer of pie filling.

NUTRITION:
216 Cal; 5g Protein; 21g Tot Fat; 8g Carb; 2g Fiber; 1g Sugar; 88mg Sodium

Ricotta Swirl
PREP TIME: 15 min **COOK TIME:** none **YIELD:** 2 Serve
INGREDIENTS:
• 3-4 teaspoons sugar-free preserves
• 1/2 cup ricotta cheese
DIRECTIONS:
• Fold the preserves into the ricotta cheese gently. Enjoy with a pinch of cinnamon!
NUTRITION:
57 Cal; 6g Protein; 2g Tot Fat; 5g Carb; 1g Fiber; 21g Sugar; 20mg Sodium

Peanut Butter Pie
PREP TIME: 15 min **COOK TIME:** 15 min **YIELD:** 6 Serve
INGREDIENTS:
Crust:
• 2 tablespoons butter, melted
• 2 tablespoons peanut butter
• 1 1/2 cups crushed Josephs Sugar-Free Almond Cookies
Filling:
• One 12-ounce container Cool Whip, thawed
• One 8-ounce package reduced-fat cream cheese
• 1 tablespoon vanilla extract
• 3/4 cup Splenda
• 1 cup creamy peanut butter
DIRECTIONS:
FOR THE CRUST: Mix the ingredients and press into a 9-inch pie dish. Preheat oven to 348°F and bake for 10 minutes, or until brown. Allow cooling fully.
TO MAKE THE FILLING: Cream cheese, peanut butter, Splenda, and vanilla extract until smooth. Lastly, fold in the whipped topping. Fill a prepared crust or individual dessert plates with the mixture. Refrigerate or freeze overnight.
NUTRITION:
133 Cal; 10g Protein; 4g Tot Fat; 6g Carb; 0g Fiber; 6g Sugar; 23mg Sodium

Vanilla Egg Custard
PREP TIME: 15 min **COOK TIME:** 35 min **YIELD:** 6 Serve
INGREDIENTS:
• 2 teaspoons vanilla extract
• pinch of salt
• Â½ cup Splenda
• 1 cup milk

• 1 can of evaporated milk
• Nutmeg
• 4 eggs, beaten
DIRECTIONS:
• Preheat your stove to 325 degrees Fahrenheit. Set 6 custard cups or ramekins aside in a large roasting pan. Combine the eggs, milk, evaporated milk, Splenda, vanilla, and salt in a mixing bowl. Into a large measuring cup, strain through a fine-mesh sieve. Grate a large quantity of nutmeg over each of the custard cups and distribute evenly.
• Bake for 25 to 35 minutes, or until the middle of the custard is just set. Remove the custards from the water bath with care and place them on a wire rack to cool. Chill before serving.
NUTRITION:
120 Cal; 8g Protein; 3g Tot Fat; 9g Carb; 0g Fiber; 7g Sugar; 27mg Sodium

Sweetened Condensed Milk
PREP TIME: 15 min **COOK TIME:** 15 min **YIELD:** 6 Serve
INGREDIENTS:
• 1 cup powdered milk (dry)
• 3/4 cup Splenda
• 4 tablespoons softened butter
• 1/2 tsp. vanilla
• 1/3 cup boiling water
DIRECTIONS:
• With a hand mixer, combine all of the ingredients until they are thick and smooth. Allow cooling slightly before serving or keeping in the refrigerator. When cold, this becomes very thick, so microwave for a few seconds and then with a few tablespoons of milk if necessary.
NUTRITION:
113 Cal; 9g Protein; 5g Tot Fat; 8g Carb; 0g Fiber; 6g Sugar; 38mg Sodium

Pecan Pie
PREP TIME: 15 min **COOK TIME:** 35 min **YIELD:** 6 Serve
INGREDIENTS:
• Whipped cream sweetened with Splenda
• 3 large eggs
• Â¾ cup Sugar-Free Maple Syrup
• Pinch of table salt
• 4 tablespoons salted butter, melted
• 1 tsp. vanilla extract
• 1/2 cup chopped pecans, plus 10 halves
• 3/4 cup Splenda Granular
DIRECTIONS:
• Preheat oven to 350 degrees Fahrenheit. beat the eggs until well combined, then add the Splenda, salt, vanilla, butter, and syrup. Pour the filling into the pie crust after adding the chopped pecans.
• Arrange the pecan halves equally on top of the custard and bake for 30 to 35 minutes, or until the edges are set, but the center is still soft. Allow it cool to room temperature before serving with Splenda-sweetened whipped cream in tiny slices.
NUTRITION:
98 Cal; 2g Protein; 9g Tot Fat; 4g Carb; 0g Fiber; 45g Sugar; 45mg Sodium

Cinnamon Caramel Custard

PREP TIME: 15 min **COOK TIME:** 30 min **YIELD:** 6 Serve
INGREDIENTS:
- 1/3 cup Splenda Granular Cinnamon
- 4 eggs, beaten
- 1/4 cup Cinnamon Bliss sauce
- 2 1/4 cups milk
- 1/2 tsp. Vanilla extract
- Pinch of salt

DIRECTIONS:
- Whisk together the eggs, salt, milk, sauce, vanilla, and Splenda until smooth. Sprinkle cinnamon on top and pour through a sieve into six (4oz) custard cups. Fill a 9x13 baking pan with 1-inch boiling water and place cups in it. Preheat oven to 325°F and bake for 25-30 minutes. Allow cooling on a wire rack after removing from the baking pan. Run a knife along the edge of the cooled custard and invert onto a dessert dish when ready to serve. Over the custard and onto the dish, drizzle Cinnamon Bliss sauce.

NUTRITION:
113 Cal; 9g Protein; 5g Tot Fat; 8g Carb; 0g Fiber; 6g Sugar; 38mg Sodium

Cheesecake Tarts with Berries

PREP TIME: 15 min **COOK TIME:** 15 min **YIELD:** 12 Serve
INGREDIENTS:
- 1 cup raspberries
- 12 wonton wrappers
- 1/2 cup Splenda
- 2 teaspoons lemon juice
- 1/2 tsp. vanilla
- 2 cups frozen whipped topping, thawed
- One 8 ounce pkg. reduced-fat cream cheese
- 1/2 cup blueberries
- Vegetable spray

DIRECTIONS:
- Preheat your stove to 350 degrees Fahrenheit. Using a vegetable spray, coat a regular-sized muffin tin. Spray the wrappers lightly with veggie spray. Preheat oven to 348°F and bake for 8.5 minutes, or until golden and crisp. Allow cooling before serving. Cream together the cream cheese, vanilla, lemon juice, and Splenda in a medium mixing bowl. Lastly, fold in the whipped topping. Fill each tart shell with 2 teaspoons of filling. Arrange the berries on top of the filling. If desired, dust with powdered sugar.

NUTRITION:
108 Cal; 6g Protein; 8g Tot Fat; 1g Carb; 1g Fiber; 1g Sugar; 103mg

Almond Shortbread

PREP TIME: 15 min **COOK TIME:** 15 min **YIELD:** 15 Serve
INGREDIENTS:
- 1/2 cup REAL butter, softened
- 1/2 cup Almond flour
- 1/2 cup Nature Sweet crystals or Splenda in a pinch
- A pinch of salt
- 1/2 cup flour

DIRECTIONS:

- With a fork, thoroughly combine all ingredients, except the butter. As you would for pie crust, add the butter and cut it into the flour mixture. It will get extremely crumbly before suddenly starting to hold together. Mix it in a bit more until it resembles a ball. Allow for a 15-minute rest period. Preheat your stove to 350°F and lightly grease a baking sheet. (Or, like genuine shortbread, press them into an 8x8 pan and score and prick with a fork.)
- Form tablespoon-sized balls by gently pressing them together and rolling them in the palm of your hand. Place on sheet and flatten to 1/4 inch thick. Bake for 8-9 minutes, or until the edges are browning. Allow cooling for a minute on the baking sheet before gently transferring to the wire rack. Allow cooling fully before serving. Keep the container sealed.

NUTRITION:
98 Cal; 2g Protein; 9g Tot Fat; 4g Carb; 0g Fiber; 45g Sugar; 45mg Sodium

Old-Fashioned Apple Crisp

PREP TIME: 15 min **COOK TIME:** 45 min **YIELD:** 10 Serve
INGREDIENTS:
- ¼ cup coconut oil, melted
- Cooking spray (nonstick)
- ¾ cup whole-wheat pastry flour
- ½ cup water
- Juice of ½ lemon
- 1 tablespoon cornstarch
- ¼ tsp. ground nutmeg
- ½ tsp. ground cinnamon
- ¾ cup old-fashioned oats
- 3 teaspoons stevia powder, divided
- ½ cup of low-fat plain Greek yogurt
- 6 apples, cut into 1-inch chunks

DIRECTIONS:
- Preheat your stove to 350 degrees Fahrenheit. Using the cooking spray, coat an 8-by-8-inch baking dish. Combine the apples, water, 112 tablespoons of stevia, cornstarch, cinnamon, nutmeg, and lemon juice in a baking dish. Mix. Preheat oven to 348°F and bake for 18 minutes. combine the oats, flour, and the remaining 112 tablespoons of stevia.
- Combine the yogurt and coconut oil in a mixing bowl. Stir until all of the flour is wet and combined. Cover the apple mixture with the oatmeal mixture in an even layer. Bake for 22 minutes, or until golden brown on top. Serve right away.

NUTRITION:
222 Cal; 22 g Protein; 9 g Tot Fat; 11 g Carb; 0 g Fiber; 0 g Sugar; 221 mg Sodium

Lemon-Blackberry Frozen Yogurt

PREP TIME: 10 min **COOK TIME:** 10 min **YIELD:** 4 Serve
INGREDIENTS:
- Fresh mint leaves, for garnish
- cups frozen blackberries
- 2 teaspoons liquid stevia
- Juice of 1 lemon
- ½ cup of low-fat plain Greek yogurt

DIRECTIONS:
- Combine the blackberries, yogurt, lemon juice, and stevia in a blender or food processor. Blend for approximately

5 minutes or until smooth. Serve with fresh mint leaves as a garnish. Serve right away or store in an airtight jar for up to 3 weeks.

NUTRITION:
68 Cal; 3 g Protein; 0 g Tot Fat; 15 g Carb; 5 g Fiber; 11 g Sugar; 12 mg Sodium

Chocolate Brownies with Almond Butter

PREP TIME: 5 min **COOK TIME:** 26 min **YIELD:** 16 Serve
INGREDIENTS:
- ½ cup agave nectar
- Cooking spray (nonstick)
- ½ cup cocoa powder
- 1 tsp. vanilla extract
- 2 large eggs
- ¼ tsp. baking soda
- ¼ cup melted coconut oil
- ½ cup almond butter
- ½ tsp. ground instant coffee
- 1 tablespoon ground flaxseed

DIRECTIONS:
- Preheat your stove to 325 degrees Fahrenheit. Using the cooking spray, coat an 8-by-8-inch glass baking dish. combine the cocoa powder, flaxseed, instant coffee, baking soda, almond butter, coconut oil, eggs, vanilla, and agave nectar. Blend on high until completely smooth. Fill the baking dish halfway with batter. Preheat oven to 348°F and bake for 23 minutes, or until a toothpick inserted in the center comes out clean. Allow 8 minutes to cool before cutting into 16 squares.

NUTRITION:
124 Cal; 3 g Protein; 9 g Tot Fat; 11 g Carb; 2 g Fiber; 9 g Sugar; 49 mg Sodium

Easy Peanut Butter Cookies

PREP TIME: 15 min **COOK TIME:** 15 min **YIELD:** 15 Serve
INGREDIENTS:
- ½ tsp. vanilla extract
- Cooking spray (nonstick)
- ½ cup stevia baking blend
- 1 large egg
- 1 cup natural smooth peanut butter

DIRECTIONS:
- Preheat your stove to 350 degrees Fahrenheit. Cooking spray or parchment paper may be used to coat a nonstick baking pan. In a medium mixing bowl, combine the peanut butter, egg, stevia, and vanilla using a hand mixer. Place the batter balls on the baking sheet in 1-inch balls.
- Flatten each ball to a thickness of approximately 14 inches. Make two crisscross pattern impressions on the cookie using a fork. Preheat oven to 348°F and bake for 12 minutes. When the cookies are golden brown, they are done. Cool for 5 minutes before transferring to a cooling rack to cool completely.

NUTRITION:
107 Cal; 4 g Protein; 9 g Tot Fat; 4 g Carb; 1 g Fiber; 2 g Sugar; 47 mg Sodium

Chocolate Chia Pudding

PREP TIME: 15 min **COOK TIME:** 60 min **YIELD:** 4 Serve

INGREDIENTS:
- ½ cup fresh raspberries, for garnish
- 2 cups unsweetened soy milk
- ¼ tsp. vanilla extract
- ¼ tsp. ground cinnamon
- ¼ cup unsweetened cocoa powder
- ½ cup chia seeds
- 10 drops liquid stevia

DIRECTIONS:
- Whisk together the stevia, soy milk, cinnamon, cocoa powder, and vanilla in a small mixing dish until thoroughly mixed. Add the chia seeds and mix well. Divide the mixture into four small serving plates. overnight, covered. Garnish with raspberries when ready to serve.

NUTRITION:
222 Cal; 22 g Protein; 9 g Tot Fat; 11 g Carb; 0 g Fiber; 0 g Sugar; 221 mg Sodium

Super food Dark Chocolates

PREP TIME: 5 min **COOK TIME:** 26 min **YIELD:** 18 Serve
INGREDIENTS:
- 1 tsp. sea salt
- 6 ounces dark chocolate chips
- ¼ cup chopped pecans
- ¼ cup unsweetened shredded coconut
- ¼ cup unsweetened dried wild blueberries
- ¼ cup pumpkin seeds (pipits), chopped

DIRECTIONS:
- Preheat oven to 350°F. Line 1 or 2 baking pans with parchment paper. Bring a big saucepan of water to a rolling boil. Reduce the heat to a low simmer and cover the boiling water with a stainless steel heat-proof bowl. Stir in the chocolate chunks until they are completely melted and smooth.
- Drizzle the melted chocolate in tiny circles on the sheet pan with a spoon (approximately 34 teaspoons of chocolate in circles about 2 inches in diameter). Fill each chocolate circle with pumpkin seeds, coconut, pecans, and dried blueberries.
- Each one should be able to contain approximately 34 tablespoons of toppings. Season with a pinch of salt. Allow the chocolates to the firm in the refrigerator or at room temperature. To ensure optimum freshness, store them in an airtight container and consume them within two weeks.

NUTRITION:
102 Cal; 3 g Protein; 7 g Tot Fat; 8 g Carb; 2 g Fiber; 6 g Sugar; 99 mg Sodium

Caramel Custard

Preparation Time: 15 Minutes **Cooking Time:** 7 Minutes
Servings: 4
Ingredients:
- 4 cups milk - 6 eggs
- 4 tablespoons sugar
- 3/4 cup sugar
- 1 teaspoon vanilla extract
- 1 pinch sea salt
- 1/4 teaspoon ground cinnamon
- Round stainless-steel pan
- 2 tablespoons water

Directions:

1. Beat the milk, eggs, sugar, cinnamon, vanilla extract and salt in the bowl until they become smooth.
2. Transfer the mixture to the steel pan.
3. Set a cup of water into Instant Pot and place the trivet inside.
4. Cover the bowl with tin foil, poke some holes in it then place it over the trivet.
5. Secure the lid and cook on Manual for 7 minutes at high pressure.
6. Boil the sugar with 2 tablespoons of water in the skillet and let it caramelize, Pour this mixture on top of custard then serve when cool.

Nutrition:
Calories: 361 Fat: 11.5g
Protein: 16.2g Carbs: 50.2g
Net Carbs: 50.1g Fiber: 0.1g

Chocolate Cheesecake

Preparation Time: 10 Minutes **Cooking Time:** 18 Minutes **Servings:** 4

Ingredients:
- 3/4 tablespoon cocoa powder
- 1/4 cup Swerve sugar Sweetener
- 1 egg
- 8 ounces (227 g) cream cheese softened
- 1 tablespoon powdered peanut butter
- 1/2 teaspoon pure vanilla extract

Directions

1. Mix the eggs and cream cheese in a blender to form a smooth mixture.
2. Add the brown sugar, peanut butter and vanilla extract to the egg mixture and blend.
3. Transfer the mixture to a greased ramekin.
4. Pour water into Instant Pot and place the trivet inside.
5. Arrange the ramekin over the trivet.
6. Secure the lid and cook on Manual function for 18 minutes at high pressure.
7. When it beeps; do a quick release and remove the lid.
8. Let the ramekin cool and refrigerate the cake for 8 hours. Serve.

Nutrition:
Calories: 224 Fat: 21.1g
Protein: 6.6g
Carbs: 17.7g
Net Carbs: 17.2g
Fiber: 0.5g

Crème Brûlée

Preparation Time: 10 Minutes **Cooking Time:** 14 Minutes **Servings:** 4

Ingredients:
- 1/4 cup superfine sugar
- 5 egg yolks
- 2 cups heavy cream
- 1 tablespoon vanilla extract
- 1/2 cup sugar

Directions

1. Beat the egg yolks, cream, vanilla extract and sugar in a large bowl.
2. Divide the mixture into 4 ramekins.
3. Set a cup of water into Instant Pot and place the trivet inside.
4. Arrange the ramekins over the trivet.
5. Secure the lid and cook on Manual function for 13 minutes at high pressure.
6. When it beeps; do a quick release and remove the lid.
7. Let the ramekin cool and refrigerate for 4 hours. Sprinkle superfine sugar on top and serve.

Nutrition
Calories: 378
Fat: 27.7g
Protein: 4.5g
Carbs: 27.6g
Net Carbs: 27.6g
Fiber: 0g

Pears with Coconut Butter

Preparation Time: 10 Minutes **Cooking Time:** 15 Minutes **Servings:** 3

Ingredients:
- 2 large pears, peeled and cut into wedges
- 2 tablespoons coconut oil
- 3 tablespoons coconut butter, melted
- 1 teaspoon cinnamon
- 1 cup water

Directions

1. Pour the water into the Instant Pot.
2. Place the pears inside the steamer basket and lower the basket into the pot.
3. Close the lid and cook for 2 minutes.
4. Quickly let the pressure and open the lid.
5. Transfer the bowl to a plate and discard the water from the pan.
6. Melt the coconut butter in the Instant Pot on Sauté and add the pears inside.
7. Sprinkle with cinnamon and cook until they become browned.
8. Serve drizzled with the melted coconut butter.
9. Enjoy!

Nutrition:
Calories: 241
Fat: 17.1g
Protein: 1.0g
Carbs: 22.0g
Net Carbs: 16.0g
Fiber: 6.0g

Green Beans with Lemon

Preparation Time: 10 Minutes **Cooking Time:** 10 Minutes **Servings:** 2

Ingredients:
- 4 ounces (113 g) trimmed green beans
- 1 teaspoon fresh lemon juice
- 1/2 teaspoon extra-virgin olive oil
- Pinch of sea salt

Directions:

1.   Steam the green beans in your instant pot for about 5 minutes for until crisp-tender.

2.   Drizzle with fresh lemon juice, olive oil and sprinkle with sea salt. Enjoy!

Nutrition

Calories: 30

Fat: 1.2g

Protein: 1.0g

Carbs: 4.0g

Net Carbs: 2.0g

Fiber: 2.0g

Peppermint Cheesecake

Preparation Time: 10 Minutes   **Cooking Time:** 34 Minutes **Servings:** 3

Ingredients:

*   1 cups organic cream cheese, softened, 1/4 cup sour cream

*   1 large organic eggs

*   1/2 cup swerve or erythritol sweetener

*   1/2 tablespoon coconut, Pinch of salt

*   1 teaspoons pure vanilla extract,

*   1/2 teaspoons pure peppermint extract

Chocolate Ganache:

*   3 ounces (85 g) unsweetened chocolate chips, melted

*   1/3 cup organic heavy cream, Pinch of salt

Crust:

*   1/2 cup almond flour

*   1 tablespoons swerve or Erythritol sweetener

*   1 tablespoons ghee or goat butter, melted

Directions

1.   Combine ingredients for crust. Press down in a spring form pan; choose pan suitable for Instant Pot. Place in freezer for 10 minutes.

2.   In a large bowl or blender, combine filling ingredients. Stir well.

3.   Pour cheesecake filling in spring form pan. Cover with aluminum foil.

4.   Add 1 cup of water, and trivet to Instant Pot. Place spring form pan on top.

5.   Close, seal the lid. Press Manual button. Cook on High 35 minutes.

6.   When done, naturally release pressure 15 minutes, then quick release remaining pressure. Remove the lid.

7.   Remove pan from pot. Cool on counter 30 minutes, then refrigerate 4 hours.

8.   In a bowl, combine chocolate ganache ingredients. Microwave 30 seconds. Stir. Repeat until smooth.

9.   Transfer cheesecake to platter. Drizzle over ganache. Serve.

Nutrition:

Calories: 454

Fat: 33.2g

Protein: 8.8g

Carbs: 30.1g

Net Carbs: 29.2g

Fiber: 0.9g

Strawberry Sorbet

Preparation Time: 10 Minutes

Cooking Time: 0 Minutes

Servings: 1 cup

Ingredients:

*   3 cups Almond Breeze Almond Coconut Milk Blend Unsweetened

*   2 cup, unthawed Strawberries, frozen, unsweetened

*   cup, sliced Banana, frozen

*   1/8 piece of Fresh Lime with skin

*   6 tsp. Organic cane sugar,

Directions:

1.   Place all ingredients into your Vitamin in the order listed. Set the blender on to Variable 1, then quickly increase the speed to Variable 10.

2.   Set to high then blend for about 30-60 seconds. Set the tamper to press the ingredients into the blades.

3.   Stop the machine as soon as the mounds form. Serve.

Nutrition:

Calories: 47

Fat: 1.1 g

Carbs: 9.1 g

Protein: 0.6 g

Pumpkin Balls

Preparation Time: 15 Minutes **Cooking Time:** 0 Minutes

Servings: 18

Ingredients:

*   1 cup almond butter

*   5 drops liquid stevia.

*   2 tbsp. coconut flour

*   2 tbsp. pumpkin puree

*   1 tsp. pumpkin pie spice

Directions:

1.   Mix pumpkin puree in a large bowl and almond butter until well combined. Add liquid stevia, pumpkin pie spice, and coconut flour and mix well.

2.   Make small balls from the mixture and place onto a baking tray in the freezer for 1 hour.

3.   Serve and enjoy.

Nutrition:

Calories: 95.1

Fat: 5.2 g

Carbs: 10.8 g

Protein: 2.3 g

Smooth Peanut Butter Cream

Preparation Time: 10 Minutes **Cooking Time:** 0 Minutes

Servings: 8

Ingredients:

*   1/4 cup peanut butter

*   4 overripe bananas, chopped.

*   1/3 cup cocoa powder

*   1/4 tsp. vanilla extract

*   1/8 tsp. salt

Directions:

1.   In the blender, add all the listed ingredients and blend until smooth. Serve immediately and enjoy.

Nutrition:

Calories: 101

Fat: 5 g

Carbs: 14 g
Protein: 3 g

Vanilla Avocado Popsicles

Preparation Time: 20 Minutes **Cooking Time**: 0 Minutes**Servings**: 6
Ingredients:
*   2 avocadoes
*   1 tsp. vanilla
*   1 cup almond milk
*   1 tsp. liquid stevia
*   1/2 cup unsweetened cocoa powder

Directions:
1.   In the blender, add all the listed ingredients and blend smoothly.
2.   Pour blended mixture into the Popsicle molds and place in the freezer until set. Serve and enjoy.

Nutrition:
Calories: 130
Fat: 12 g
Carbs: 7 g
Protein: 3 g

Cocoa Chocolate Chips Cookies

Preparation Time: 20 Minutes **Cooking Time:** 11 Minutes **Servings:** 12
Ingredients:
*   12 tablespoons butter, melted
*   1/2 cup light brown sugar
*   1 cup granulated sugar
*   1 large egg
*   1 large egg yolk
*   teaspoon vanilla extract
*   1 3/4 cups all-purpose flour
*   1/4 cup unsweetened cocoa powder
*   1/2 teaspoon salt
*   1/2 teaspoon baking soda
*   1 1/2 cups semisweet chocolate chips

Directions:
1.   Merge melted butter with brown sugar and granulated sugar until smooth. Cool slightly and beat in egg and egg yolk. Beat in vanilla.
2.   Merge the flour, cocoa, salt, and baking soda. Slowly beat into the butter and sugar mixture until well blended.
3.   Chill the dough for at least 1 hour, or until firm.
4.   Heat oven to 350°.
5.   With a cookie scoop or tablespoon, scoop mounds of dough onto a silicone-lined or greased baking sheet, leaving about 1 1/2 to 2 inches between cookies. Bake for 12 to 15 minutes, until set.
6.   Cool on baking sheet on a rack, then remove cookies to rack to cool completely.
7.   Makes 2 to 3 dozen cookies.

Nutrition:
Calories: 490.3
Fat: 21.7 g
Carbs: 58.7 g
Protein: 3.0 g

Amazing Rice Pudding

Preparation Time: 10 Minutes **Cooking Time:** 45 Minutes **Servings:** 12
Ingredients:
*   3 cups cooked white rice
*   cups skim milk
*   tbsp. light margarine
*   1/2 cup sugar
*   1/2 cup raisins
*   Tsp. vanilla extract
*   1/2 tsp. nutmeg
*   Tsp. cinnamon

Directions:
1.   Cook the rice.
2.   Let the rice cool for a few minutes. In a medium sized pot, merge the rice, milk, margarine, sugar, raisins, and vanilla.
3.   Cook until the liquid is mostly absorbed. Stir frequently to keep the rice from sticking to the bottom of the pot.
4.   Attach the cinnamon and nutmeg, stirring well.
5.   Cook another 5 minutes.
6.   Serve

Nutrition:
Calories: 137.8
Fat: 1.0 g
Carbs: 28.1 g
Protein: 3.2 g

Mini Molten Lava Cakes

Preparation Time: 15 Minutes **Cooking Time:** 20 Minutes **Servings:** 36
Ingredients:
*   Butter, unsalted, 170 grams
*   Semisweet chocolate, 1 cup chips (6 oz. package)
*   Egg, fresh, 3 larges
*   Cocoa, dry powder, unsweetened, 3 tbsp.
*   Granulated Sugar, 0.5 cup
*   Flour, white, 0.33 cup

Directions:
1.   Pre-heat oven to 350.
2.   Melt chocolate and butter
3.   Sift flour and cocoa in separate bowl.
4.   Mix sugar and eggs in another bowl until it turns a lighter color.
5.   Mix chocolate mixture to egg and sugar mixture. Blend in flour and cocoa.
6.   Put into ramekins or muffin pan (grease muffin pan).
7.   Bake until top starts to split a little.
8.   Inside will be deliciously gooey!

Nutrition:
Calories: 78.7
Fat: 5.7 g
Carbs: 6.9 g
Protein: 1.0 g

Raspberry Compote

Preparation Time: 10 Minutes **Cooking Time:** 20 Minutes **Servings:** 12

Ingredients:
- 2 cups raspberries, fresh or frozen (thawed)
- 3 tbsp. honey
- juice of 1/2 an orange (preferably a blood orange)
- Pinch salt
- 2 tbsp. cold water
- 1tsp. cornstarch

Directions:
1. Set raspberries, honey, orange juice and salt in a small saucepan.
2. Place to a low simmer over medium heat and cook, stirring occasionally, until the berries are mostly broken down, 3 to 5 minutes.
3. Whisk together the cold water and cornstarch until smooth and stir into the cooking mixture.
4. Cook until mixture thickens.
5. Set to at least room temperature before serving. Store in fridge.

Nutrition:
Calories: 33.5
Fat: 0.1 g
Carbs: 8.5 g
Protein: 0.3 g

Chocolate Popsicle

Preparation Time: 20 Minutes **Cooking Time:** 10 Minutes **Servings:** 6

Ingredients:
- 4 oz. unsweetened chocolate, chopped.
- 6 drops liquid stevia
- 1 1/2 cups heavy cream

Directions:
1. Add heavy cream into the microwave-safe bowl and microwave until it just begins the boiling. Add chocolate into the heavy cream and set aside for 5 minutes.
2. Add liquid stevia into the heavy cream mixture and stir until chocolate is melted. Pour mixture into the Popsicle molds and place in freezer for 4 hours or until set. Serve and enjoy.

Nutrition:
Calories: 198 Fat: 21 g
Carbs: 6 g Protein: 3 g

Raspberry Ice Cream

Preparation Time: 10 Minutes **Cooking Time:** 0 Minutes **Servings:** 2

Ingredients:
- 1 cup frozen raspberries
- 1/2 cup heavy cream
- 1/8 tsp. stevia powder

Directions:
1. Blend all the listed fixings in a blender until smooth. Serve immediately and enjoy.

Nutrition:
Calories: 144
Fat: 11 g

Carbs: 10 g
Protein: 2 g

Chocolate Frosty

Preparation Time: 20 Minutes **Cooking Time:** 0 Minutes **Servings:** 4

Ingredients:
- 2 tbsp. unsweetened cocoa powder
- 1 cup heavy whipping cream
- 1 tbsp. almond butter
- 5 drops liquid stevia.
- 1 tsp. vanilla

Directions:
1. Add cream into the medium bowl and beat using the hand mixer for 5 minutes. Add remaining ingredients and blend until thick cream forms.
2. Pour in serving bowls and place them in the freezer for 30 minutes. Serve and enjoy.

Nutrition:
Calories: 137
Fat: 13 g
Carbs: 3 g
Protein: 2 g

Wrapped Pears with Vanilla Bean Sauce

Preparation Time: 35 Minutes **Cooking Time:** 2 hours 5 Minutes **Servings:** 4

Ingredients:
- 3 cups water
- 3/4 cup sugar
- 1/2 vanilla bean,
- 4 Bartlett or Bosc pear cored and peeled.
- 1/2 cup heavy cream
- 1/2 of a 17.3-ounce package Pepperidge Farm Puff Pastry Sheets (1 sheet), thawed
- 1cup fresh raspberries

Directions:
1. Warmth the water, sugar and vanilla bean in a 2-quart saucepan over low heat until the sugar is dissolved, stirring occasionally.
2. Attach the pears to the saucepan and cook for 10 minutes or until the pears are tender, turning occasionally. Detach the pears from the saucepan. Secure and refrigerate for 1 hour or until the pears are cold.
3. Stir the cream into the saucepan. Cook until the mixture is reduced to about 3/4 cup, stirring often. Detach the vanilla bean and scrape the seeds into the saucepan. Remove the saucepan from the heat.
4. Heat the oven to 400F.
5. Set the pastry sheet on a lightly floured surface. Divide the pastry sheet crosswise into 8 (3/4-inch wide) strips. Garnish the strips with water and sprinkle with additional sugar.
6. Set the ends of 2 pastry strips together. Set the wrapped pears onto a baking sheet. Loosely cover the wrapped pears with aluminum foil.
7. Bake. Spoon the vanilla sauce onto 4 plates. Top each with 1 pear and garnish with the raspberries.

Nutrition:
Calories: 571

Fat: 21 g
Carbs: 96.1 g
Protein: 4.5 g

Chocolate Almond Butter Brownie

Preparation Time: 10 Minutes **Cooking Time:** 16 Minutes **Servings:** 4

Ingredients:
- 1 cup bananas, overripe
- 1/2 cup almond butter, melted.
- 1 scoop protein powder
- 2 tbsp unsweetened cocoa powder

Directions:
1. Warm air fryer to 325 F. Grease air fryer baking pan and set aside. Blend all fixings in a blender until smooth.
2. Pour batter into the prepared pan and place in the air fryer basket and cook for 16 minutes. Serve and enjoy.

Nutrition:
Calories: 82
Fat: 2 g
Carbs: 11 g
Protein: 7 g

Peanut Butter Fudge

Preparation Time: 10 Minutes **Cooking Time:** 10 Minutes **Servings:** 20

Ingredients:
- 1/4 cup almonds toasted and chopped.
- 12 oz. smooth peanut butter
- 15 drops liquid stevia
- 3 tbsp. coconut oil
- 4 tbsp. coconut cream
- Pinch of salt

Directions:
1. Line baking tray with parchment paper. Dissolve coconut oil in a pan over low heat. Add peanut butter, coconut cream, stevia, and salt in a saucepan. Stir well.
2. Pour fudge mixture into the prepared baking tray and sprinkle chopped almonds on top. Place the tray in the refrigerator for 1 hour or until set. Slice and serve.

Nutrition:
Calories: 131
Fat: 12 g
Carbs: 4 g

Banana Chocolate Cake

Preparation Time: 15 Minutes **Cooking Time:** 35 Minutes **Servings:** 16

Ingredients:
- 2 very ripe medium bananas
- 1/4 cups all-purpose flour
- 3/4 cup sugar
- 1/4 cup unsweetened cocoa powder
- 1/3 cup canola oil
- 1/3 cup water
- 1teaspoon baking soda
- 1teaspoon white vinegar
- 1/4 teaspoon salt

- 1/3 cup semisweet chocolate chips

Directions:
1. Warmth oven to 350
2. Press bananas or blend with electric beater.
3. Blend in wet ingredients and brown sugar.
4. Sift dry ingredients together then add to wet.
5. Blend well.
6. Sprinkle chocolate chips over batter.
7. Bake until toothpick inserted in the center comes out clean. Cool completely, about 45 minutes.

Nutrition:
Calories: 142.5
Fat: 5.8 g
Carbs: 24.9 g
Protein: 1.7 g

Blueberry Muffins

Preparation Time: 15 Minutes **Cooking Time:** 25 Minutes **Servings:** 12

Ingredients:
- 2 eggs
- 1/2 cup fresh blueberries
- 1 cup heavy cream
- 2 cups almond flour
- 1/4 tsp. lemon zest
- 1/2 tsp. lemon extract
- 1 tsp. baking powder
- 5 drops stevia
- 1/4 cup butter, melted.

Directions:
1. Heat the cooker to 350 F. Line muffin tin with cupcake liners and set aside. Add eggs into the bowl and whisk until mix.
2. Add remaining ingredients and mix to combine, then pour the mixture into the prepared muffin tin and bake for 25 minutes. Serve and enjoy.

Nutrition:
Calories: 190
Fat: 17 g
Carbs: 5 g
Protein: 5 g

Chia Pudding

Preparation Time: 20 Minutes **Cooking Time:** 0 Minutes **Servings:** 2

Ingredients:
- 4 tbsp. chia seeds
- 1 cup unsweetened coconut milk
- 1/2 cup raspberries

Directions:
1. Add raspberry and coconut milk into a blender and blend until smooth. Pour mixture into the glass jar. Add chia seeds in a jar and stir well.
2. Seal the jar with a lid and shake well and place in the refrigerator for 3 hours.
3. Serve chilled and enjoy.

Nutrition:
Calories: 360
Fat: 33 g

Carbs: 13 g
Protein: 6 g

Lean Green Smoothie

Preparation Time: 10 Minutes **Cooking Time:** 0 Minutes
Servings: 1
Ingredients:
• cup frozen tropical fruit mix (papaya, pineapple, guava)
• 1/2 cup chilled green tea, unsweetened
• 1/2 cup plain low-fat yogurt
• 1tbsp.. green powder
• 2tbsp flax seed (or chia seeds)
• 1tbsp vanilla protein powder (whey or soy)
• a pinch of fresh mint (optional)
• sweeten to taste (nutrition count includes 2 tsp. agave)

Directions:
1. Combine in a blender until smooth, about 30 seconds. Makes about 14 ounces.
2. It can substitute either cultured soy or more tea and ice, to make this vegan or less calories.

Nutrition:
Calories: 403
Fat: 8.9 g
Carbs: 48.9 g
Protein: 34.8 g

Light Ice Cream Sandwich Cake

Preparation Time: 10 minutes **Cooking Time:** 2 hours
Servings: 16
Ingredients:
• Low fat,. Hy-Vee brand could be a good one.
• Light, fat free hot fudge topping
• Light Cool Whip 12 oz. tub

Directions:
1. Set your whipped topping. Set a 9x13 pan with the ice cream sandwiches, you will have to cut them to cover the whole bottom of the pan.
2. Warmth the fudge and spread over the ice cream sandwiches.
3. Secure the whole thing with Cool Whip and refreeze.

Nutrition:
Calories: 173.8
Fat: 3.8 g
Carbs: 37.9 g
Protein: 3.2 g

Carrot Gelatin Salad

Preparation Time: 15 minutes **Cooking Time:** 5 hours
Servings: 8
Ingredients:
• (6 ounce) package lemon flavored gelatin mix
• can crushed pineapple, drained with juice
• 4 large carrots, shredded.

Directions:
1. In a large bowl, set the lemon gelatin according to package directions using reserved pineapple juice in place of some of the water. Refrigerate until thickened, about 1 hour.

2. When the gelatin has thickened, set in pineapple and shredded carrot. refrigerate at least 4 hours.

Nutrition:
Calories: 54.8
Fat: 0.1 g
Carbs: 12.8 g
Protein: 0.6 g

Vegan Chocolate Almond Milk Ice Cream Fudgsicle Style

Preparation Time: 10 minutes **Cooking Time:** 0 minutes
Servings: 8
Ingredients:
• 2 cups unsweetened almond milk
• 1/2 cup Cocoa, dry powder, unsweetened
• 1/2tsp Vanilla Extract
• 300 grams avocados
• 1 cup coconut sugar

Directions:
1. Set everything into a blender and puree.
2. Freeze it in a plastic bag, squishing it together as it freezes..

Nutrition:
Calories: 183.5
Fat: 8.0 g
Carbs: 31.0 g
Protein: 2.2 g

Avocado Pudding

Preparation Time: 20 Minutes **Cooking Time:** 0 Minutes
Servings: 8
Ingredients:
• 2 ripe avocados pitted and cut into pieces.
• 1 tbsp. fresh lime juice
• 14 oz. coconut milk
• 2 tsp. liquid stevia
• 2 tsp. vanilla

Directions:
1. Inside the blender, Add all ingredients and blend until smooth. Serve immediately and enjoy.

Nutrition:
Calories: 317
Fat: 30 g
Carbs: 9 g
Protein: 3 g

Strawberry Granita

Preparation Time: 10 minutes **Cooking Time:** 3 hours
Servings: 8
Ingredients:
• 3 cups sliced fresh strawberries.
• 1/2 cup sugar
• 1/2 cup warm water
• 2 TBS fresh lemon juice = 1 oz.

Directions:
1. In a blender dissolve the sugar with the water. Once dissolved add in the strawberries and the lemon juice.

2.   Puree until smooth. Pour into an 8 X 8 dish. Freeze for 3 hours. Stir completely.

3.   Freeze for another 5 hours or overnight. Let sit on counter around 10 minutes. Grate with the tines of a fork and serve in 1 cup dishes.

Nutrition:
Calories: 68.0
Fat: 0.2 g
Carbs: 17.2 g
Protein: 0.4 g

Peanut Butter Coconut Popsicle

Preparation Time: 15 Minutes **Cooking Time:** 0 Minutes
Servings: 12
Ingredients:
- 1/2 cup peanut butter
- 1 tsp. liquid stevia
- 2 cans unsweetened coconut milk

Directions:
1.   In the blender, add all the listed ingredients and blend until smooth. Pour mixture into the Popsicle molds and place in the freezer for 4 hours or until set. Serve!

Nutrition:
Calories: 155
Fat: 15 g
Carbs: 4 g
Protein: 3 g

Brownie Bites

Preparation Time: 20 minutes **Cooking Time:** 0 minutes
Servings: 13
Ingredients:
- 1/4 cup unsweetened chocolate chips
- 1/4 cup unsweetened cocoa powder
- 1 cup pecans, chopped.
- 1/2 cup almond butter
- 1/2 tsp. vanilla
- 1/4 cup monk fruit sweetener
- 1/8 tsp. pink salt

Directions:
1.   Add pecans, sweetener, vanilla, almond butter, cocoa powder, and salt into the food processor and process until well combined.
2.   Transfer brownie mixture into the large bowl.
3.   Add chocolate chips and fold well. Make small round shape balls from brownie mixture and place onto a baking tray. Place in the freezer for 20 minutes. Serve and enjoy.

Nutrition:
Calories: 108 Fat: 9 g
Carbs: 4 g Protein: 2 g

Peanut Butter Brownie Ice Cream Sandwiches

Preparation Time: 20 Minutes **Cooking Time:** 20 Minutes **Servings:** 18 ice cream sandwiches
Ingredients:
Brownies
- 1/2 cup Coconut oil or butter
- 1/2 cup Crazy Richard's Creamy Peanut Butter
- 2 cups semi-sweet chocolate chips
- 4 eggs
- 2/3 cup granulated sugar
- 1/2 cup unsweetened cocoa powder
- 1/2tsp pure vanilla extract
- 1/2 tsp. sea salt

Filling:
- 3 cups ice cream
- 1/4 to 1/2 cup creamy peanut butter
- Optional drizzle:
- 1/2 cup chocolate chips
- TBS Peanut butter

Directions:
1.   Warmth oven to 350 degrees F
2.   Set and grease two 8x8" square baking pans
3.   In a mixing bowl, dissolve together butter, peanut butter and chocolate chips. Stir until smooth.
4.   Attach the eggs and stir until smooth.
5.   Attach sugar, sea salt, vanilla, and cocoa powder and mix until the batter is smooth.
6.   Set mixture evenly between the two prepared 8x8" baking pans.
7.   Bake until the edges and top of the brownie looks set and feels firm to the touch.
8.   Detach the brownies from the oven and let them cool in the baking pans.
9.   While the brownies are cooling, detach 3 cups of ice cream from the freezer and let it sit at room temperature to soften.
10.   Once the brownies are completely cool, detach ONE batch of brownies from its baking pan.
11.   Set the pan of brownies with peanut butter in the freezer to harden for at least 15 minutes.
12.   Detach the brownies from the freezer and spread softened ice cream over the peanut butter layer.
13.   Set the baking pan in the freezer to harden for at least 5 hours or overnight.
14.   Detach the brownie ice cream sandwiches from the freezer and place on a cutting board.
15.   Divide the sandwiches into 9 pieces, and then cut each of those 9 pieces in half, with a large, sharp knife.
16.   If desired, set topping by melting chocolate chips and peanut butter together, then drizzle as desired on the cut ice cream sandwiches.

Nutrition:
Calories: 257
Fat: 18.5 g
Carbs: 21.4 g
Protein: 6.8 g

Homemade Bounty Bars

Preparation Time: 1 hour **Cooking Time:** 0 minutes
Servings: 12 bars
Ingredients:
- 3 cups unsweetened shredded coconut
- 1 cup sweetened condensed milk
- 15 oz. semisweet chocolate

Directions:

1. In a medium bowl, merge coconut and sweetened condensed milk to make a thick and sticky paste.
2. With your hands, form some rectangles with the paste. Set firmly to make sure the rectangles will keep their shape. After 3 or 4 rectangles, clean your hands and do not dry them completely.
3. Set the coconut bars on a baking sheet lined with parchment paper and put in the freezer for about 20 minutes.
4. In the meantime, divide the chocolate into pieces and put 2/3 of it in a microwave safe bowl.
5. Microwave, stir, then repeat in 15 seconds intervals, until the chocolate has melted completely.
6. If you prefer to dissolve chocolate on the stove top, place a heatproof bowl over a small saucepan filled with simmering water. On low heat, stir chocolate until dissolved, ensuring the chocolate does not contact water and steam while melting.
7. Attach 1/3 remaining chocolate and keep stirring until it is fully melted.
8. Using one fork, detach the rectangle from the melted chocolate.
9. With the other fork, remove excess chocolate and arrange your homemade bounty on a lined baking sheet.
10. Set a few hours for the chocolate cover to set and ENJOY your homemade bounty bars!

Nutrition:
Calories: 440
Fat: 30 g
Carbs: 37 g
Protein: 5 g

Tiramisu Protein Pancakes

Preparation Time: 15 Minutes **Cooking Time:** 10 Minutes **Servings:** 1
Ingredients:
• 1/3 cup rolled oats.
• scoop (30g) vanilla protein powder
• Tablespoons ground flax seed
• 1/2 teaspoon sodium-free baking powder
• 2egg white
• 1/4 cup strong brewed cold coffee
• 1/2 teaspoon vanilla extract
• 1/4 teaspoon coffee extract
For the Sweet "Cream" Filling:
• 1/3 cup low-fat no-salt-added cottage cheese.
• 1/2 large banana
• 1/8 teaspoon coffee extract
• unsweetened cocoa powder for dusting

Directions:
For the pancakes:
1. Warmth a skillet over medium heat.
2. set oats into flour.
3. Merge oat flour, protein powder, ground flax, and baking powder in a bowl.
4. In a separate bowl, set egg white until frothy.
5. Attach coffee to egg white, add to dry ingredients.
6. Incorporate flour
7. Let butter sit 5 minutes
8. Forme 3 medium-sized pancakes.

9. Cook until golden brown with crisp edges.
For the Sweet "Cream" Filling:
1. Merge cottage cheese, banana, and extract in a small food processor or blender and blend until smooth.

Nutrition:
Calories: 465
Fat: 9.8 g
Carbs: 45.1 g
Protein: 51.0 g

Mixed Berry Popsicles

Preparation Time: 4 hours to freeze **Cooking Time:** 0 minutes **Servings:** 12
Ingredients:
• 1 cup fresh blackberries
• 1 cup fresh blueberries
• 1 cup fresh raspberries
• 2 cups strawberries, sliced
• 2 tablespoons fresh lemon juice
• 2 tablespoons raw honey, or sweetener substitute

Directions:
1. blend ingredients until smooth.
2. Pour blended mixture into the popsicle molds and place in the freezer for 4 hours or until set.

Nutrition: Calories: 50 - Fat: 0 g - Protein: 0.4 g - Carbs: 10 g - Fiber: 2 g - Sugar: 8 g

Choco Frosty

Preparation Time: 30 minutes to freeze **Cooking Time:** 0 minutes **Servings:** 2
Ingredients:
• 1 teaspoon vanilla
• ½ teaspoon liquid stevia
• 2 tablespoons unsweetened cocoa powder
• ⅔ cup unsweetened almond milk
• ¾ cup fat-free heavy whipping cream, or heavy cream substitute

Directions:
1. Add whipping cream into a bowl and mix with immersion blender until soft peaks form.
2. Add remaining ingredients and continue blending until denser peaks form.
3. Place in freezer for at least 30 minutes.
4. After 15 minutes, remove the mixture from the freezer, stir, and return to freezer until the desired consistency is reached.

Nutrition: Calories: 338 - Fat: 33 g - Protein: 3 g - Carbs: 8 g - Fiber: 4 g - Sugar: 3 g

Cheesecake Fat Bombs

Preparation Time: 2 hours to freeze **Cooking Time:** 0 minutes **Servings:** 12
Ingredients:
• 4 oz. low-fat cream cheese
• 1 teaspoon vanilla
• 1 tablespoon erythritol
• 2 oz. coconut oil
• 2 oz. fat-free heavy cream, or heavy cream substitute
Directions:

1. beat all ingredients using an immersion blender until creamy.
2. Pour batter into a mini cupcake liner and place in refrigerator until set. Serve and enjoy.
Nutrition: Calories: 101 - Fat: 10 g - Protein: 1 g - Carbs: 1 g - Sugar: 1 g

Matcha Ice Cream
Preparation Time: 3-4 hours to freeze **Cooking Time:** 0 minutes **Servings:** 4
Ingredients:
- ½ teaspoon vanilla
- 2 tablespoons granular sweetener
- 1 teaspoon matcha powder
- 1 cup fat-free heavy whipping cream, or heavy whipping cream substitute

Directions:
1. Add all ingredients into a glass jar.
2. Seal jar with lid and shake for 4-5 minutes until mixture double.
3. Place in refrigerator for 3-4 hours. Serve chilled and enjoy.
Nutrition: Calories: 196 - Fat: 19 g - Protein: 1 g - Carbs: 4 g - Sugar: 3 g

Moist Avocado Brownies
Preparation Time: 10 minutes **Cooking Time:** 35 minutes **Servings:** 8
Ingredients:
- 2 avocados, mashed
- 2 eggs
- 1 teaspoon baking powder
- 2 tablespoons granulated sweetener
- ⅓ cup sugar-free chocolate chips, melted
- 4 tablespoons coconut oil, melted
- ⅔ cup unsweetened cocoa powder
- Cooking spray

Directions:
1. Preheat the oven to 325 °F.
2. mix together all dry ingredients.
3. mix together avocado and eggs until well combined.
4. Slowly add dry mixture to the wet one, along with melted chocolate and coconut oil. Mix well.
5. Pour batter in greased baking pan and bake for 30-35 minutes. Slice and serve.
Nutrition: Calories: 196 - Fat: 8 g - Protein: 4 g - Carbs: 17 g - Sugar: 10 g

Mix Berry Sorbet
Preparation Time: 2 hours to chill **Cooking Time:** 0 minutes **Servings:** 2
Ingredients:
- ½ cup raspberries, frozen
- ½ cup blackberries, frozen
- ½ teaspoon liquid stevia
- 6 tablespoons water

Directions:
1. blend ingredients until smooth.

2. Pour blended mixture into a container and place in refrigerator until harden.
3. Serve chilled and enjoy.
Nutrition: Calories: 63 - Fat: 1 g - Protein: 2 g - Carbs: 12 g - Fiber: 2 g - Sugar: 6 g

Chia Almond Pudding
Preparation Time: 1-2 hours to chill **Cooking Time:** 0 minutes **Servings:** 4-6
Ingredients:
- ⅓ cup chia seeds
- ½ teaspoon vanilla
- 4 tablespoons erythritol
- ¼ cup unsweetened cocoa powder
- 2 cups unsweetened almond milk
- 2 tablespoons almonds, toasted, and crushed (optional)

Directions:
1. Add almond milk, vanilla, sweetener, and cocoa powder into a blender and blend until well combined.
2. Pour blended mixture into a bowl. Add chia seeds and whisk for 1-2 minutes.
3. Pour pudding mixture into the serving bowls and place in fridge for 1-2 hours.
4. Top with crushed almonds, if desired, and serve.
Nutrition: Calories: 170 - Fat: 10 g - Protein: 5 g - Carbs: 14 g - Fiber: 7 g - Sugar: 3 g

Chia Raspberry Pudding
Preparation Time: 8 hours to chill **Cooking Time:** 0 minutes **Servings:** 2
Ingredients:
- ¼ teaspoon vanilla
- ¾ cup unsweetened almond milk
- 1 tablespoon erythritol
- ¼ cup chia seeds
- ½ cup raspberries, mashed
- 2 tablespoons proteins collagen peptides (optional)

Directions:
1. stir ingredients until well combined.
2. Place in refrigerator for overnight. Serve chilled and enjoy.
Nutrition: Calories: 162 - Fat: 6 g - Protein: 4 g - Carbs: 13 g - Fiber: 9 g - Sugar 3 g

Pear-Cranberry Pie with Oatmeal Streusel
Preparation Time: 15 minutes **Cooking Time:** 1 hour **Servings:** 12
Ingredients:
- 1 refrigerated pie crust, unbaked
For the Streusel:
- ¾ cup oats
- ¼ cup stevia
- ½ teaspoon cinnamon
- ½ teaspoon ground ginger
- ¼ teaspoon nutmeg
- 1 tablespoon light unsalted butter, or margarine, cubed
For the Filling:

- 3 cup pears, cubed
- 2 cup cranberries
- ⅓ cup stevia
- 2 ½ tablespoons cornstarch

Directions:
1. Set oven to 350 °F.
2. Combine all the streusel ingredients in a food processor and blend into a coarse crumb.
3. Mix all the filling ingredients in a large bowl and toss to combine.
4. Transfer filling into pie crust, and top with streusel mix.
5. Bake for about 1 hour, or until golden brown.

Nutrition: Calories: 249 - Fat: 8 g - Protein: 2 g - Carbs: 40 g - Fiber 4 g - Sugar 25 g

Blueberry Frozen Yogurt No Bake Cake

Preparation Time: 8 hours to freeze **Cooking Time:** 0 minutes **Servings:** 12

Ingredients:
- 1 cup barley, wheat cereal
- 3 cup fat-free plain Greek yogurt
- 10 oz. frozen blueberries
- 1 cup fat-free milk

Directions:
1. Set a parchment paper on a baking tray. Spread cereal evenly over the bottom of the tray.
2. Add milk, blueberries and yogurt to a blender, and process into a smooth mixture.
3. Use yogurt mixture to top cereal, wrap with foil, and place to freeze for about 8 hours, or until firm.
4. Slightly thaw, slice into portions and serve.

Nutrition: Calories: 228 - Fat: 3 g - Carbs 23 g - Fiber 4 g - Sugar 7 g

Chocolate Almond Ginger Mousse

Preparation Time: 3 hours to chill **Cooking Time:** 0 minutes **Servings:** 6

Ingredients:
- 1 ⅓ cup low-fat milk, cold
- 1 fat-free and sugar-free chocolate instant pudding package
- 1 cup low-fat whipped cream
- ¼ teaspoon dried ginger
- 1 tablespoon almonds, sliced

Directions:
1. Pour cold milk into a mixing bowl and, beating steadily with wire whisk, add the pudding mix and dried ginger. Keep whisking for 2 minutes. Fold in the cool whip topping.
2. Spoon into pudding cups, refrigerate for at least 3 hours. Garnish with sliced almonds just before serve.

Nutrition: Calories: 302 - Fat: 25 g - Protein: 4 g - Carbs: 21 g - Fiber: 9 g - Sugar: 7 g

Apple Crisp

Preparation Time: 20 minutes **Cooking Time:** 35 minutes **Servings:** 8

Ingredients:
- 4 apples, hard and crisp, cored, and sliced

- ½ lemon, juiced
- 2 tablespoons water
- 2 tablespoons agave nectar or 1 tablespoon raw honey
- ¾ cup old-fashioned rolled oats
- 2 tablespoons light unsalted butter, or margarine, cold
- ½ teaspoon cinnamon
- ½ teaspoon vanilla extract
- ½ cup walnuts, chopped
- Cooking spray

Directions:
1. Heat oven to 350 °F.
2. Place sliced apples in the bottom of a greased square cake pan.
3. Pour the water, lemon juice, vanilla, and agave nectar over the apples.
4. stir together the oats, butter and cinnamon. Use a pastry cutter or two knives to cut in the butter mixture until it resembles coarse breadcrumbs.
5. Stir in the chopped nuts.
6. Add the mixture over the apples and coat them completely.
7. Cover pan with tin foil and place in the oven for 20 minutes.
8. Remove tin foil from pan and continue baking for another 10-15 minutes until topping is golden brown.

Nutrition: Calories: 331 - Fat: 14 g - Protein: 3 g - Carbs: 61 g - Fiber: 4 g - Sugar: 34 g

Red Energy Wonders

Preparation Time: 2 hours to chill **Cooking Time:** 0 minutes **Servings:** 8

Ingredients:
- ⅓ cup all-natural almond butter
- 1 ⅓ cup unsweetened coconut, shredded, and divided into 1 cup portion and a ⅓ cup portion
- ½ cup rolled oats
- ½ cup strawberries
- ½ cup almonds
- 4 dates, pitted

Directions:
1. Place the 1 cup portion of coconut and all the rest of the ingredients in a food processor. At high speed, process until smooth and fully mixed.
2. Pour the remaining coconut onto a plate.
3. With a spoon, scoop out 1 tablespoon of the mixture and form it into a ball. Roll the ball around in the coconut, then place it on a plate lined with parchment paper.
4. Place the plate in the fridge for at least 2 hours before serve.

Nutrition: Calories: 102 - Fat: 7 g - Protein: 6 g - Carbs: 11 g - Fiber: 3 g - Sugar: 8 g

Chocolate Protein Pudding Pops

Preparation Time: 4 hours to freeze **Cooking Time:** 0 minutes **Servings:** 6-8

Ingredients:
- 1 (3.9 oz.) package chocolate-flavored instant pudding

141

- 2 cups low-fat milk, cold
- 2 scoops chocolate protein powder

Directions:

1. In a medium bowl, whisk the pudding mix, milk, and protein powder for at least 2 minutes.
2. Spoon into ice pop molds or paper cups. Insert an ice pop stick into the center of each mold or cup.
3. Freeze for 4 hours, or until firm. Remove from the molds or cups before serve.

Nutrition: Calories: 98 - Fat: 4 g - Protein: 12 g - Carbs: 10 g - Fiber: 0 g - Sugar: 7 g

Lemon Mousse

Preparation Time: 4 hours to chill **Cooking Time:** 0 minutes **Servings:** 4

Ingredients:

- 1 ½ cup boiling water
- 1 (6 oz.) package sugar-free lemon-flavored gelatin
- 2 cups ice cubes
- 1 ½ cup fat-free whipped topping
- Fresh fruit, for serving (optional)

Directions:

1. combine the boiling water and gelatin. Stir for at least 2 minutes, or until the gelatin is completely dissolved.
2. Add the ice cubes, and stir until melted. Refrigerate for 5-10 minutes until thickened.
3. Fold in the whipped topping. Divide into four portions and refrigerate until firm, about 4 hours.

4. Garnish with fresh fruit before serve, if desired.

Nutrition: Calories: 85 - Fat: 6 g - Protein: 1 g - Carbs: 6 g - Fiber: 0 g - Sugar: 3 g

Watermelon-Basil Granita

Preparation Time: 3-4 hours to freeze **Cooking Time**: 0 minutes **Servings:** 6

Ingredients:

- 1 lime, juiced
- ¼ medium watermelon, peel removed, roughly chopped
- ½ cup fresh basil leaves, finely chopped
- ⅛ cup raw sugar, or sugar substitute (optional)

Directions:

1. combine the watermelon chunks, lime juice, and sugar (if using). Blend on high until smooth.
2. Pour the watermelon mix into a baking dish, and stir in the basil leaves. Freeze for 1 hour.
3. Remove from the freezer and, using a fork, scrape the frozen areas until broken apart.
4. Return the dish to the freezer, and continue this process every half hour for at least 2-3 hours, or until the granita resembles coarse crystals.
5. Before serve, scrape the frozen mixture again with a fork.

Nutrition: Calories: 56 - Fat: 0 g - Protein: 1g - Carbs: 12 g - Fiber: 1 g - Sugar: 10 g

Conclusion

It's chock-full of delectable dishes that will help you stick to your new way of life. This cookbook offers all the information and recipes you'll need to lose weight the healthy way, whether your doctor has informed you that you need to lose weight or it's just a goal of yours.

The Gastric Sleeve Bariatric Cookbook is a guide for people who have had gastric sleeve surgery to ensure they eat a well-balanced, nutrient-dense, low-calorie diet. It assists in ensuring that a healthy diet is followed and that all of the necessary nutrients are ingested.

Because you'll have lost so much of your stomach after gastric sleeve surgery, it's critical to stick to a healthy eating plan. This means you'll need to stick to a calorie budget of less than 1,000 each day. It also means that if you don't eat foods with high nutritional value, you might not obtain all of the vitamins and minerals your body requires. This book is chock-full of nutrient-dense, calorie-dense dishes.

It will give you the meals that your body requires to stay healthy and make you feel good about yourself. It also includes a variety of recipes for various occasions. There's a dessert recipe, a snack recipe, a breakfast recipe, and more in this collection. Each dish has a set of nutritional objectives in mind and is designed to help you achieve them. It's quite straightforward: read the book and help to make the world a healthier and happier place.

You'll be able to create dinner in no time using some of the recipes in this book. You'll be able to eat your favorite dinner with your family at the table.

You can count on this book for fantastic party food if you're heading to a party, going out for a night on the town, or having company over. You can bring something nutritious and tasty and leave the junk food at home.

Made in the USA
Coppell, TX
17 November 2021